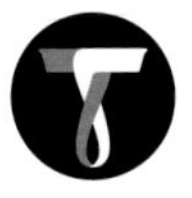

TROPE
PUBLISHING
Co.

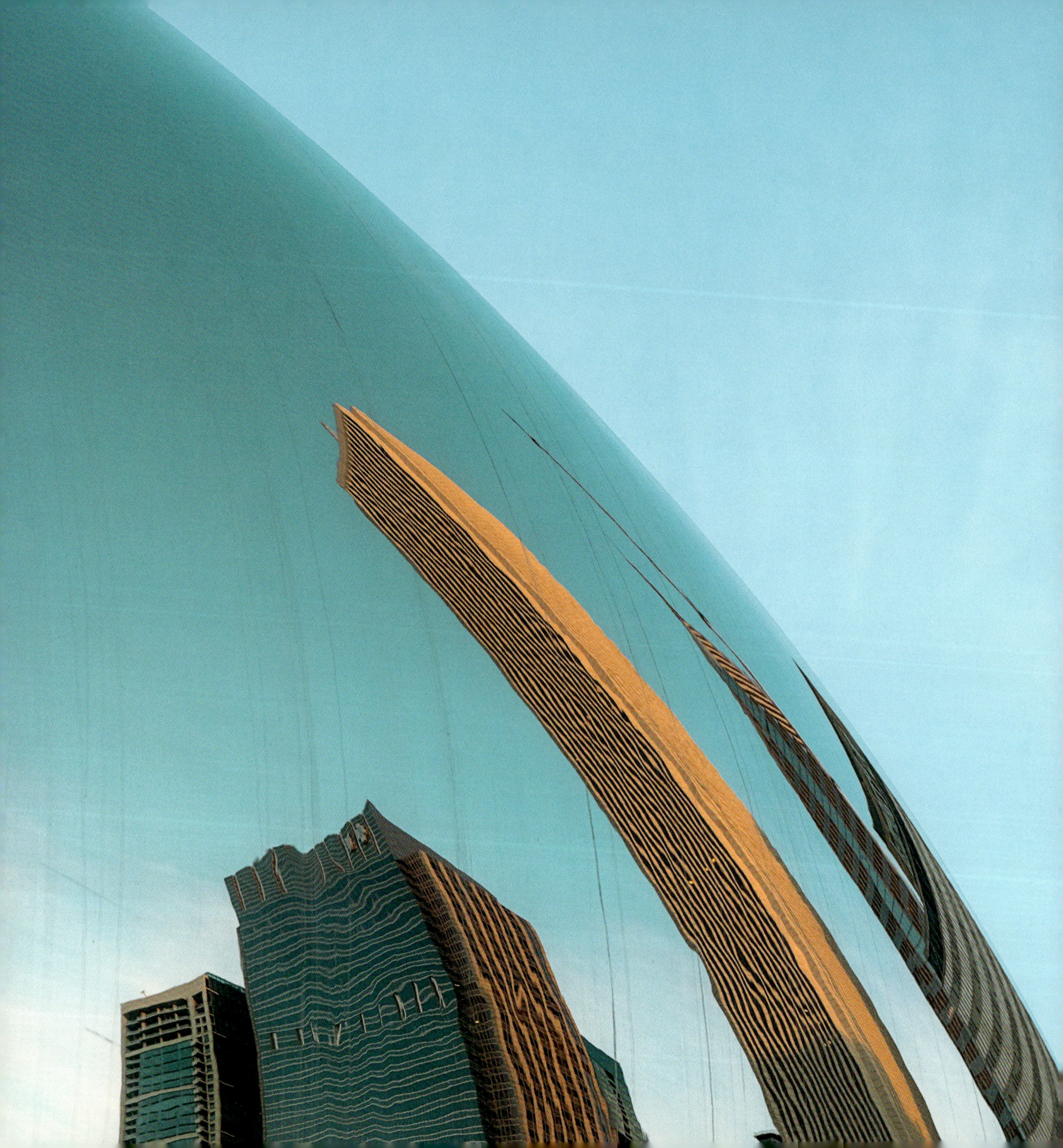

CHICAGO IN
COLOR

JUDIT
PRAT MARTÍ

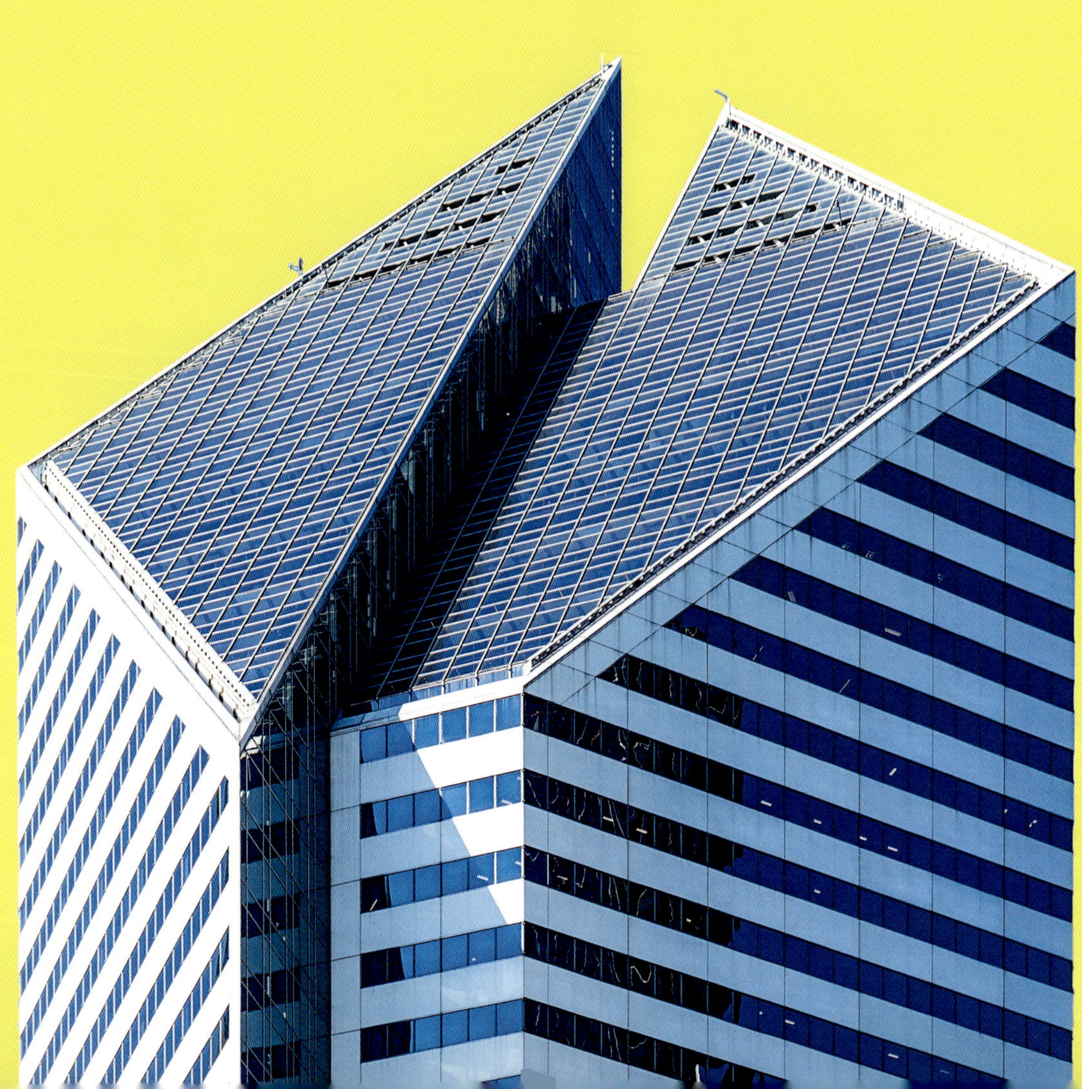

To those of you with whom I have been lucky
enough to share my time in Chicago,
these pictures belong to you.

To Chicago, for welcoming me with open arms.
Here I have felt free and loved.

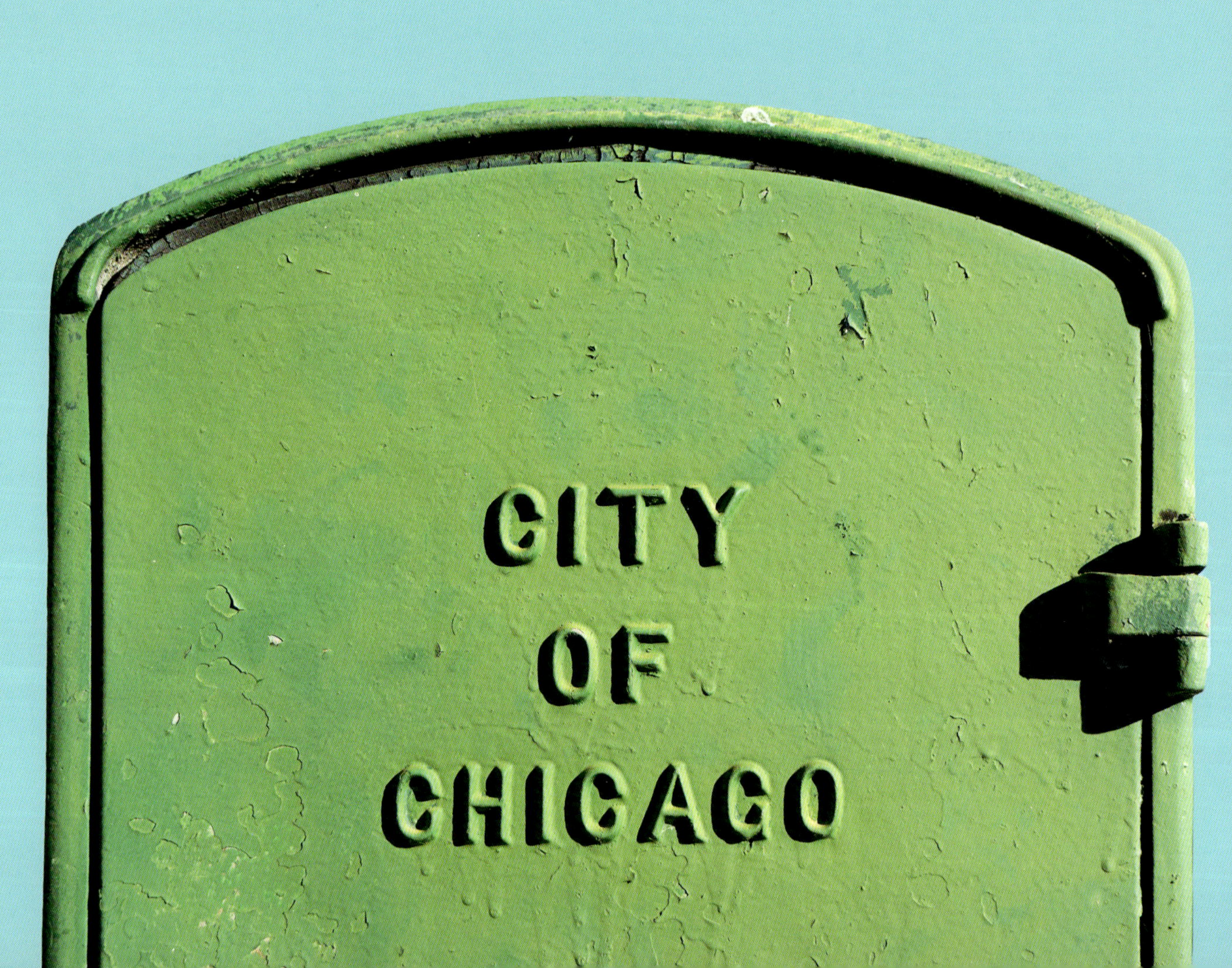

CITY
OF
CHICAGO

Introduction

In October 2019, I arrived in Chicago, leaving behind my hometown of Terrassa, a city near Barcelona. I came to Chicago because I was offered the opportunity to join the University of Chicago's Astronomy and Astrophysics Department, a chance I am truly grateful for. Since then, one of my passions has been to explore and understand Chicago from all its perspectives.

Initially, I had preconceived notions about the city of Chicago. I was full of biases and fears about living in a new (and American) city. I was also very excited.

Through my years living in Chicago, I have shaped my own opinions of the city and its neighborhoods, perspectives that are very different from the ones I had when I first arrived.

In my photography, I strive to capture the essence of the seemingly mundane, finding the beauty in the everyday. I believe that beauty is not limited to the traditionally celebrated subjects; it is pervasive, awaiting recognition in the most unexpected places. Viewing Chicago with this perspective transforms each day into an adventure, converting every journey through the city into a discovery of its hidden charms. In this book, I hope to capture this beauty using color as a medium to convey the spirit of Chicago.

Ultimately, I hope that *Chicago in Color* fosters a deeper appreciation for our city, encouraging a spirit of exploration in both longtime Chicagoans and newcomers alike. My aspiration is that this dive through the city not only shows its vibrant diversity but also helps to bridge connections amongst the different communities and neighborhoods, bringing Chicago closer together.

You are all invited to see Chicago through a new, minimalist, and colorful perspective. I hope you enjoy the journey.

I prefer living in color.

– David Hockney

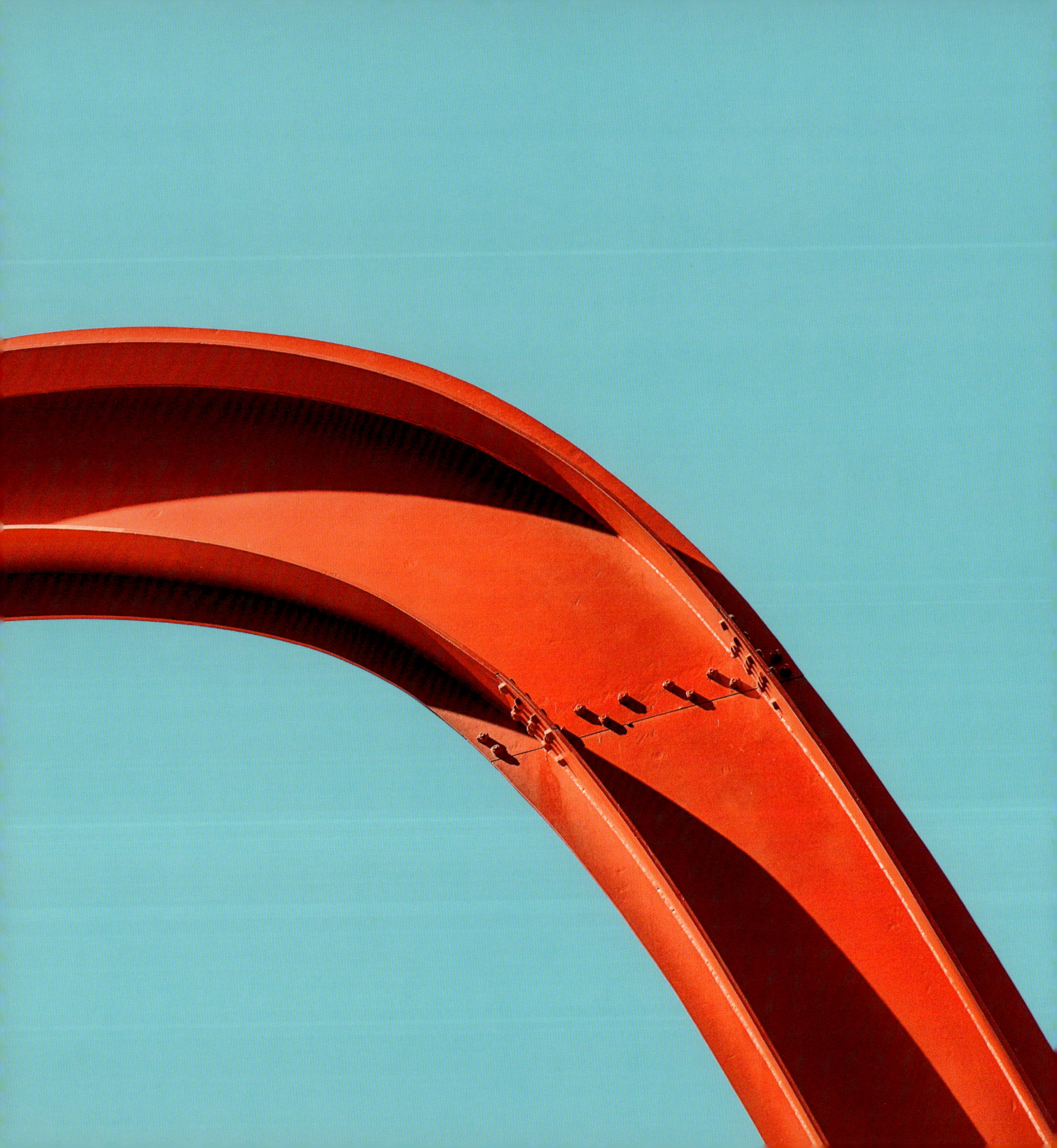

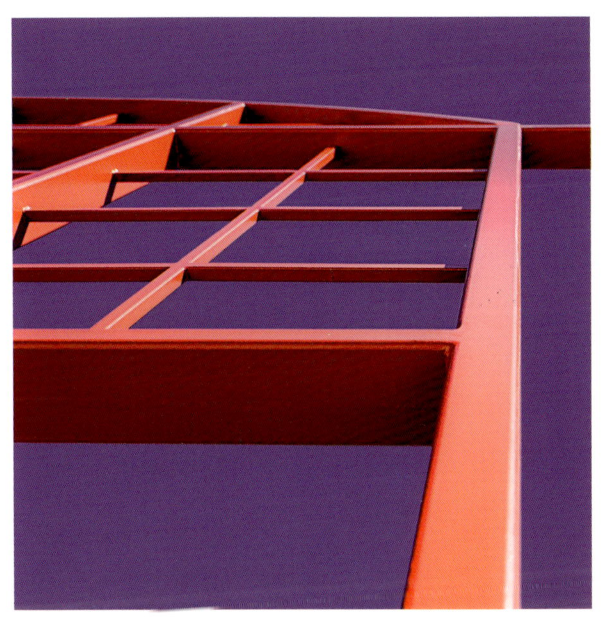

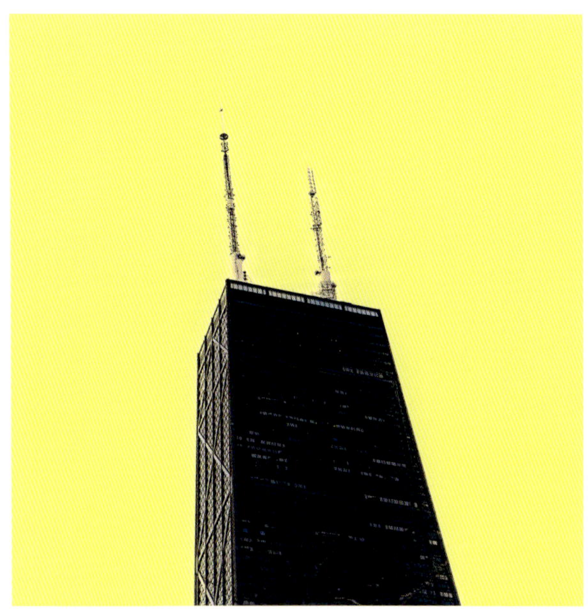

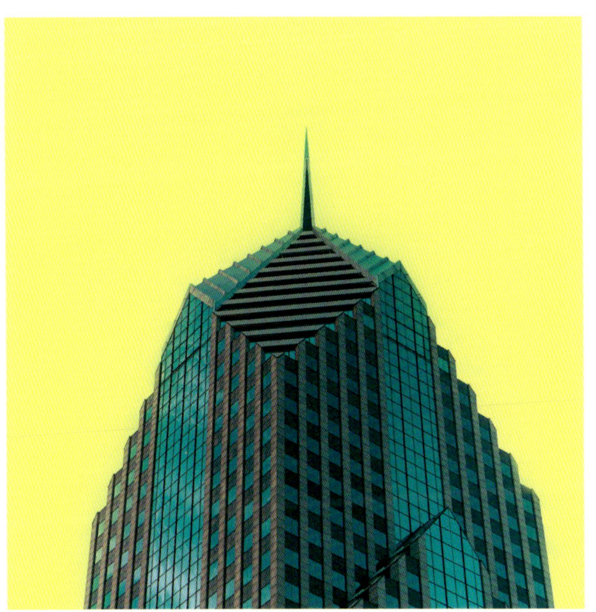

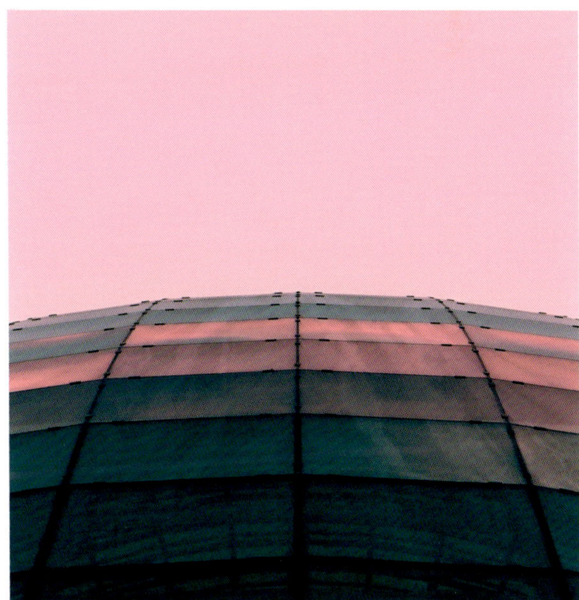

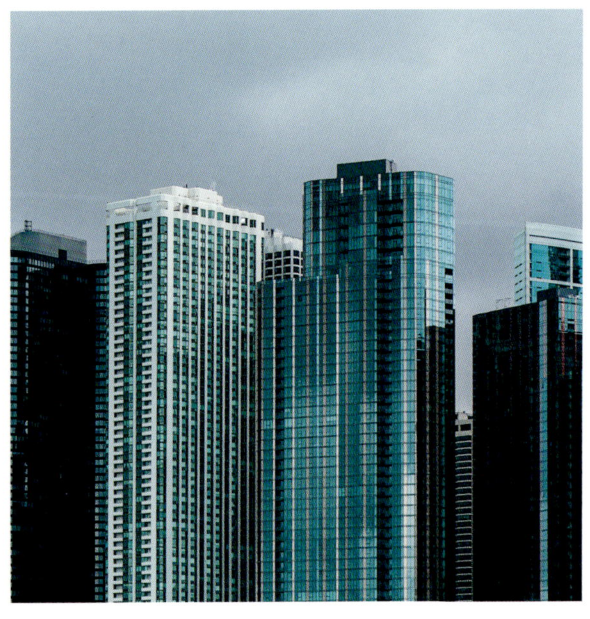

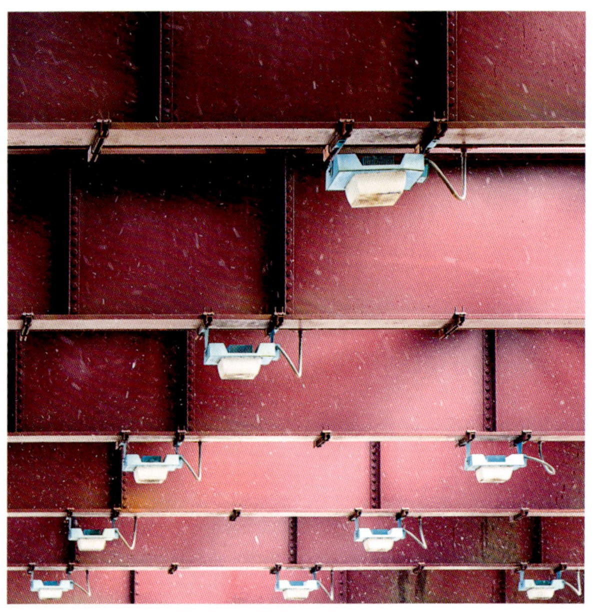

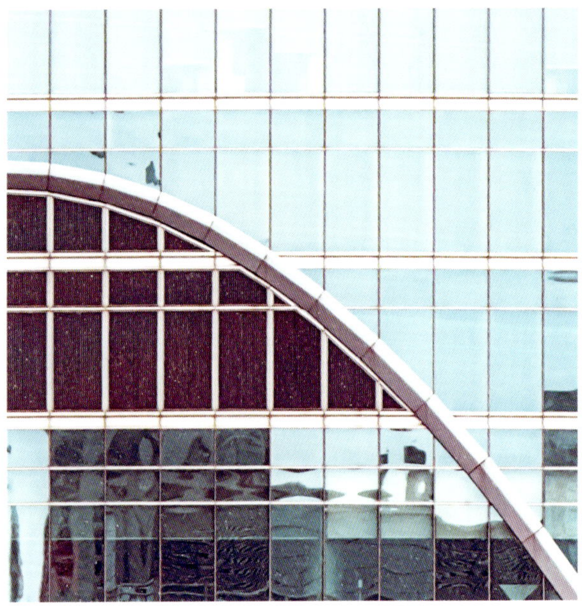

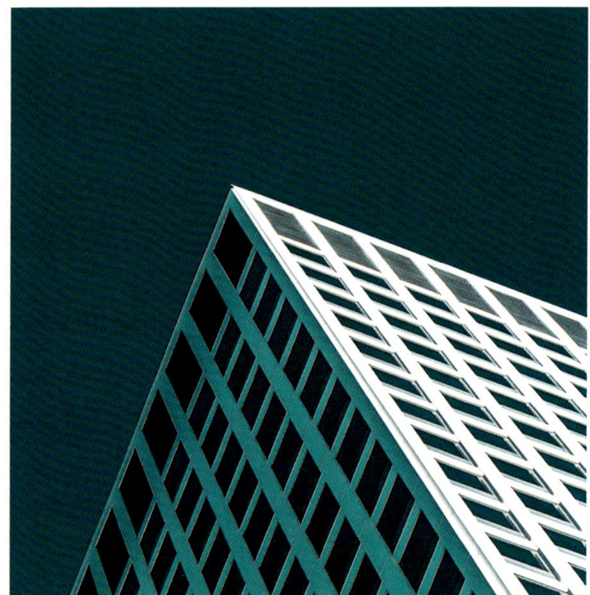

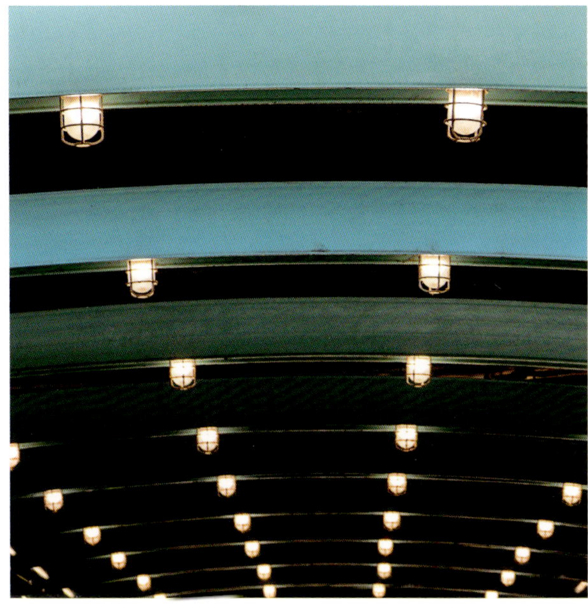
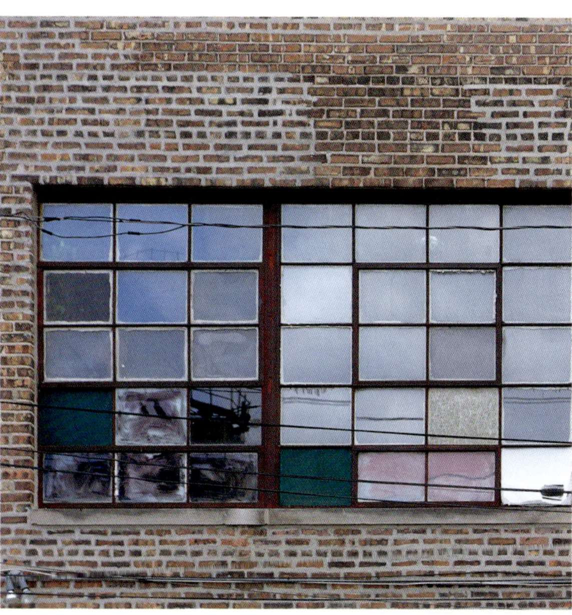
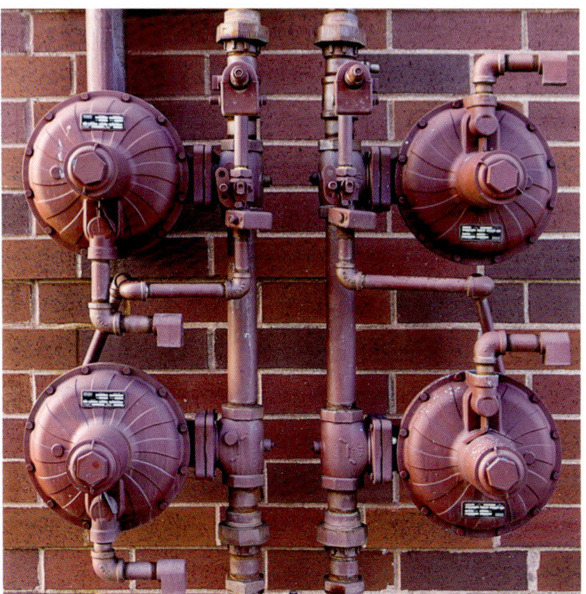
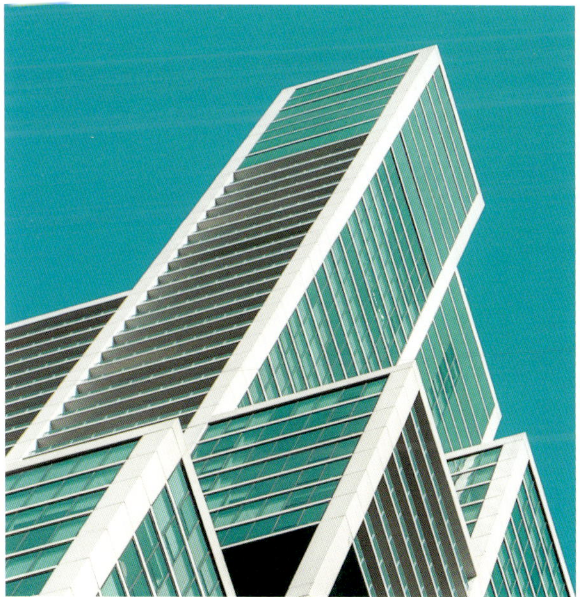

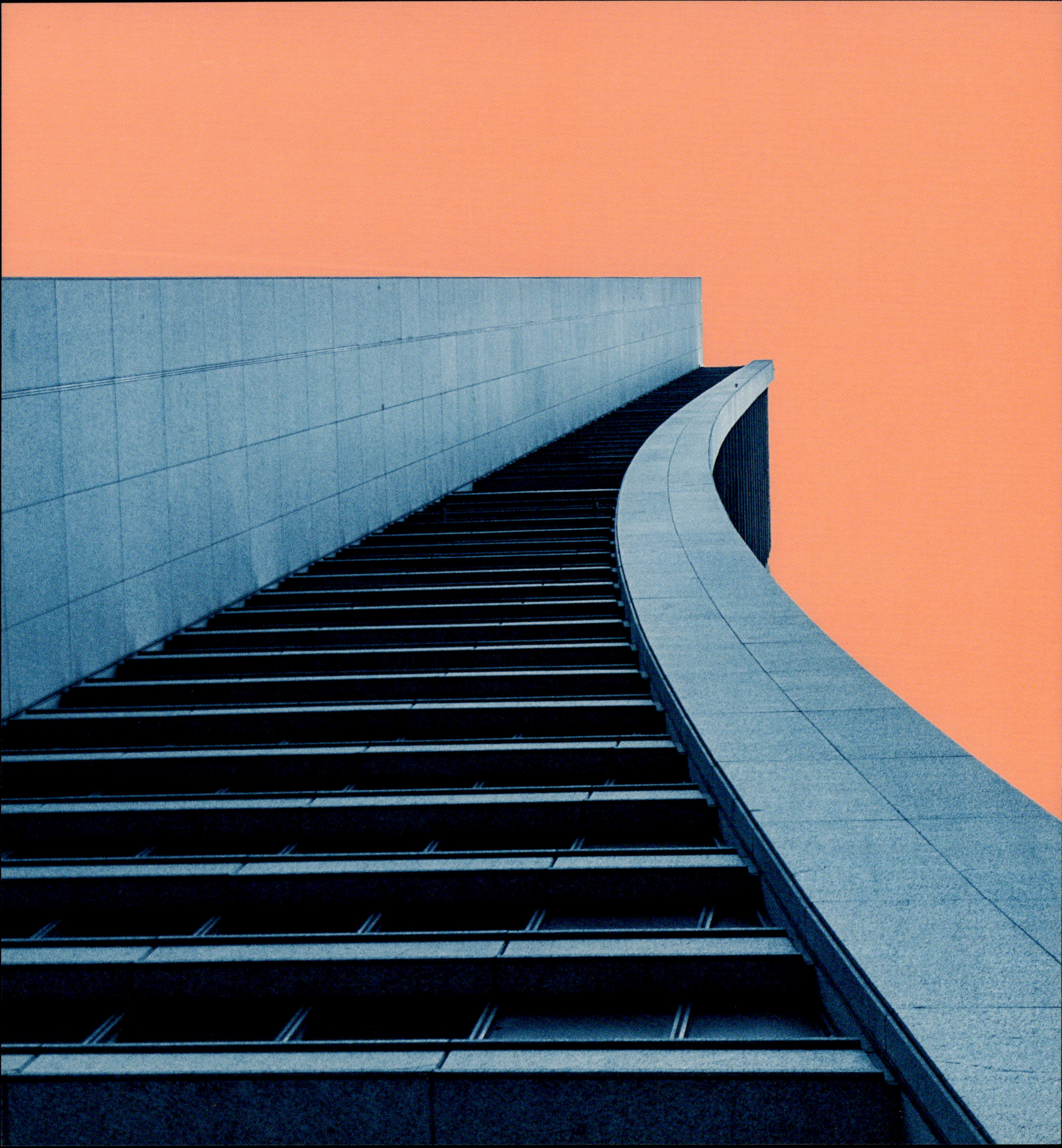

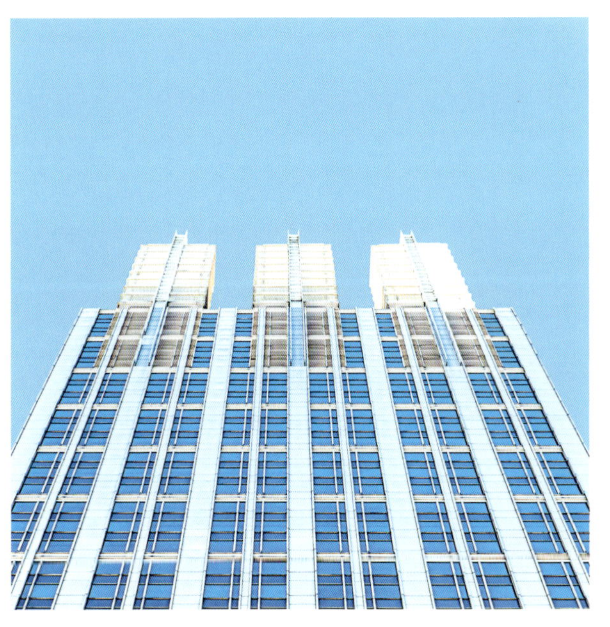

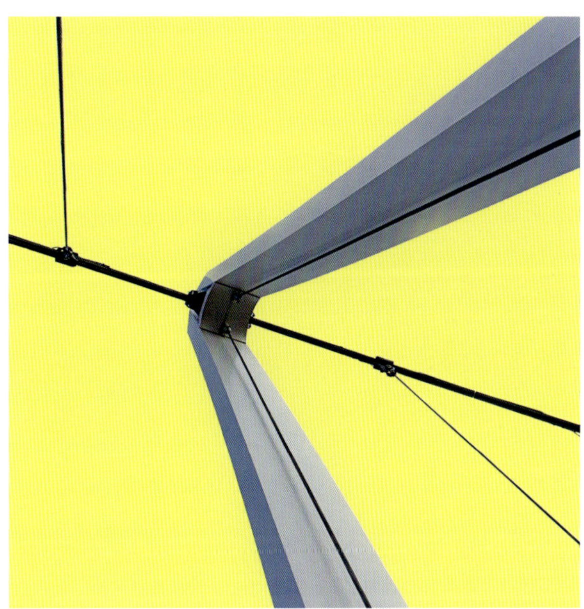

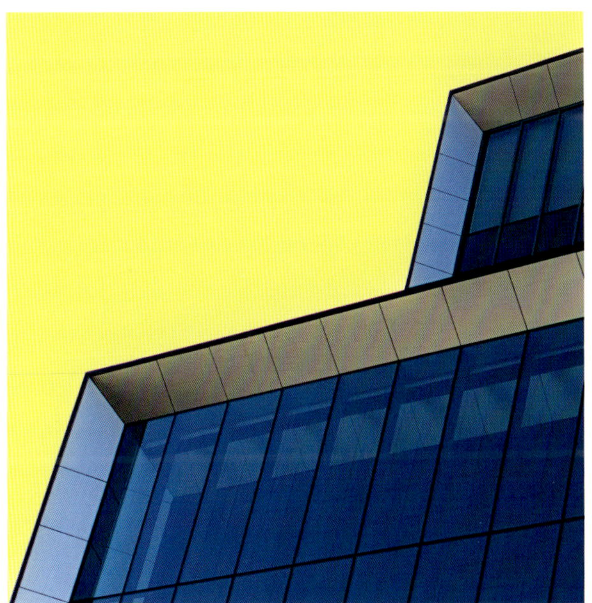

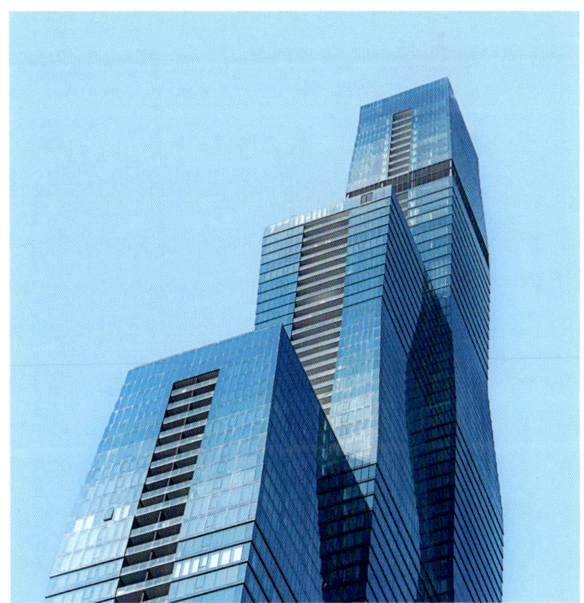

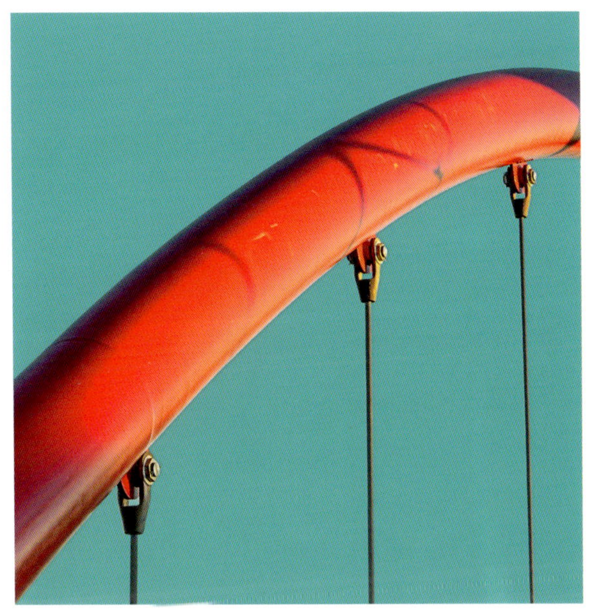
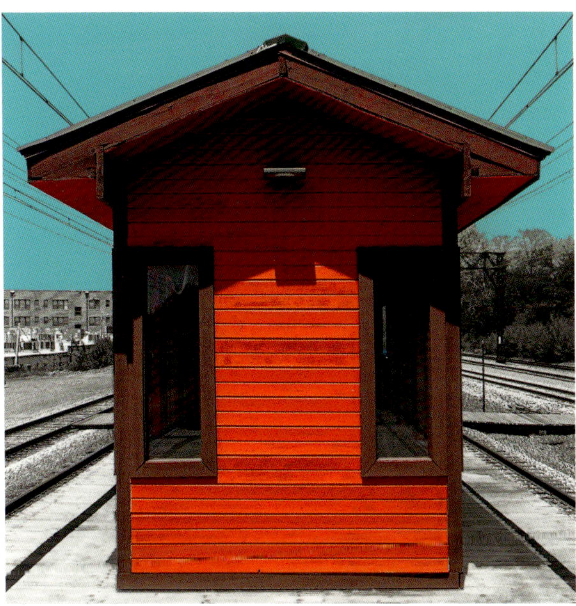
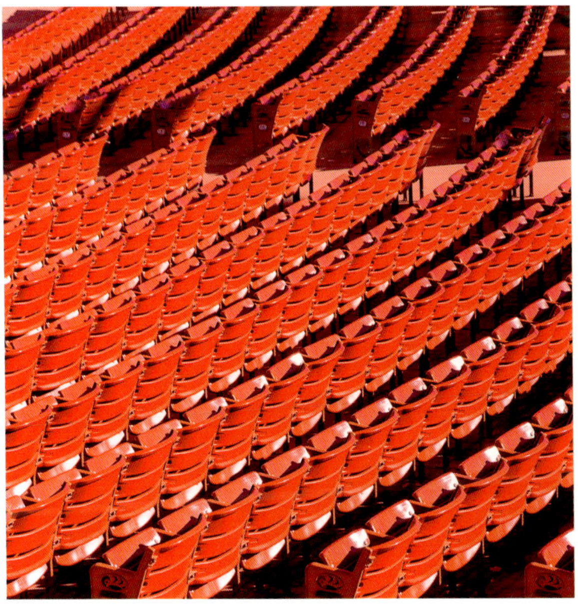
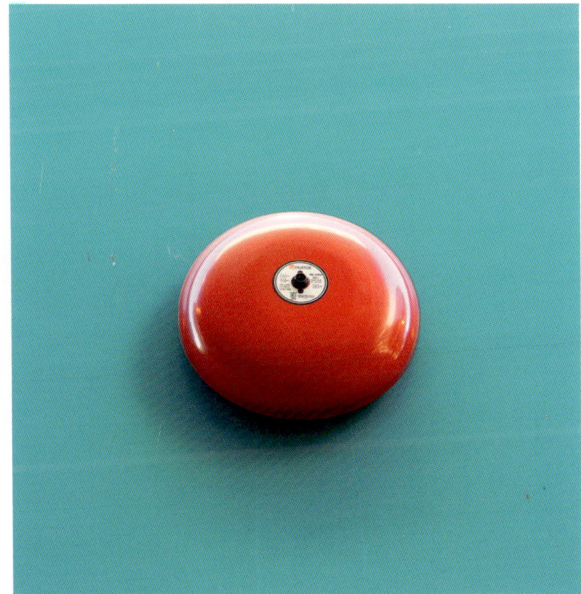

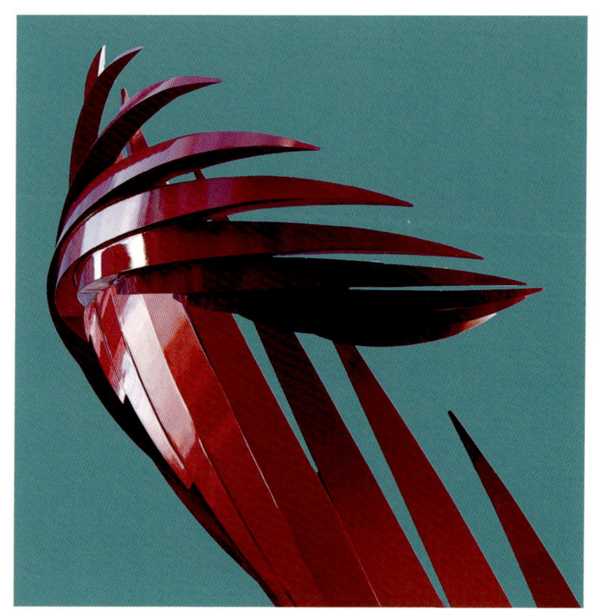
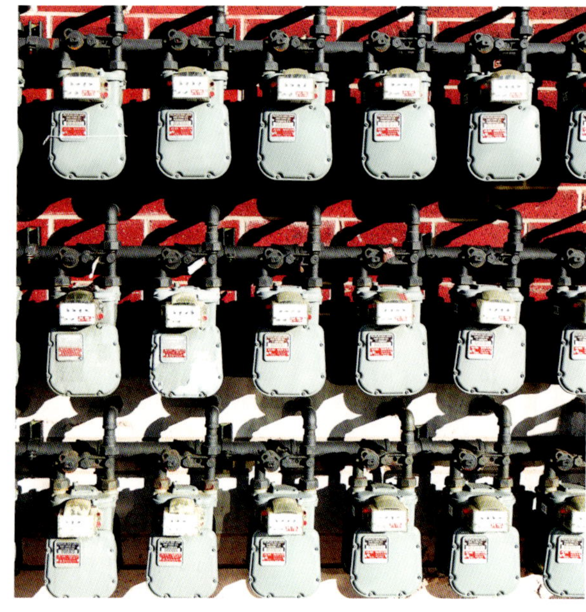
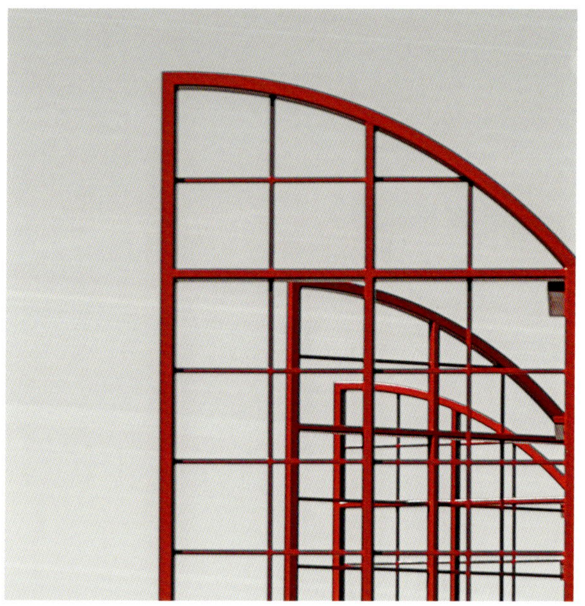
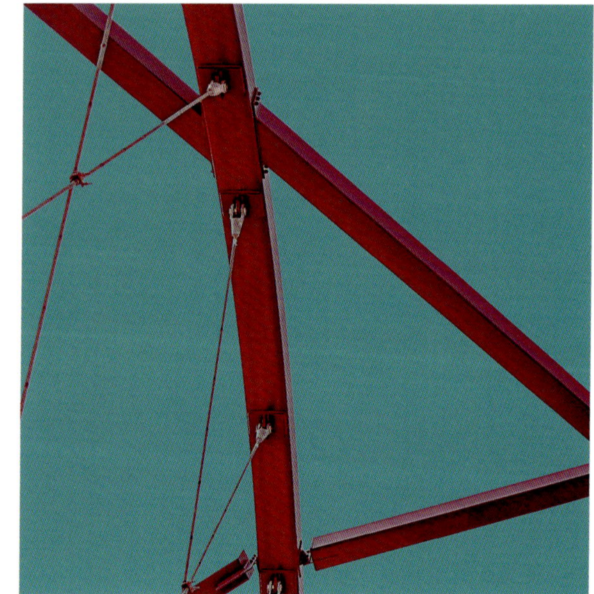

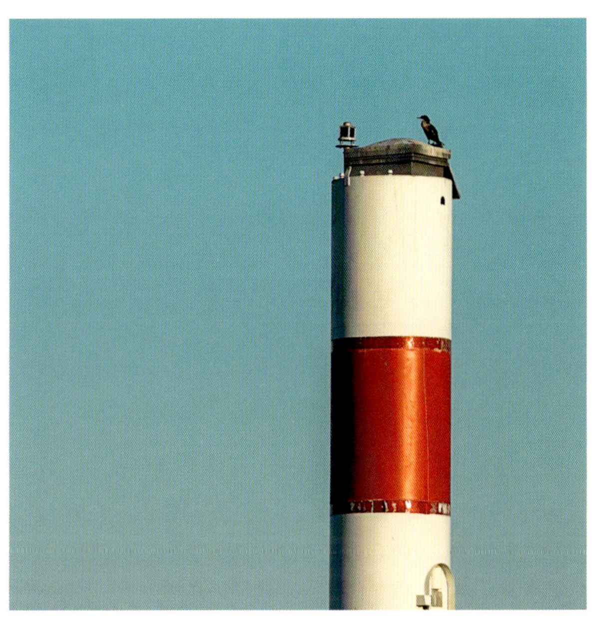
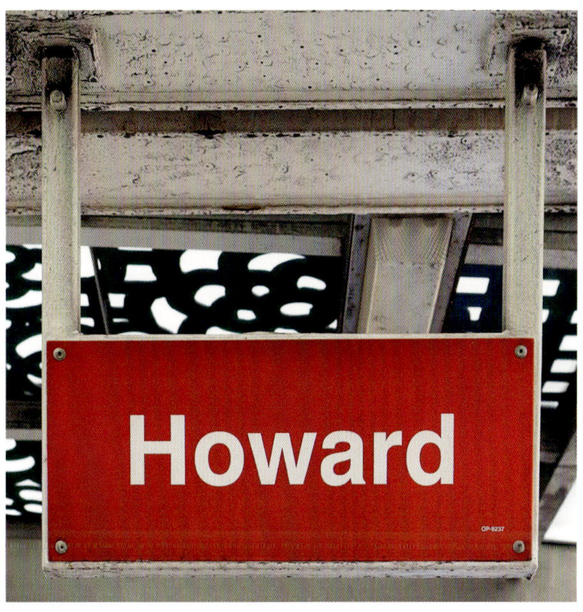

Howard

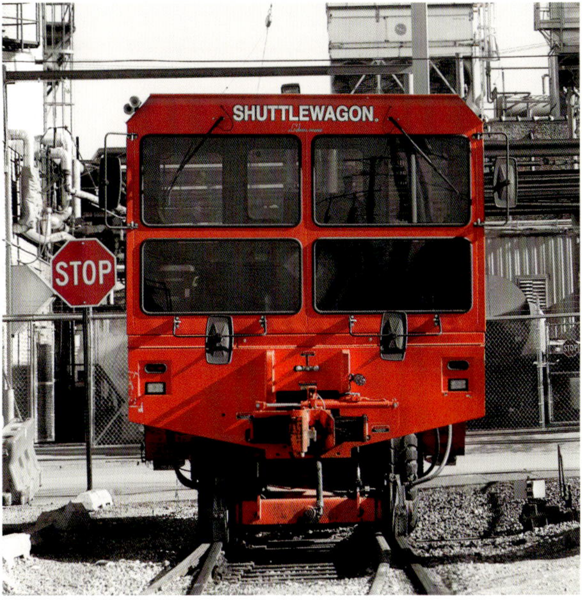

SHUTTLEWAGON.
STOP

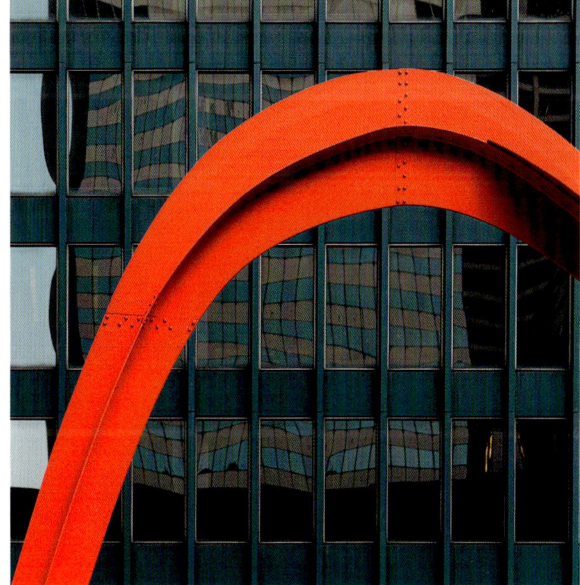

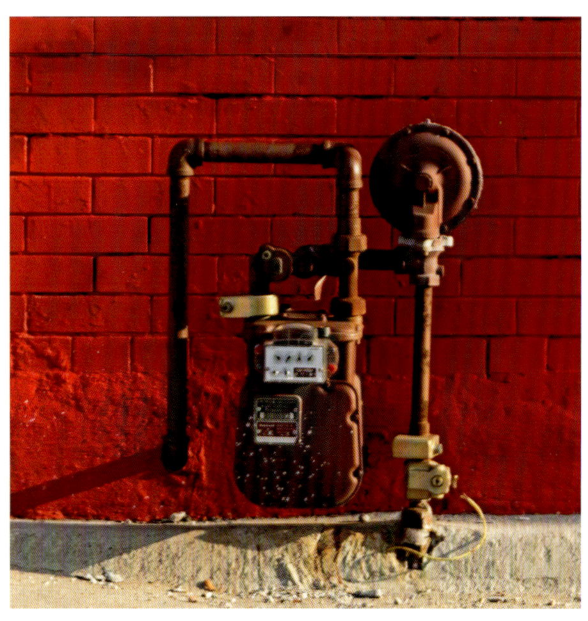
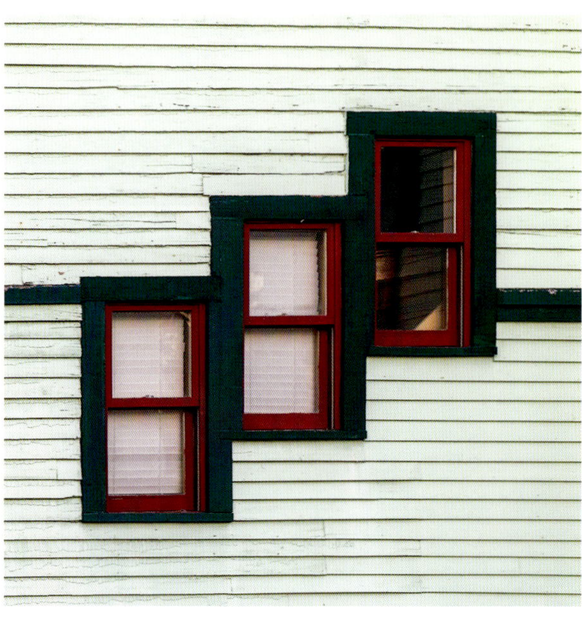
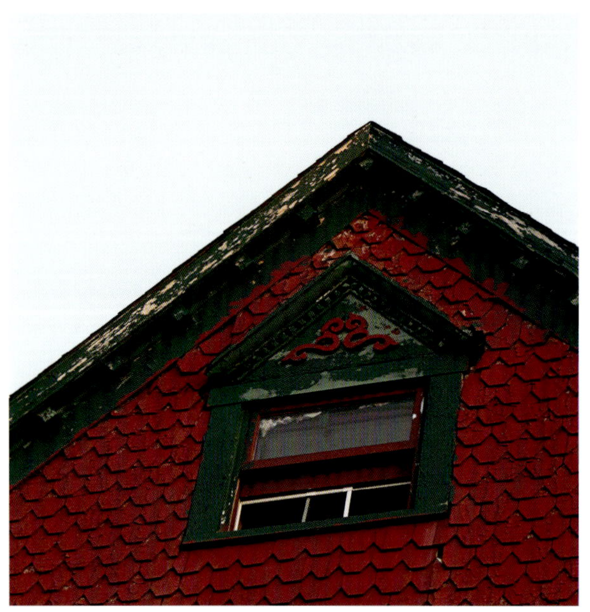
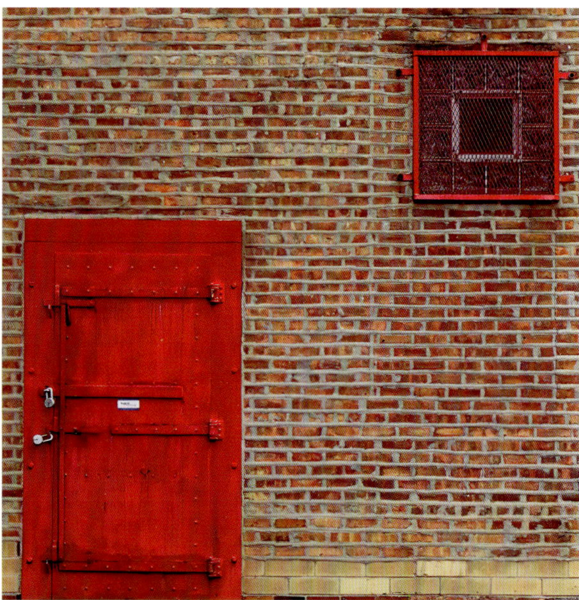

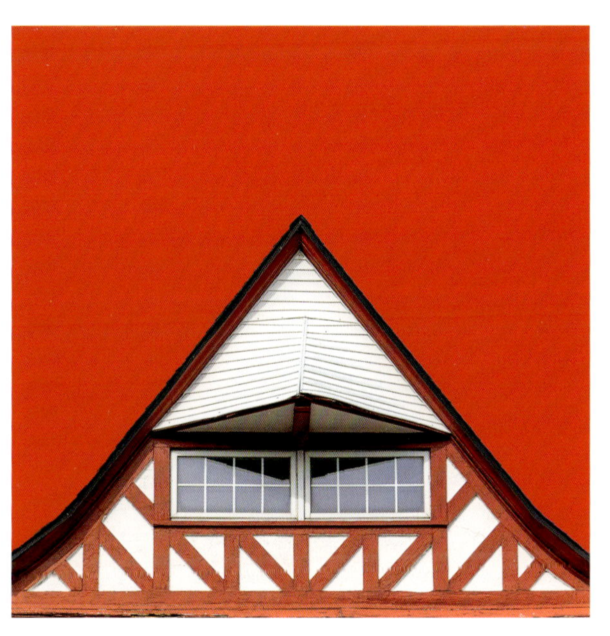
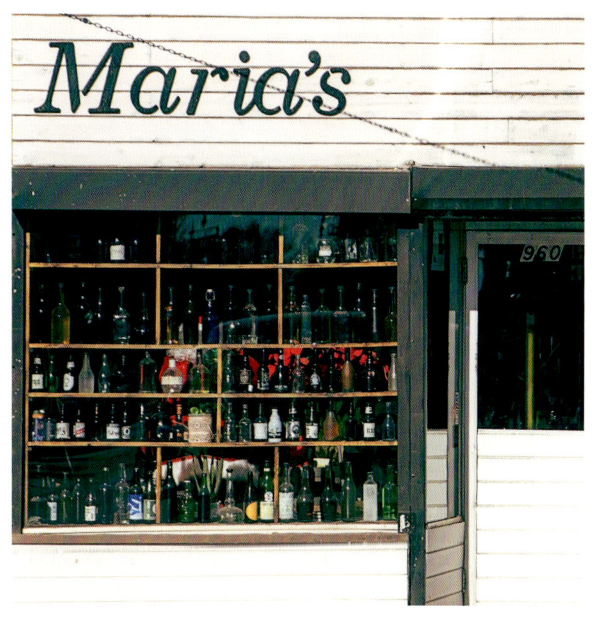
Maria's
960
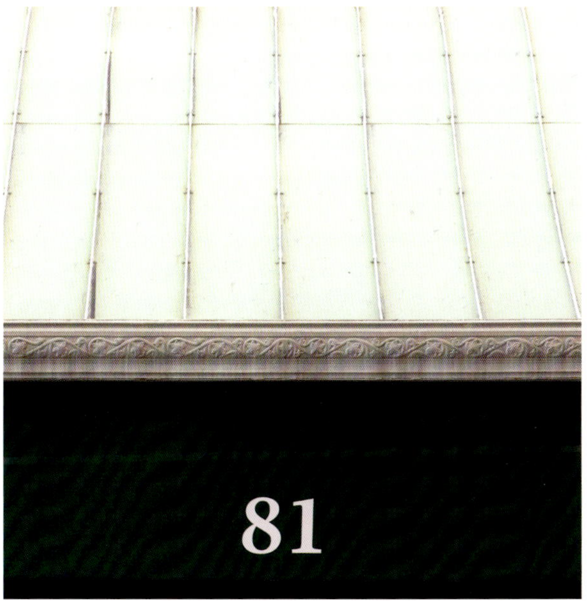
81
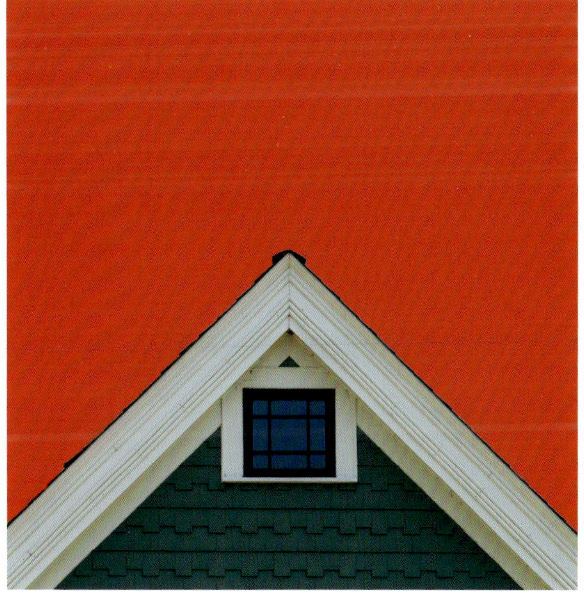

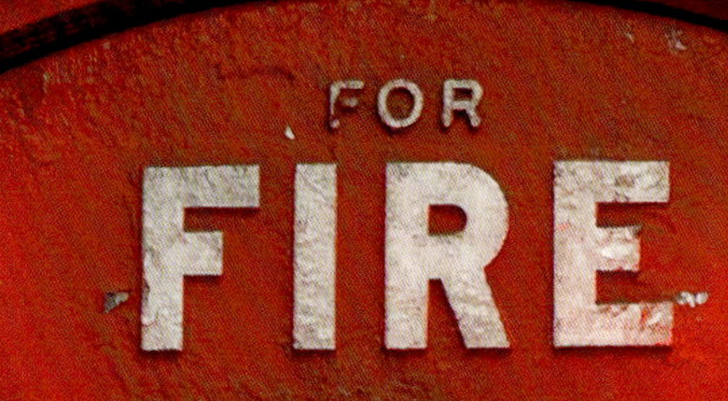

GAMEWELL
FOR
FIRE

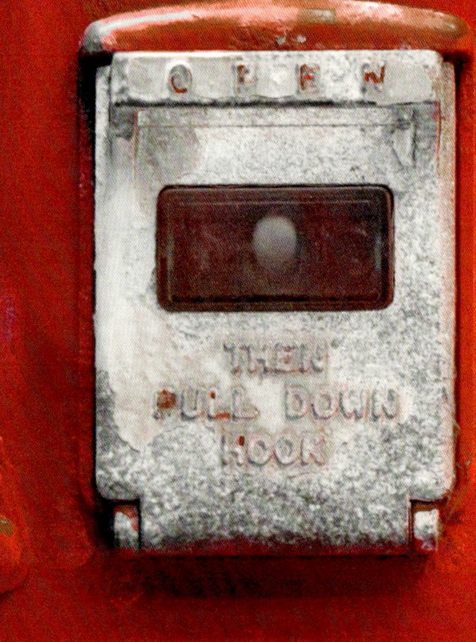

OPEN
THEN
PULL DOWN
HOOK
THE · GAMEWELL · CO
MEDWAY · MASSACHUSETTS

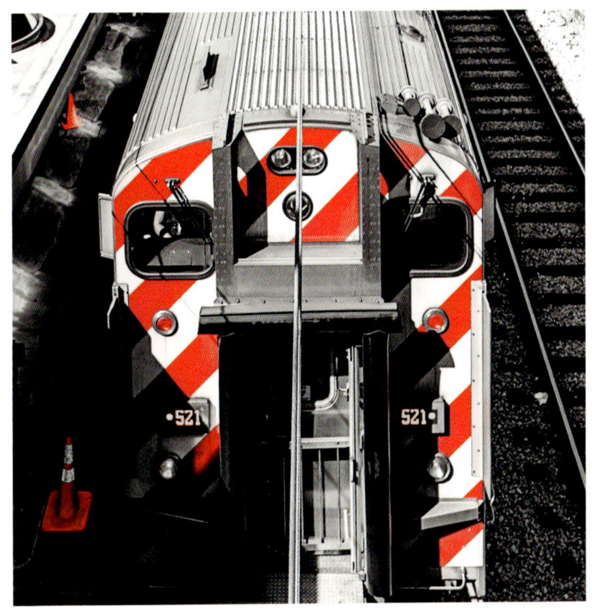
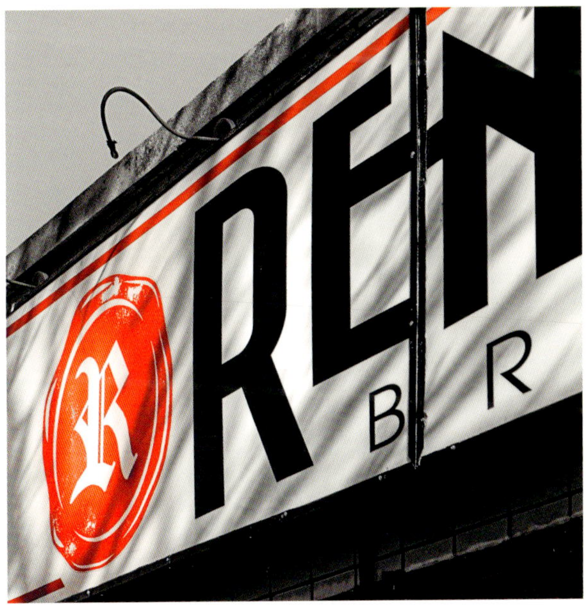
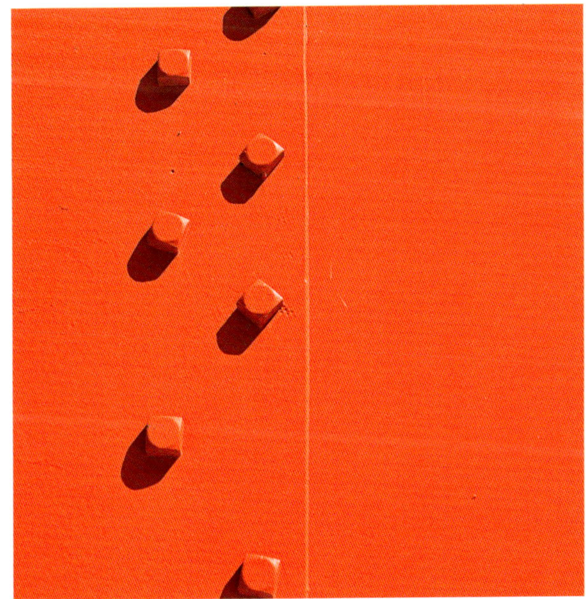

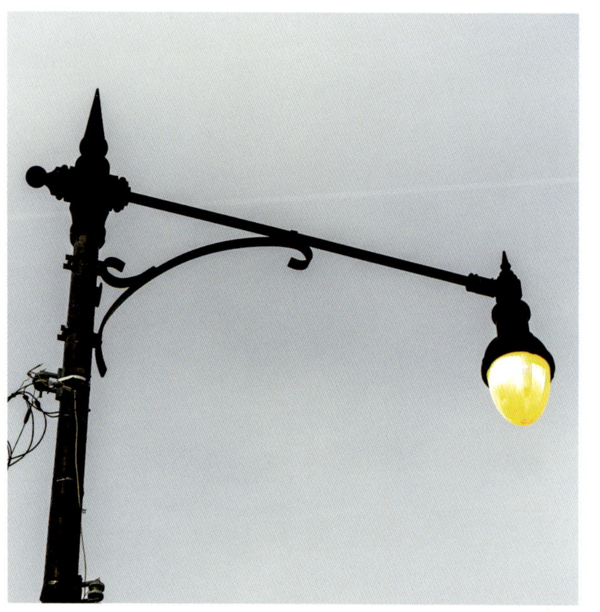
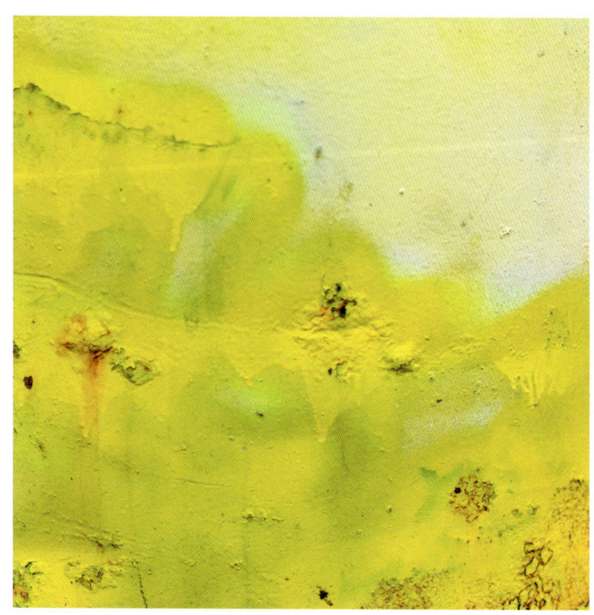
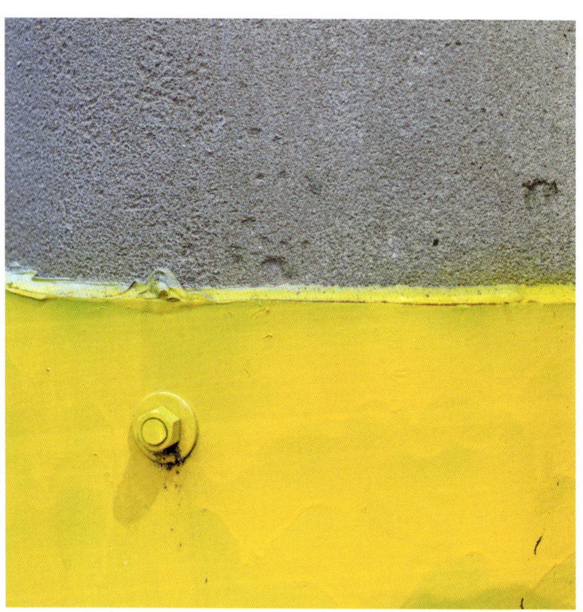
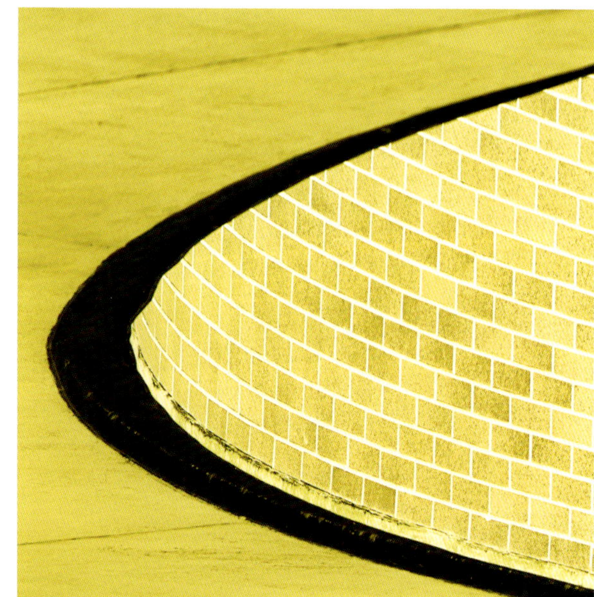

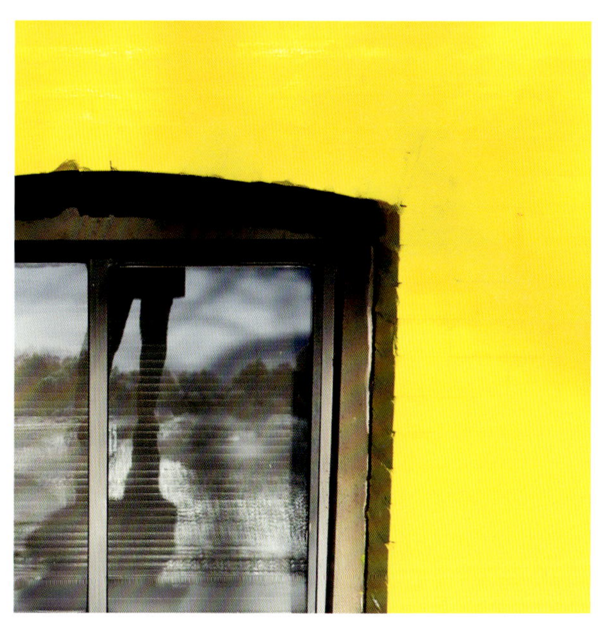
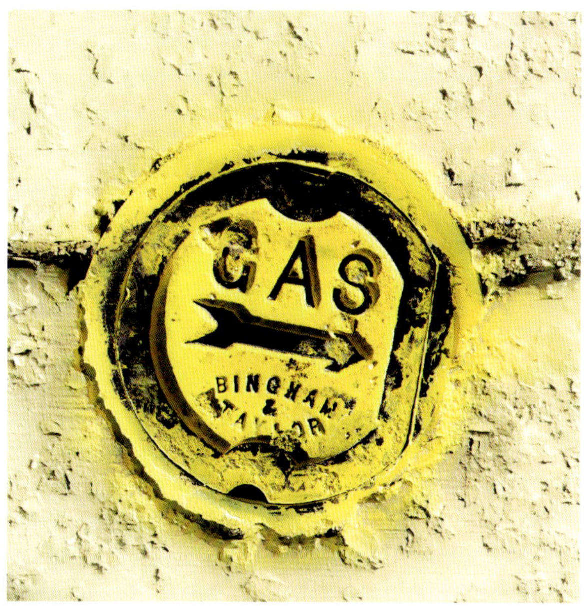

GAS
BINGHAM
&
TAYLOR

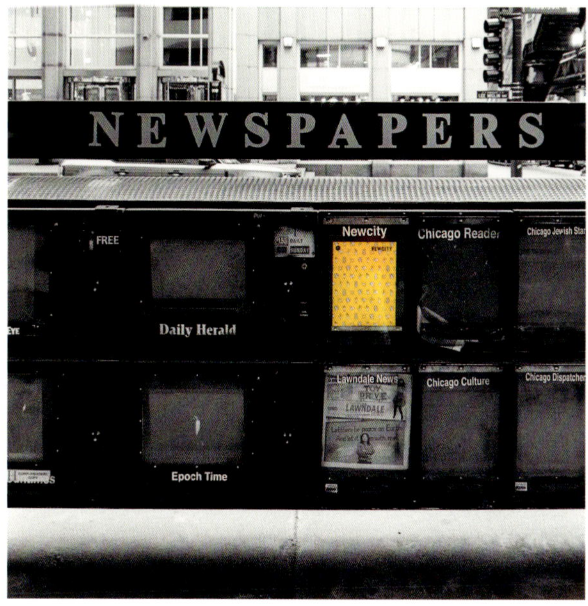

NEWSPAPERS
FREE
Newcity
Chicago Reader
Chicago Jewish Star
Daily Herald
Lawndale News
Chicago Culture
Chicago Dispatcher
Epoch Time

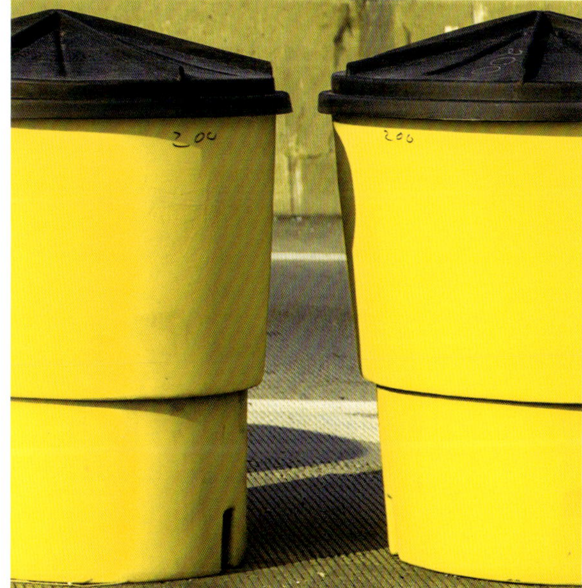

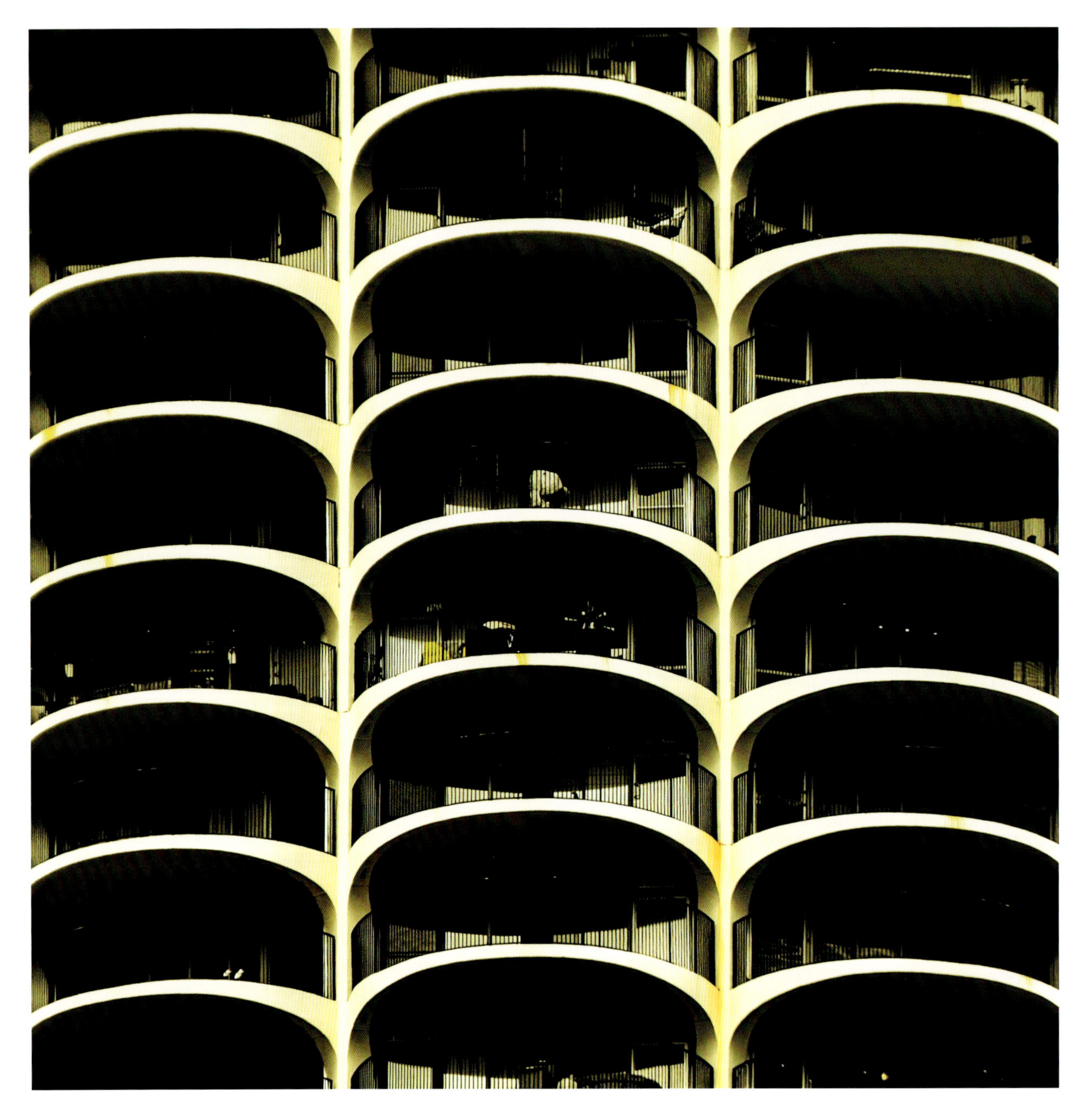

I try to apply colors like
words that shape poems,
like notes that shape music.

– Joan Miró

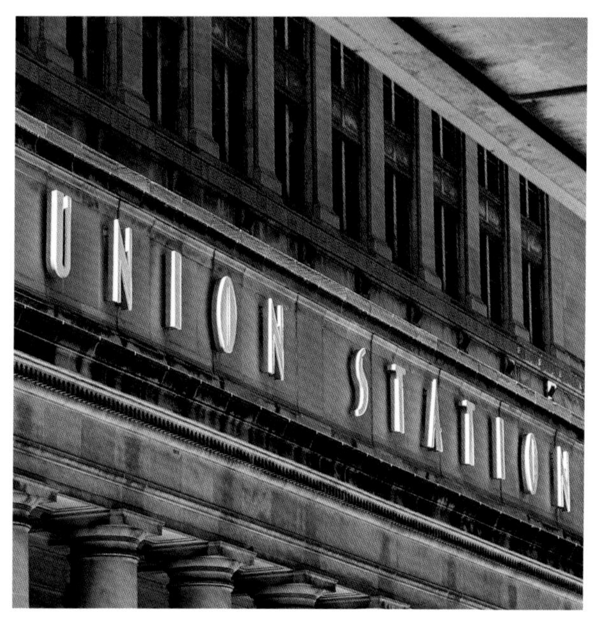

UNION STATION

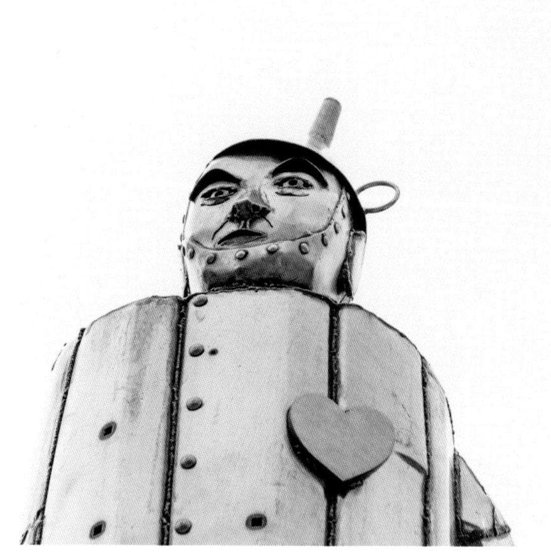

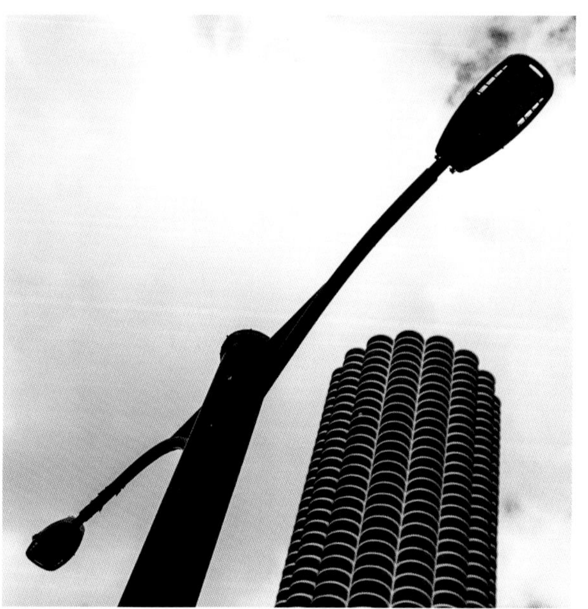

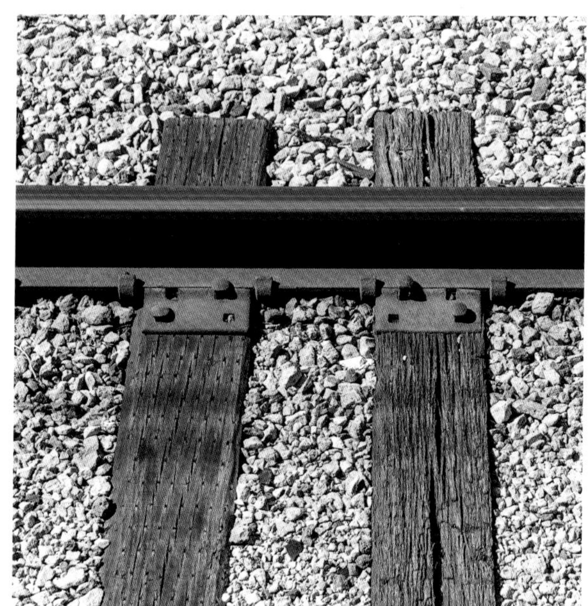

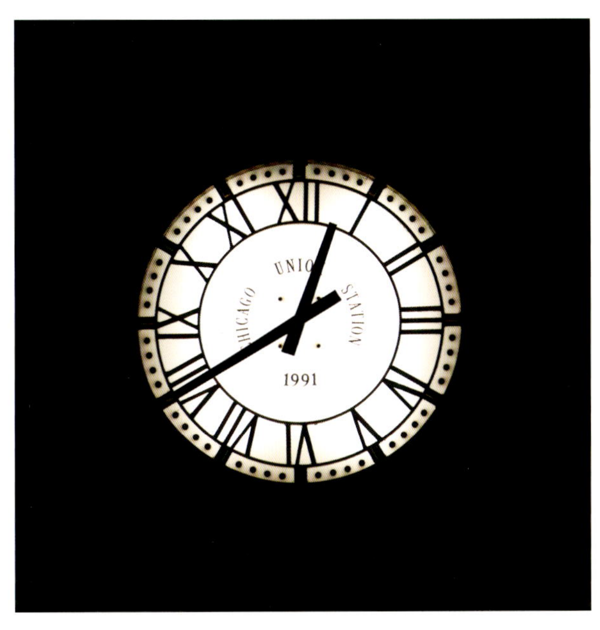
CHICAGO UNION STATION
1991

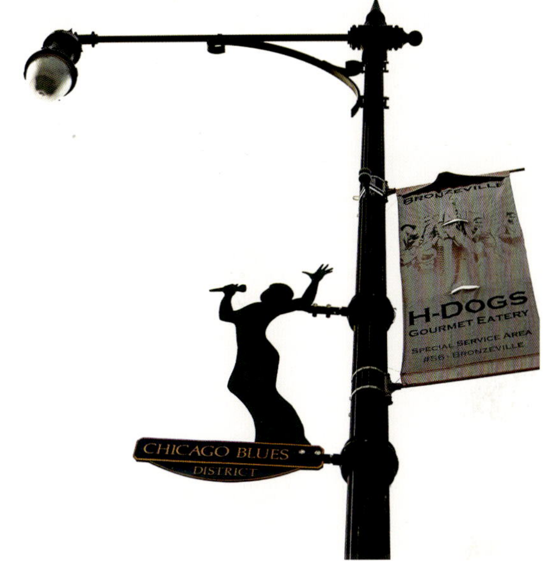
BRONZEVILLE
H-DOGS
GOURMET EATERY
SPECIAL SERVICE AREA
#56 · BRONZEVILLE
CHICAGO BLUES
DISTRICT

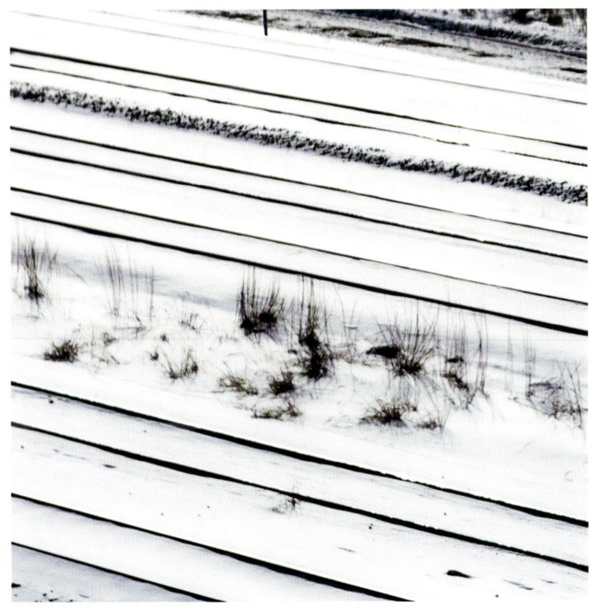

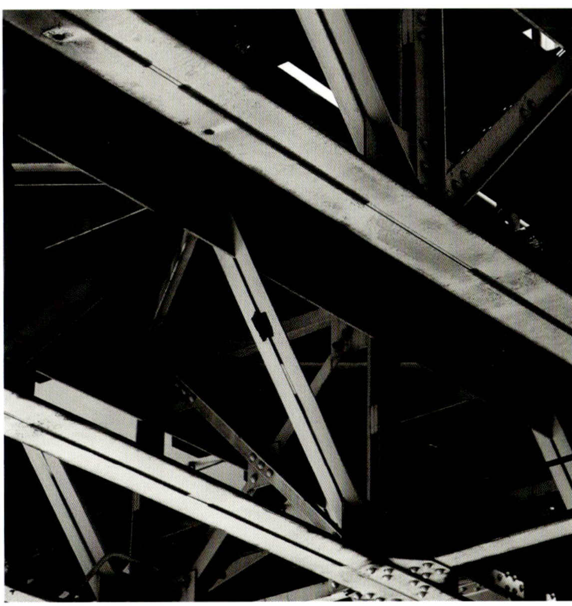

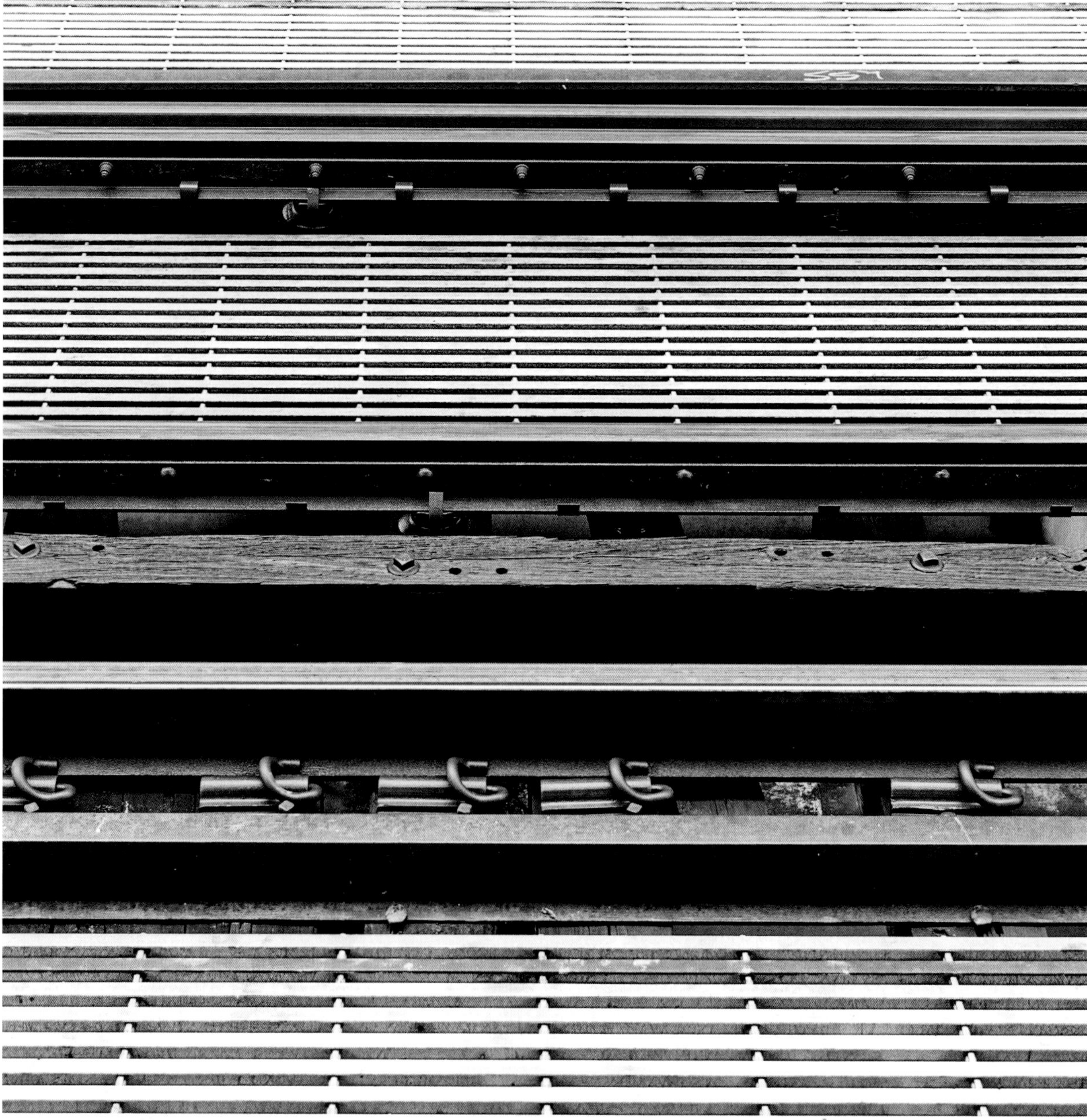

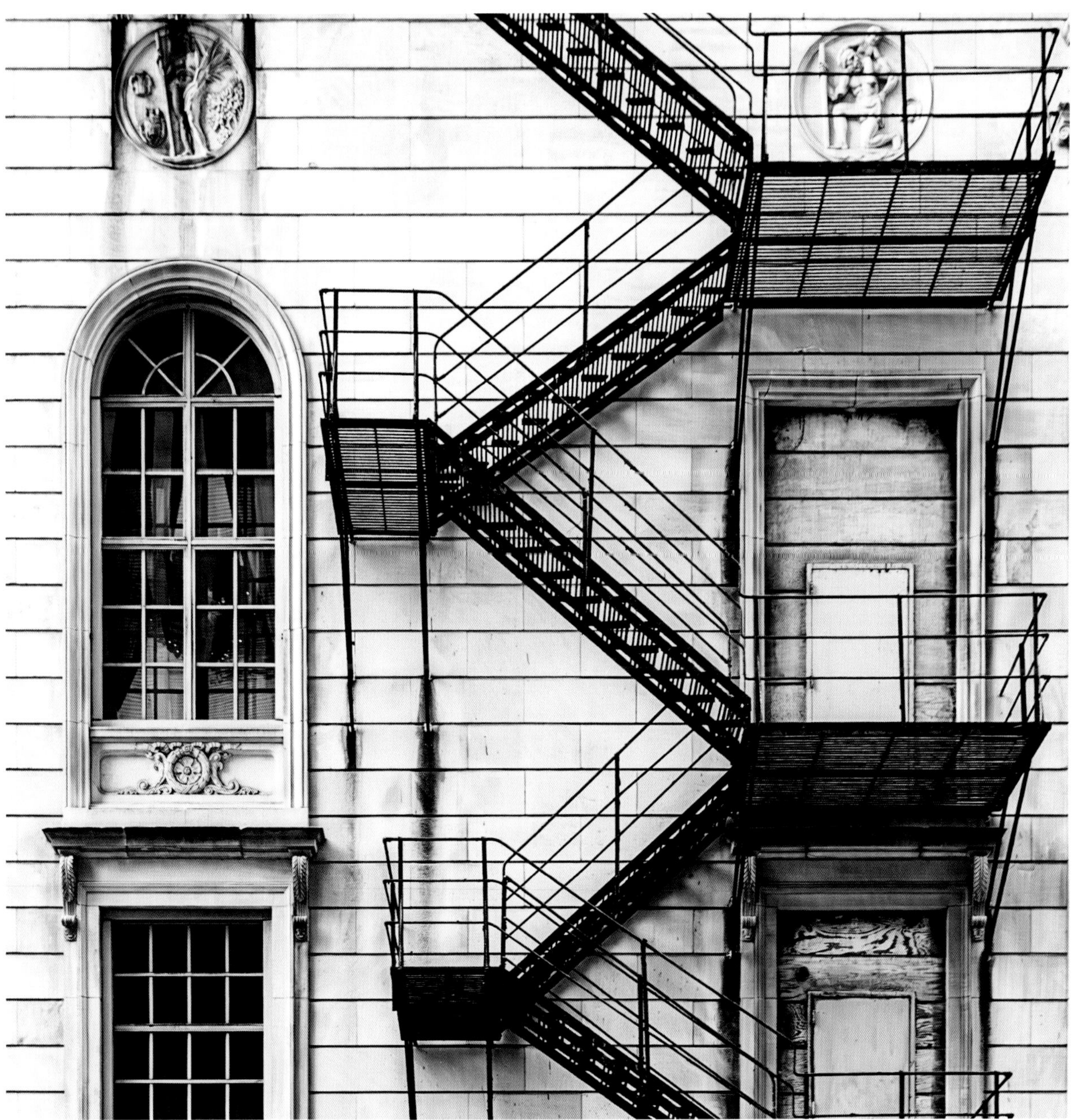

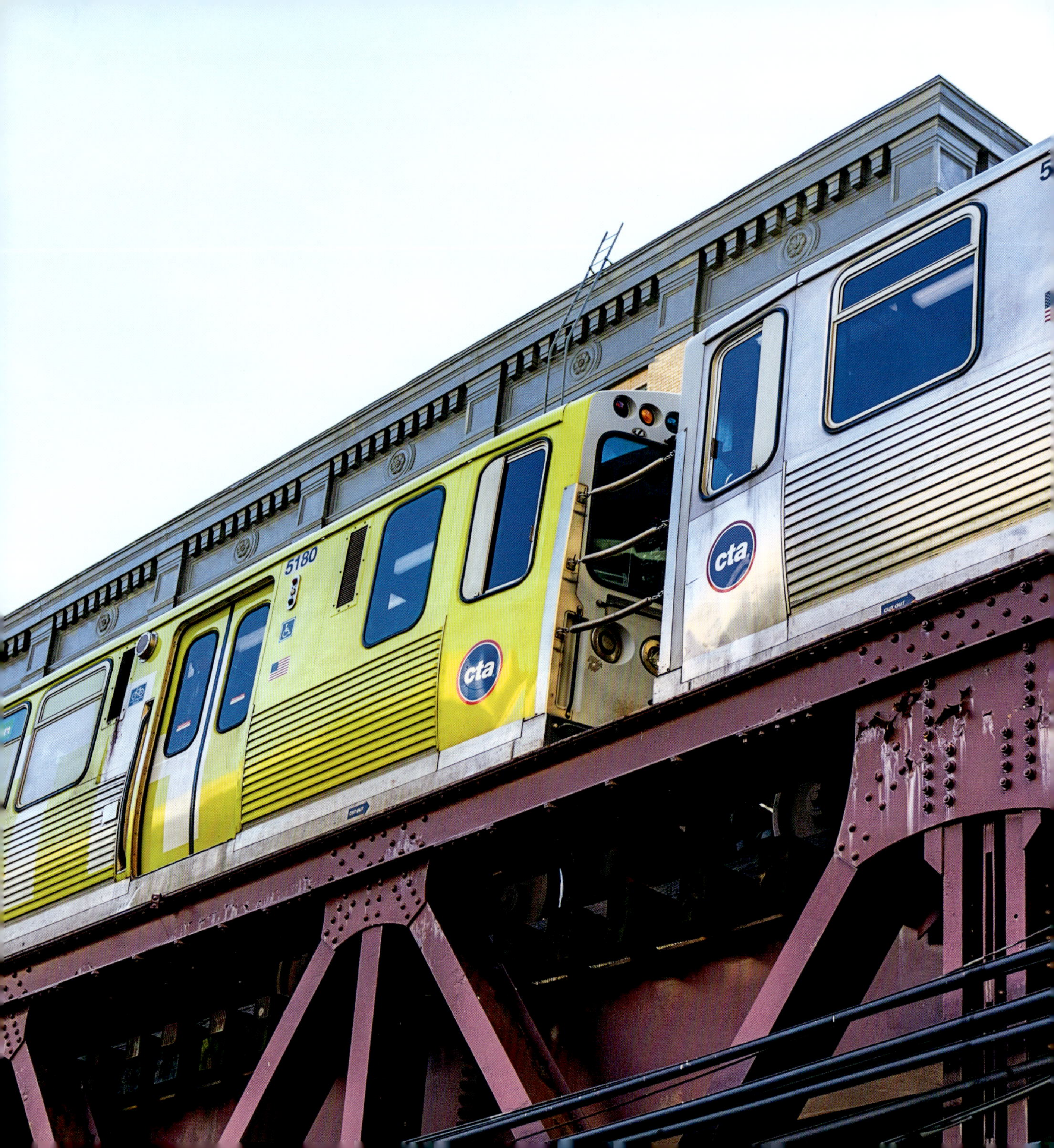

5180
cta
cta

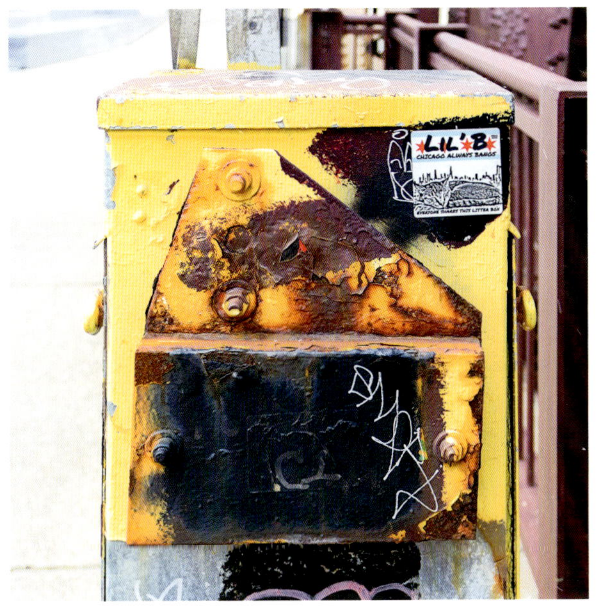

LIL B
CHICAGO ALWAYS BANGS

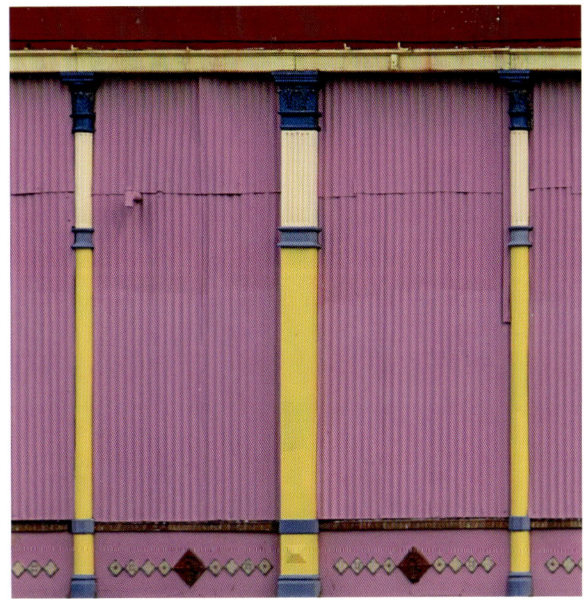

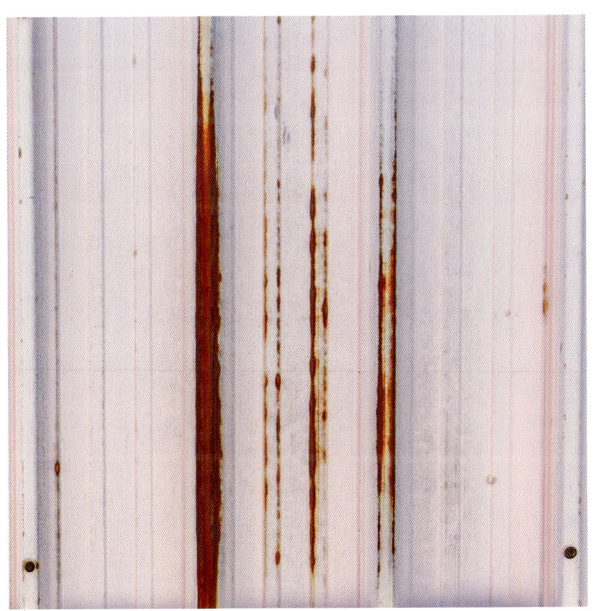

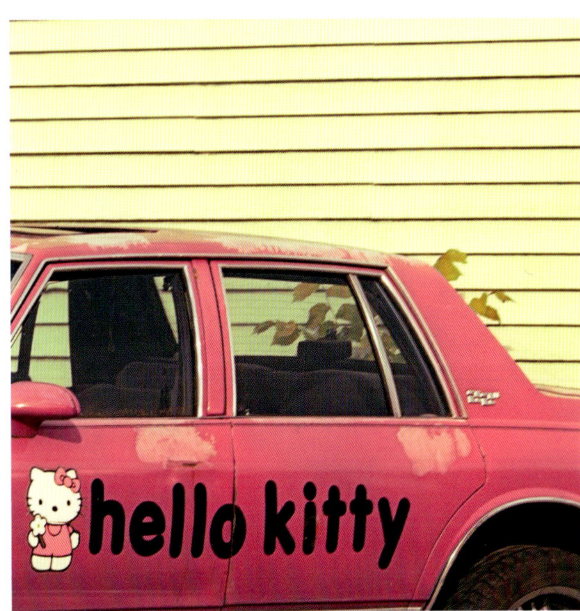

hello kitty

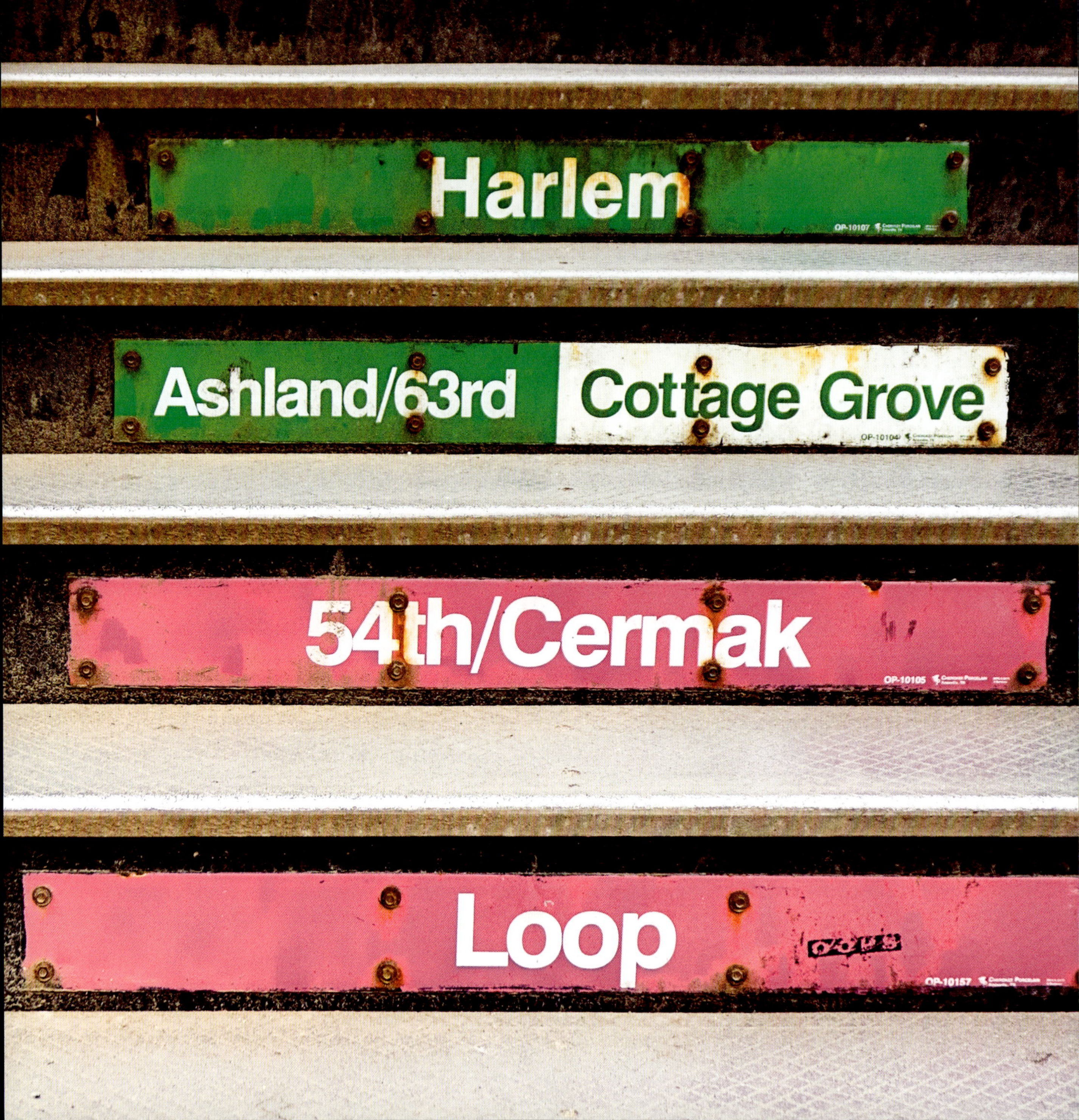

Harlem
Ashland/63rd
Cottage Grove
54th/Cermak
Loop

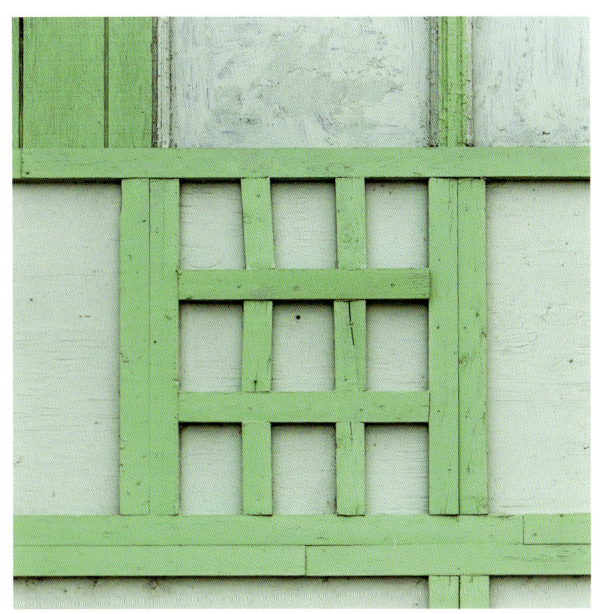
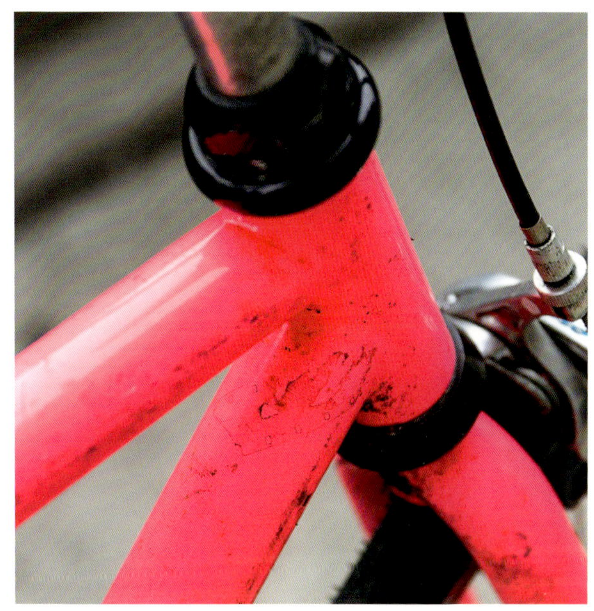
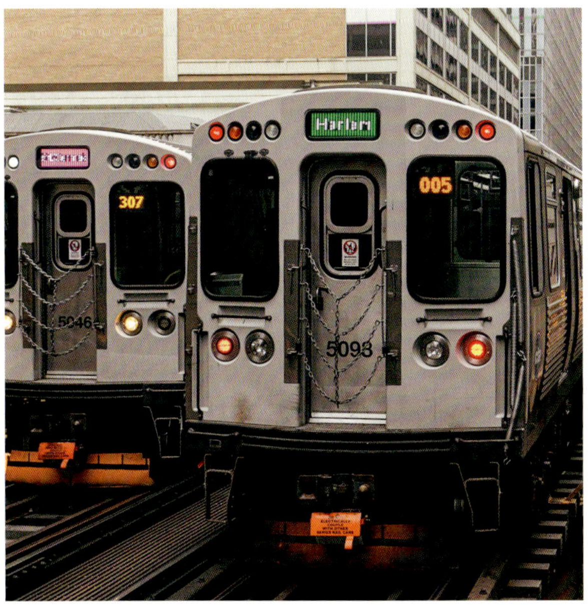
Harlem
307
005
5046
5093
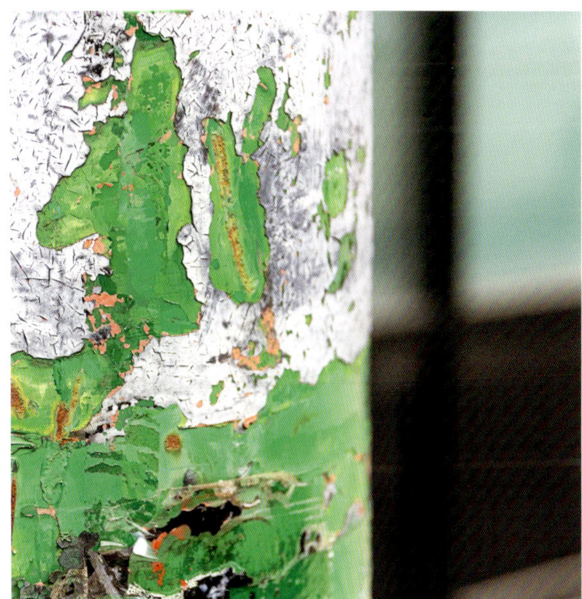

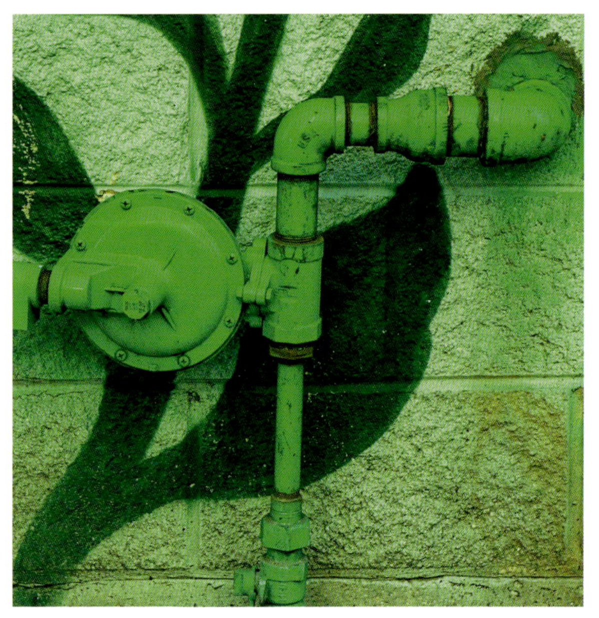
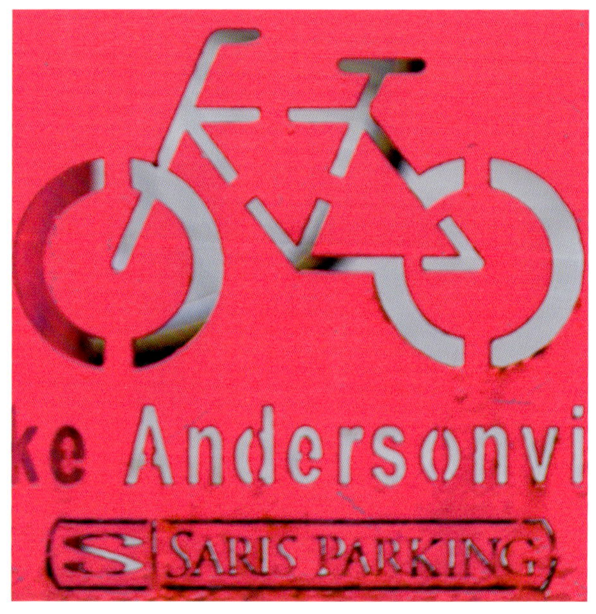

ke Andersonvi
SARIS PARKING

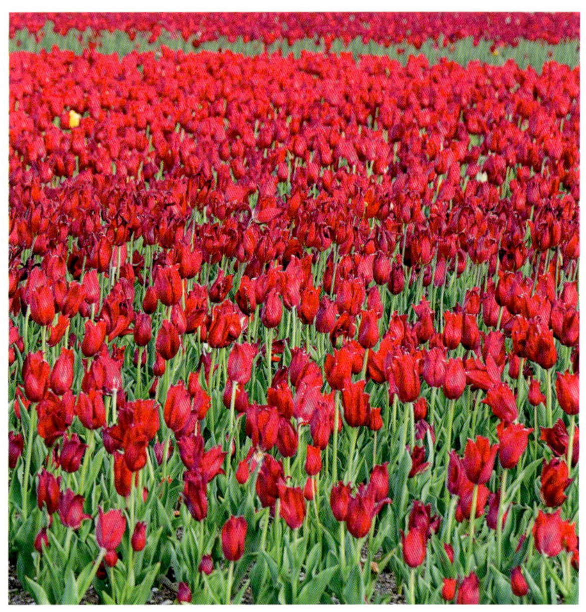
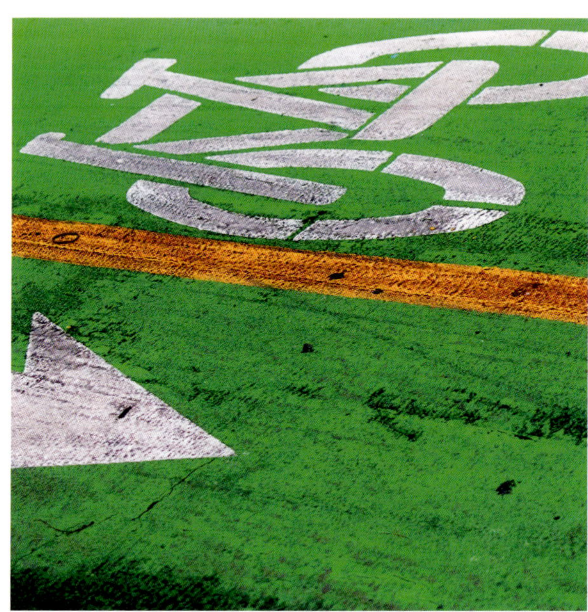

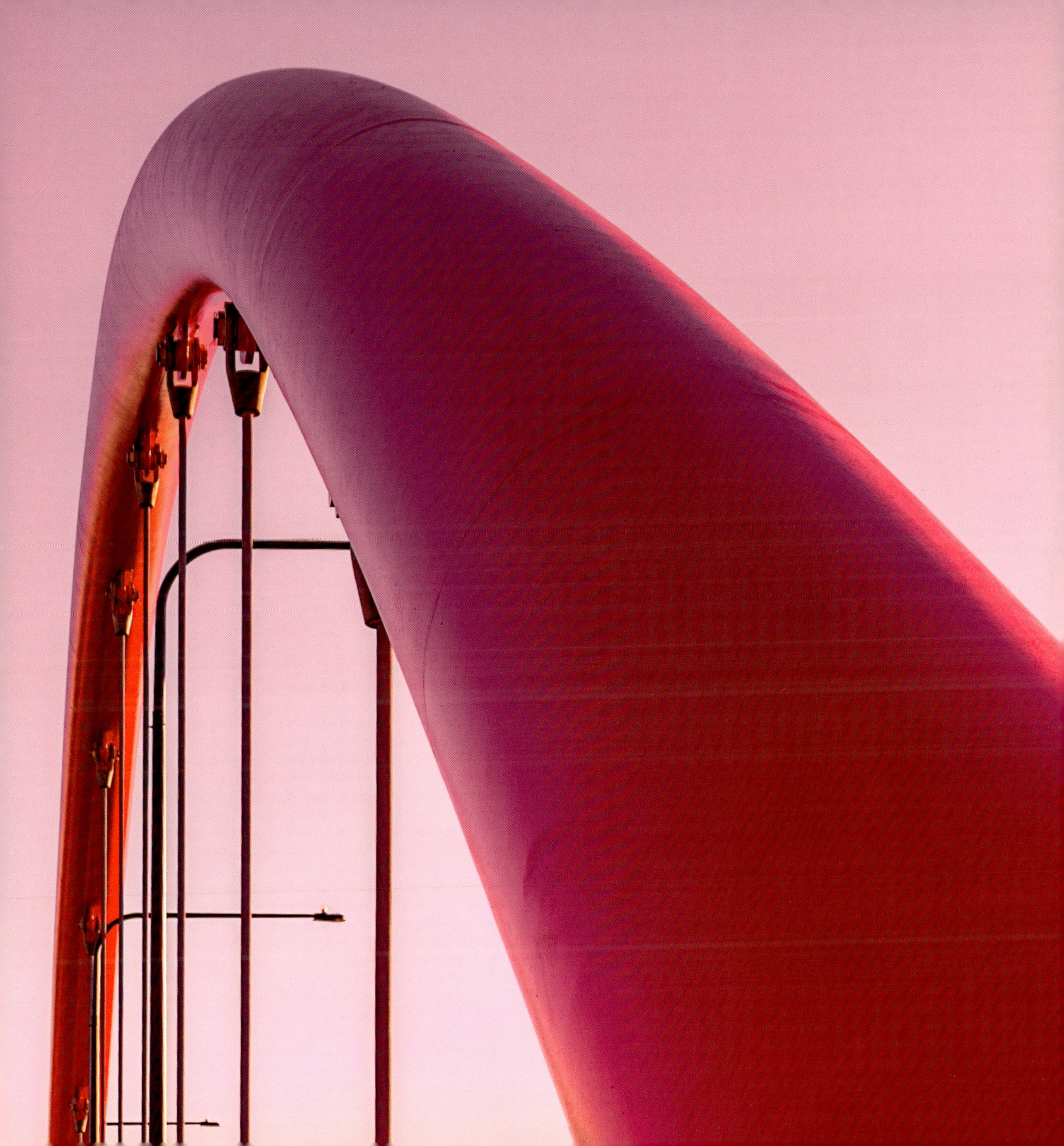

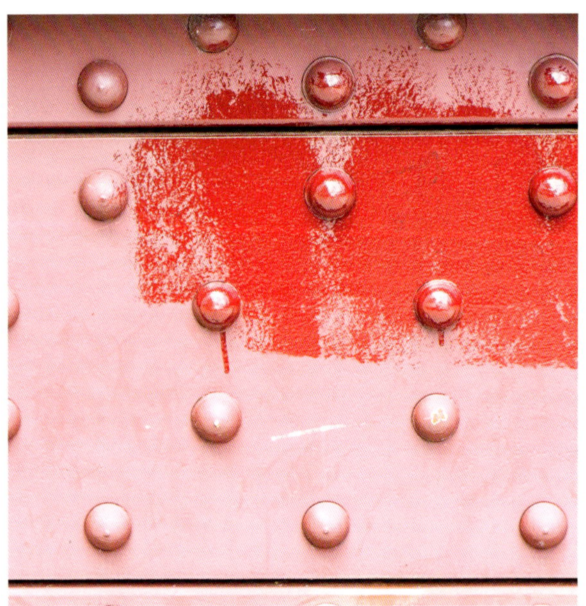
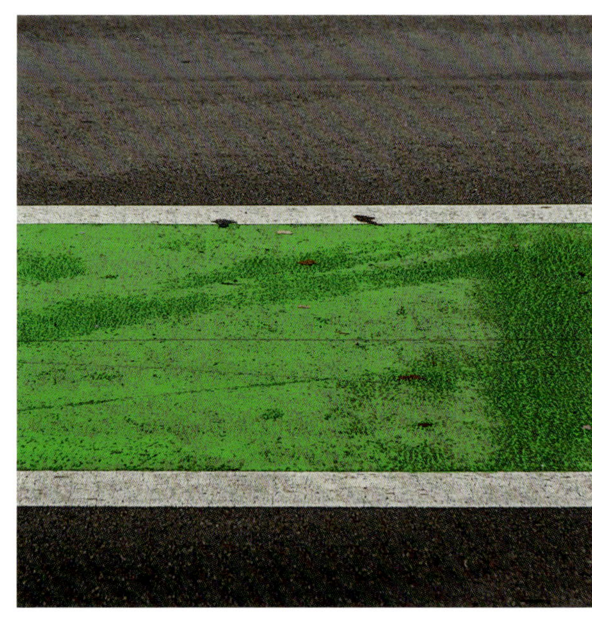
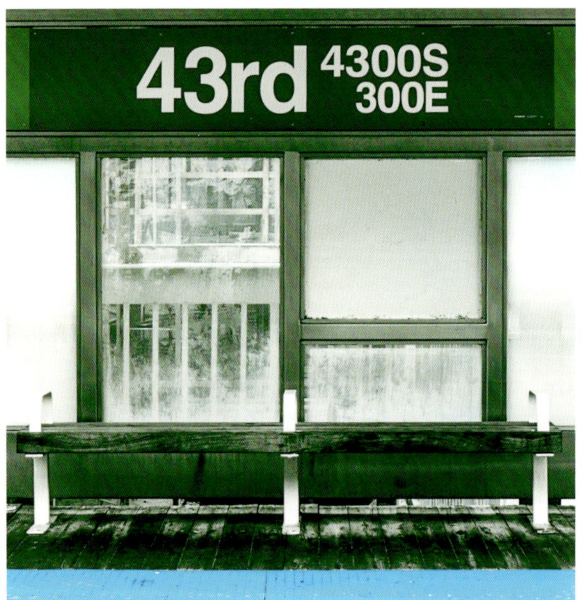

43rd 4300S 300E

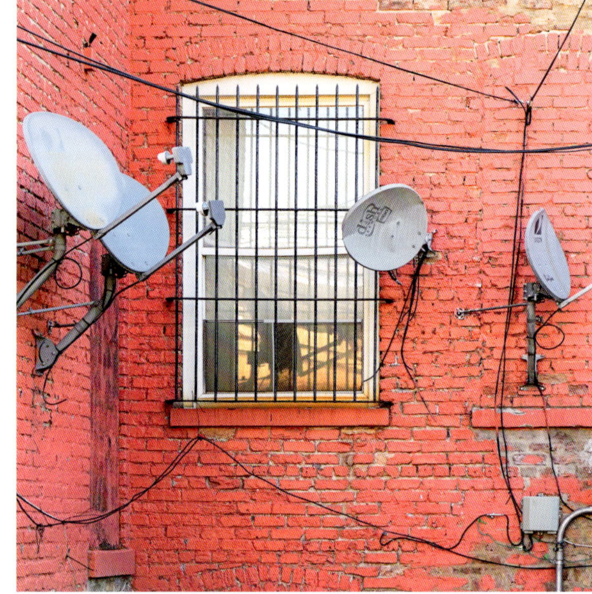

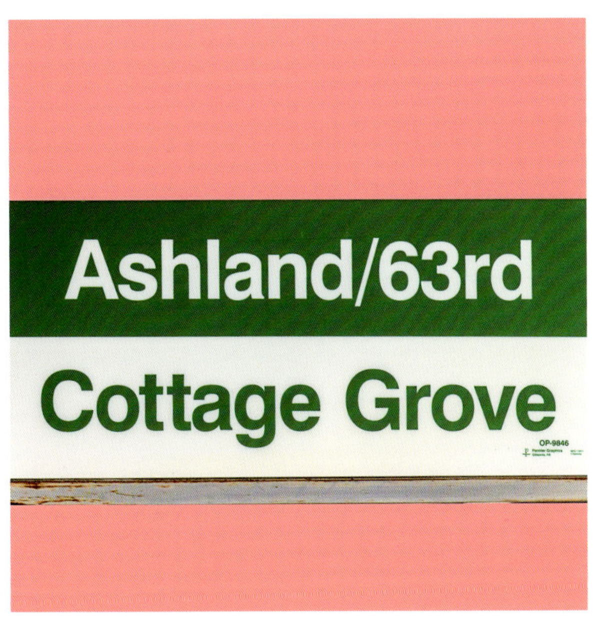
Ashland/63rd
Cottage Grove
OP-9846

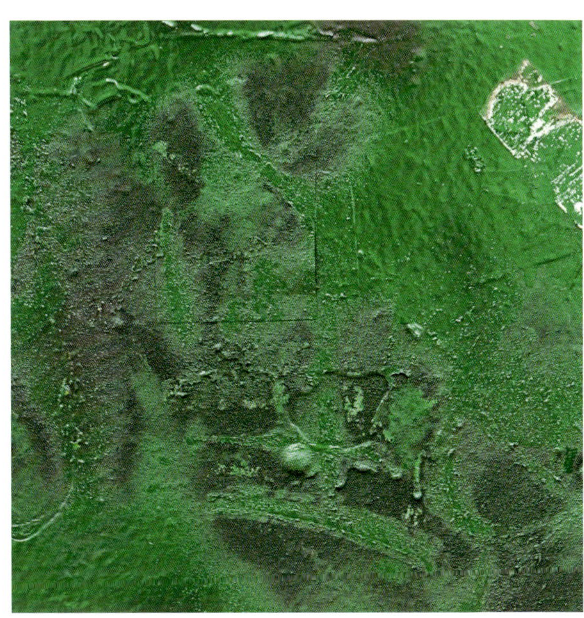

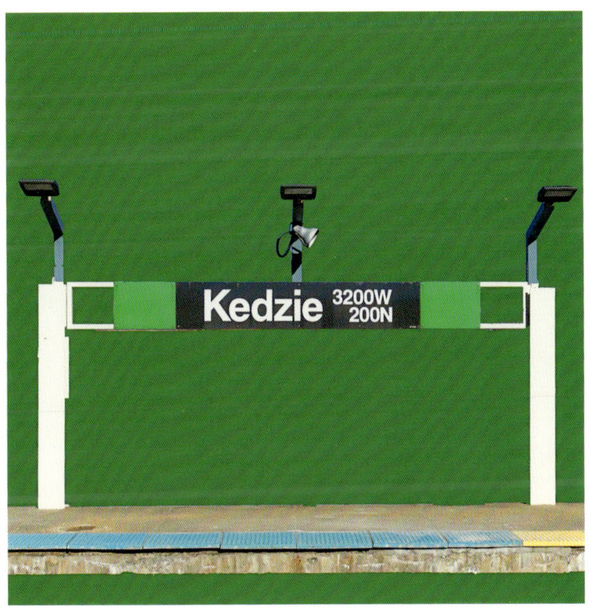
Kedzie 3200W
200N

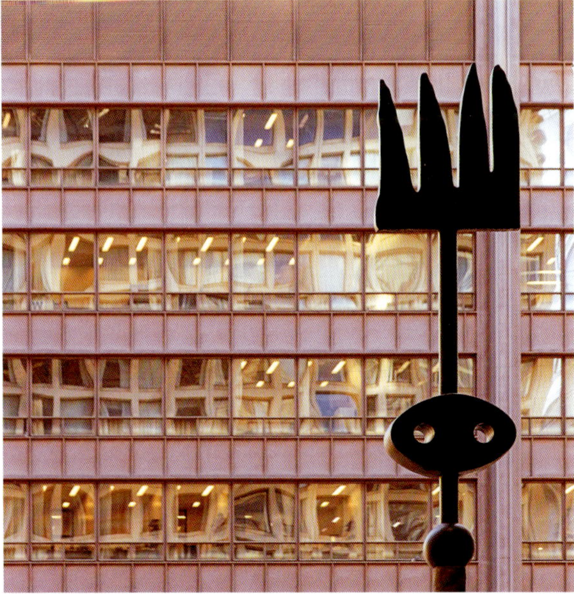

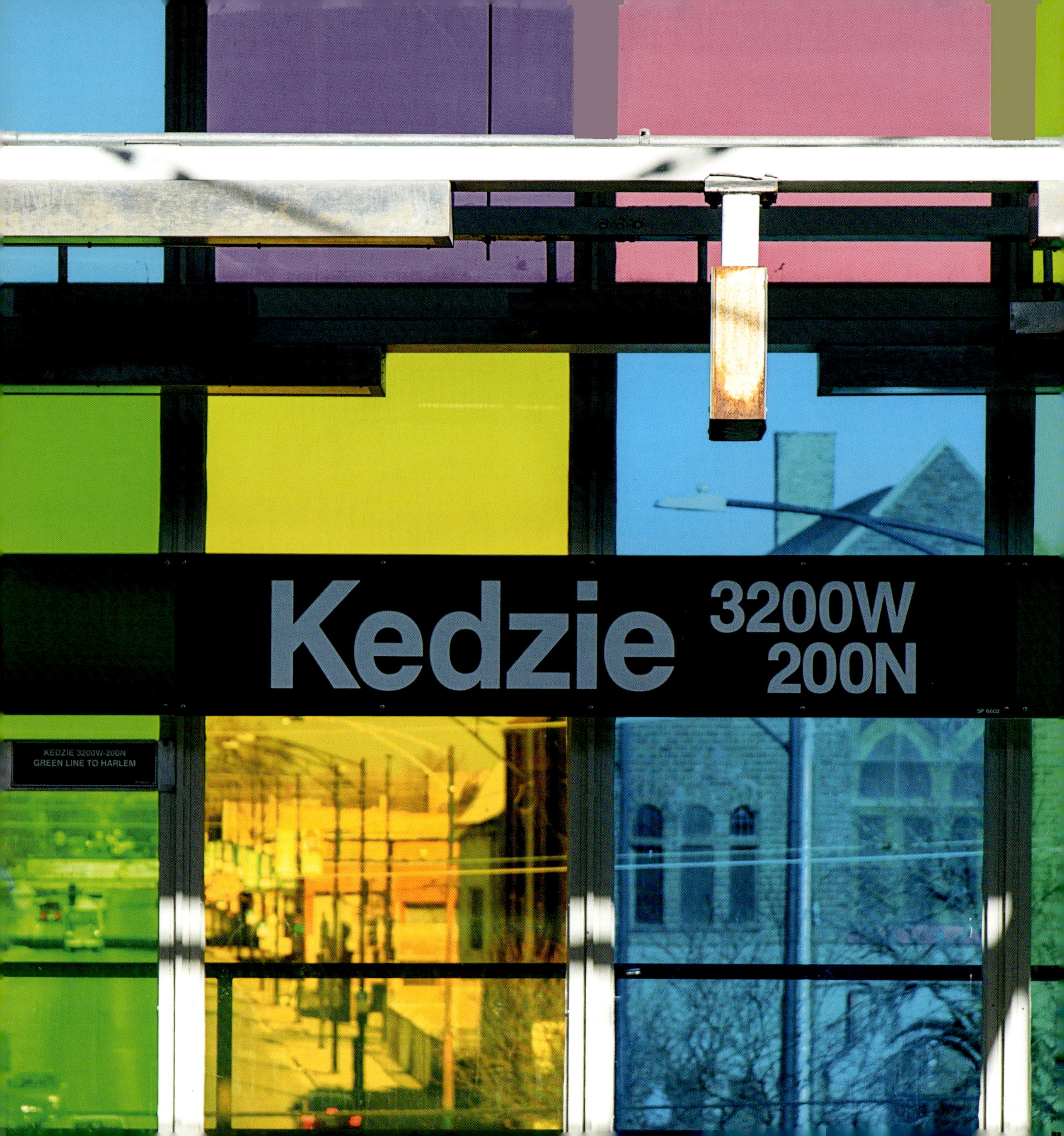

Kedzie 3200W 200N
SP 6602
KEDZIE 3200W-200N
GREEN LINE TO HARLEM

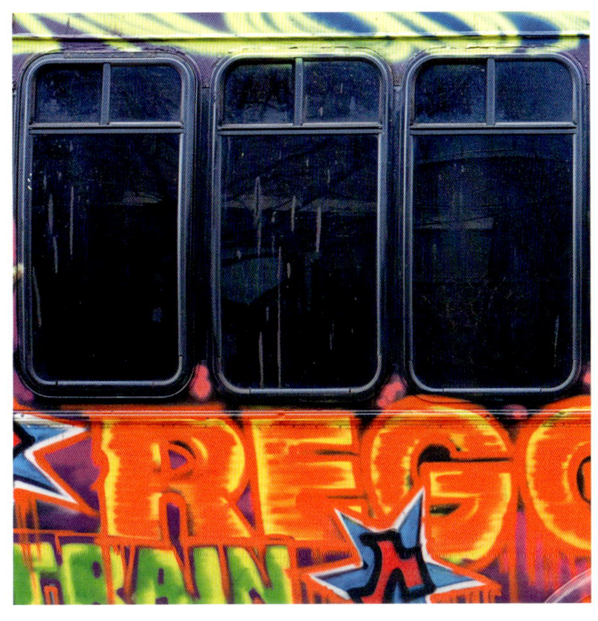
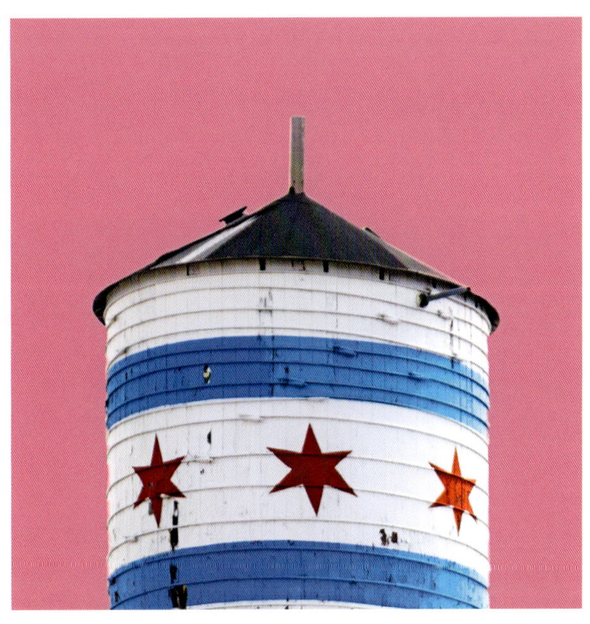
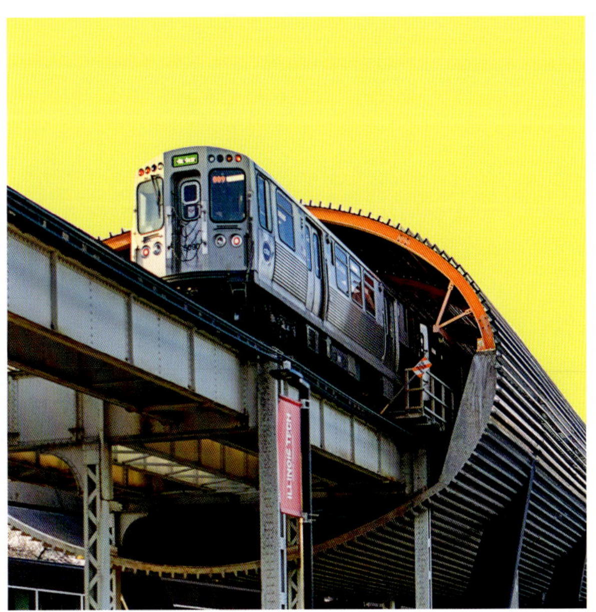
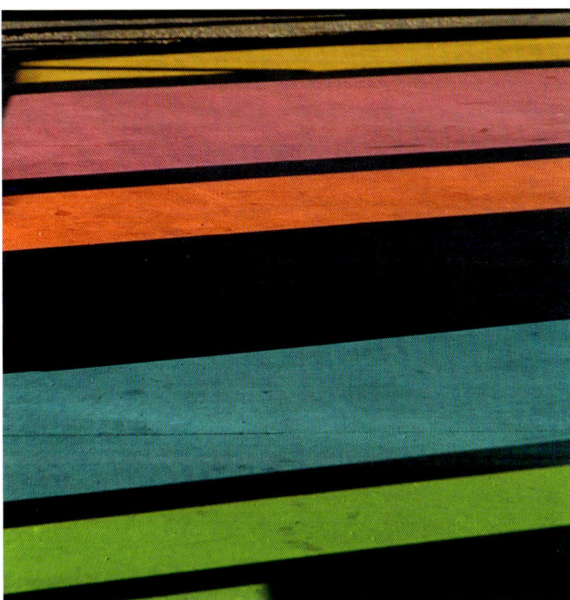

Colors, like features, follow the changes of the emotions.

— Pablo Picasso

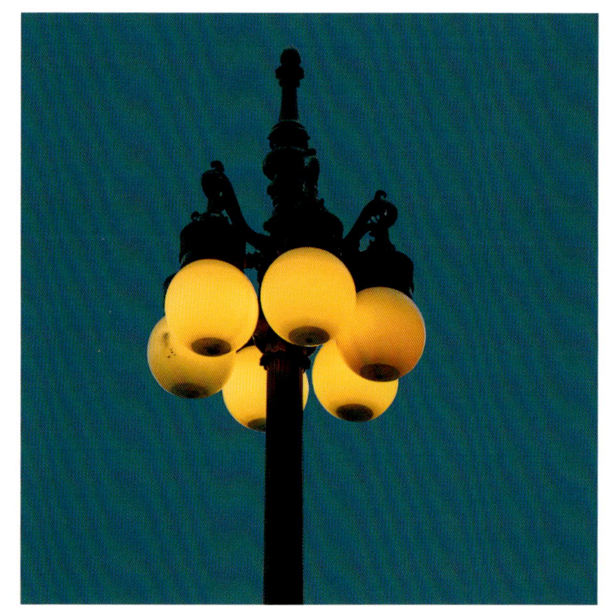
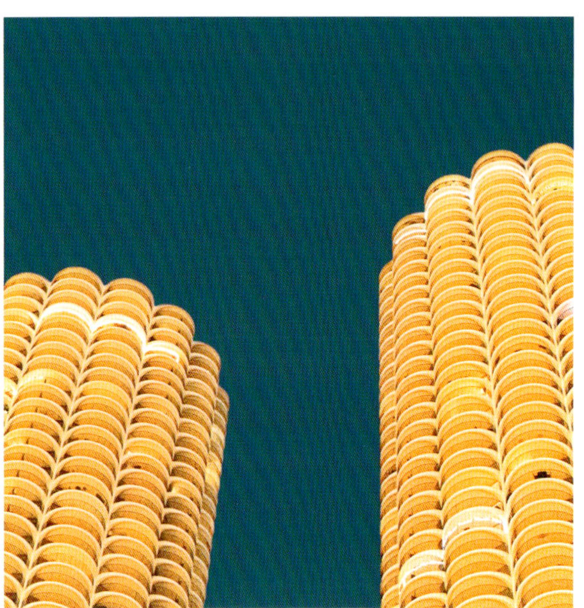
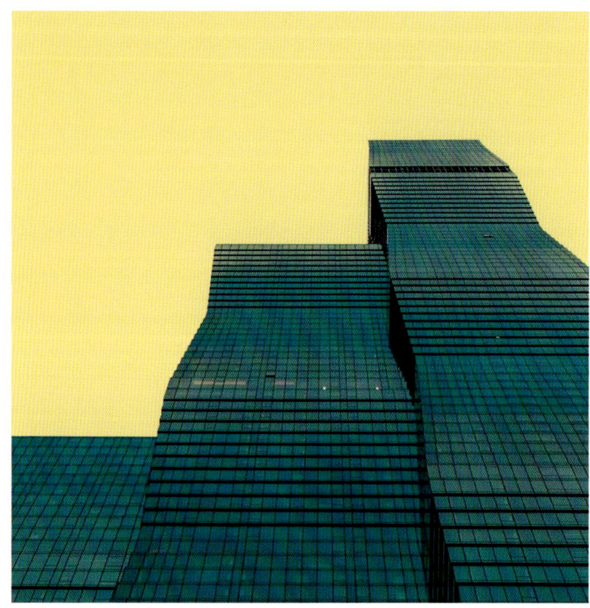

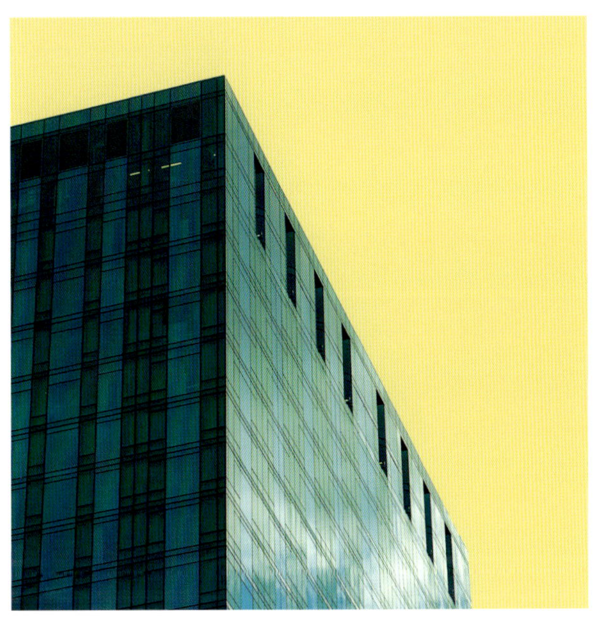
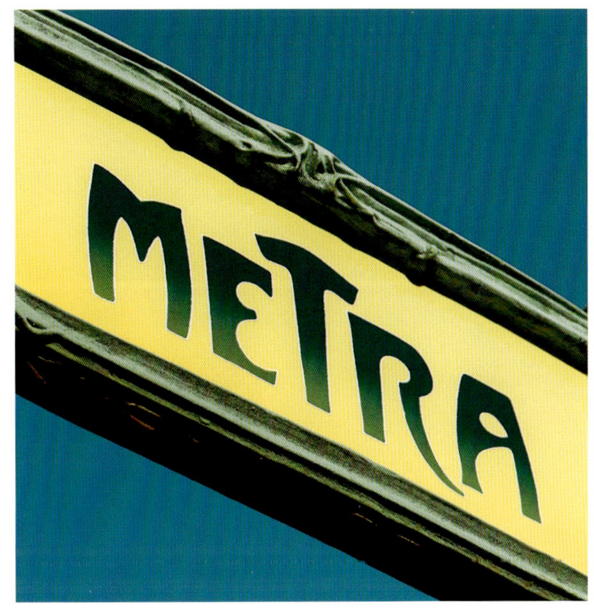
METRA
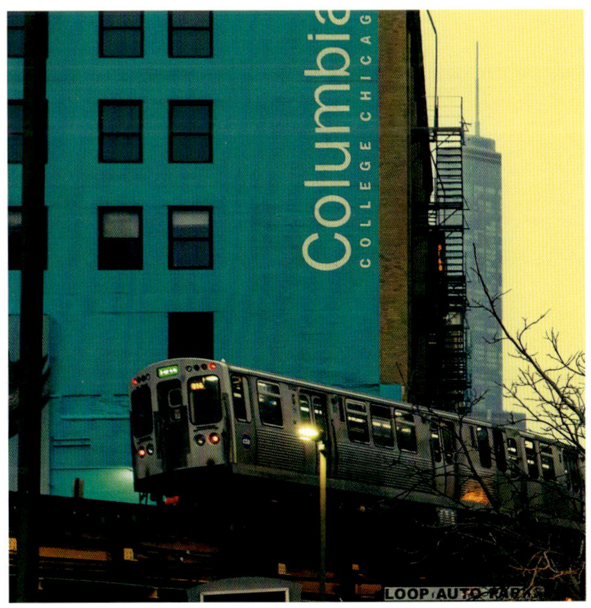
Columbia
COLLEGE CHICAG
LOOP AUTO PARK
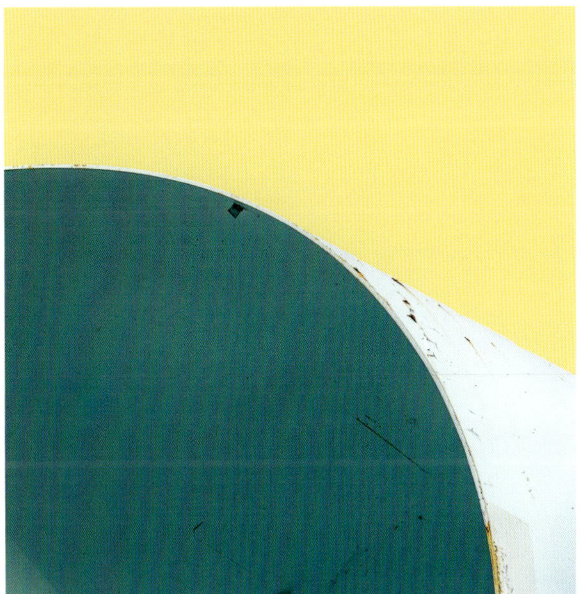

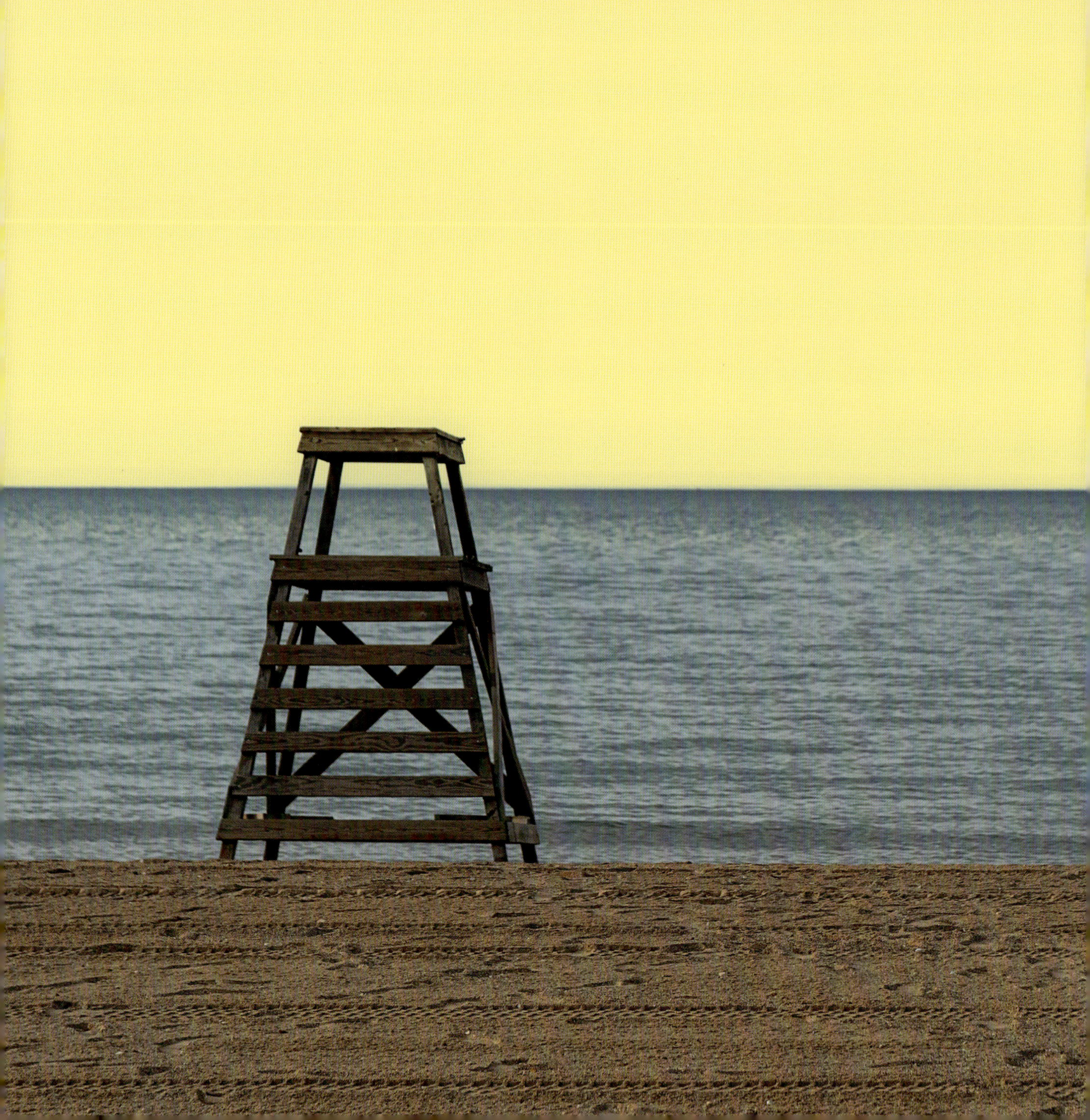

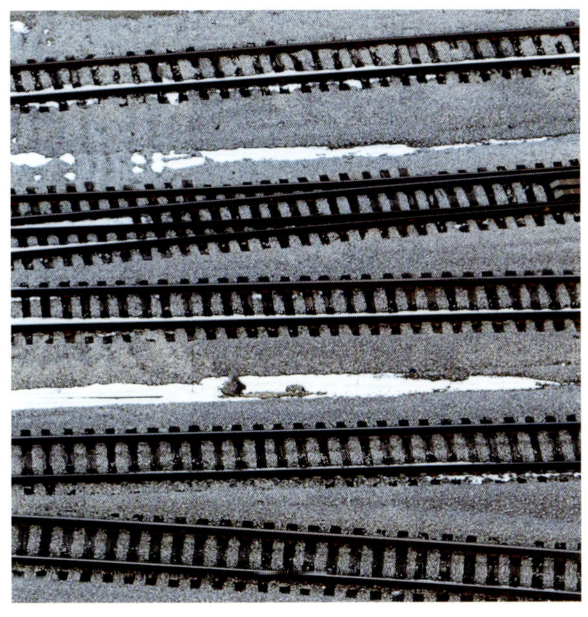
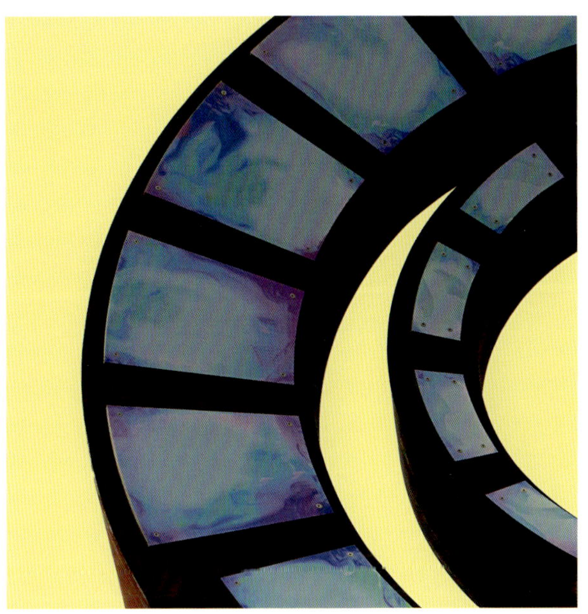
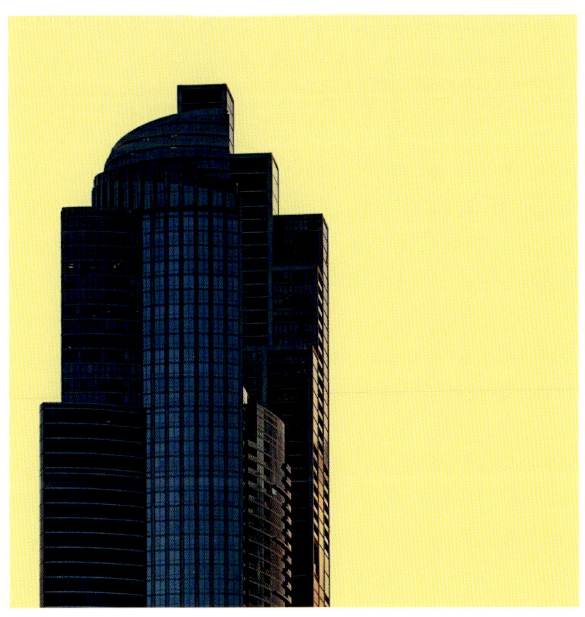
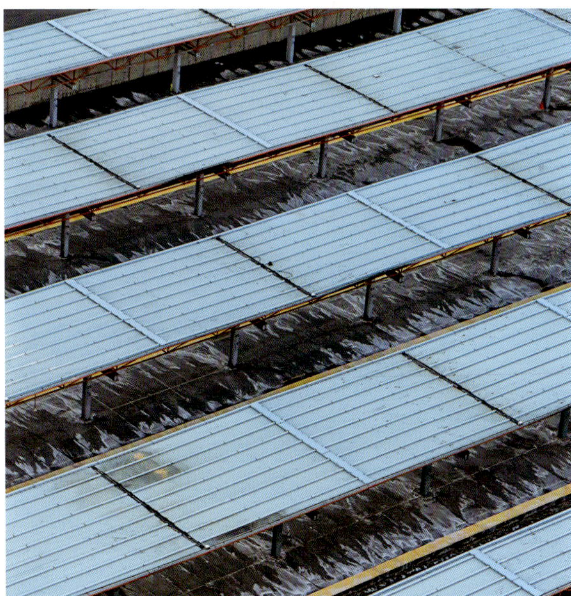

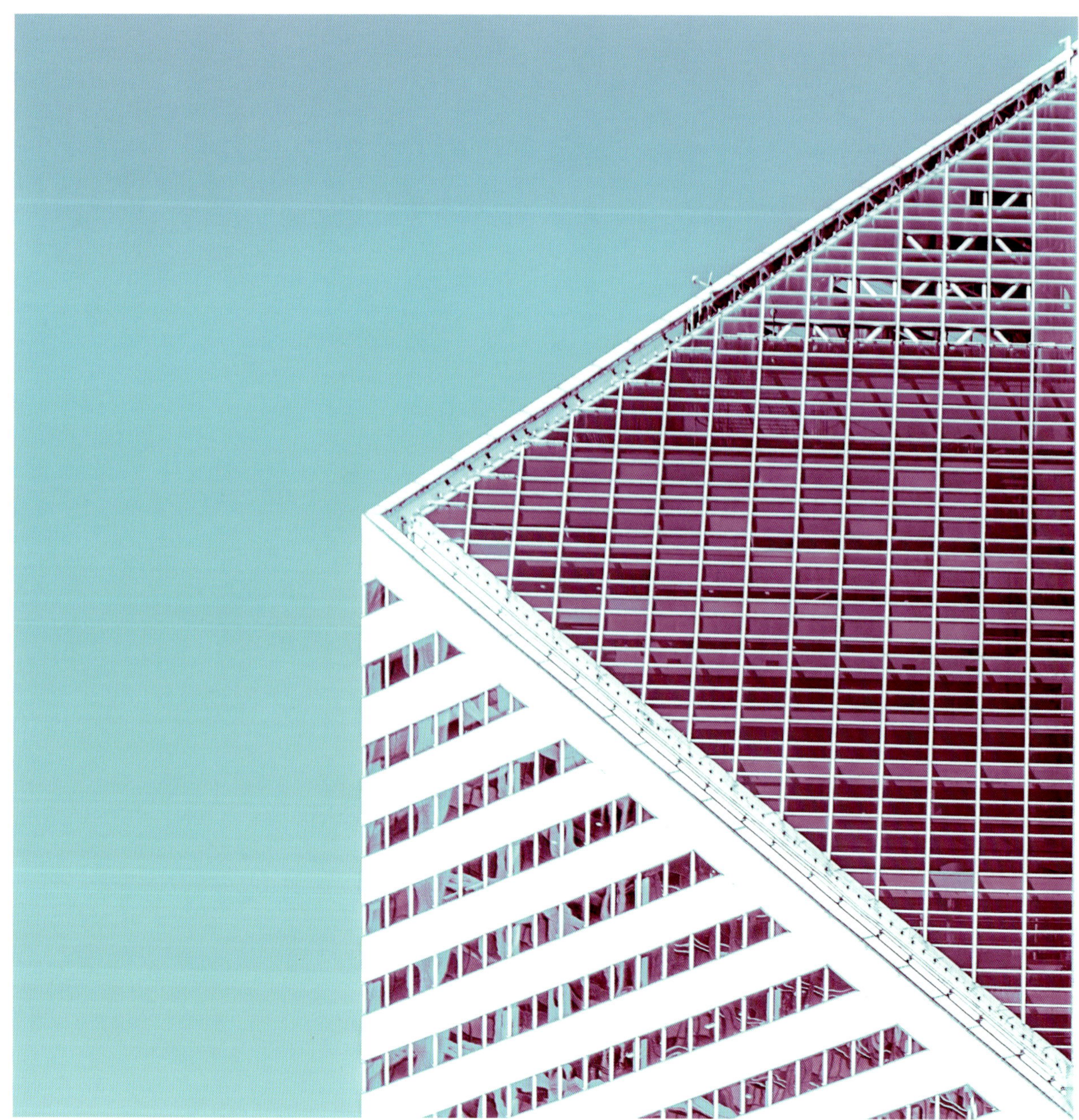

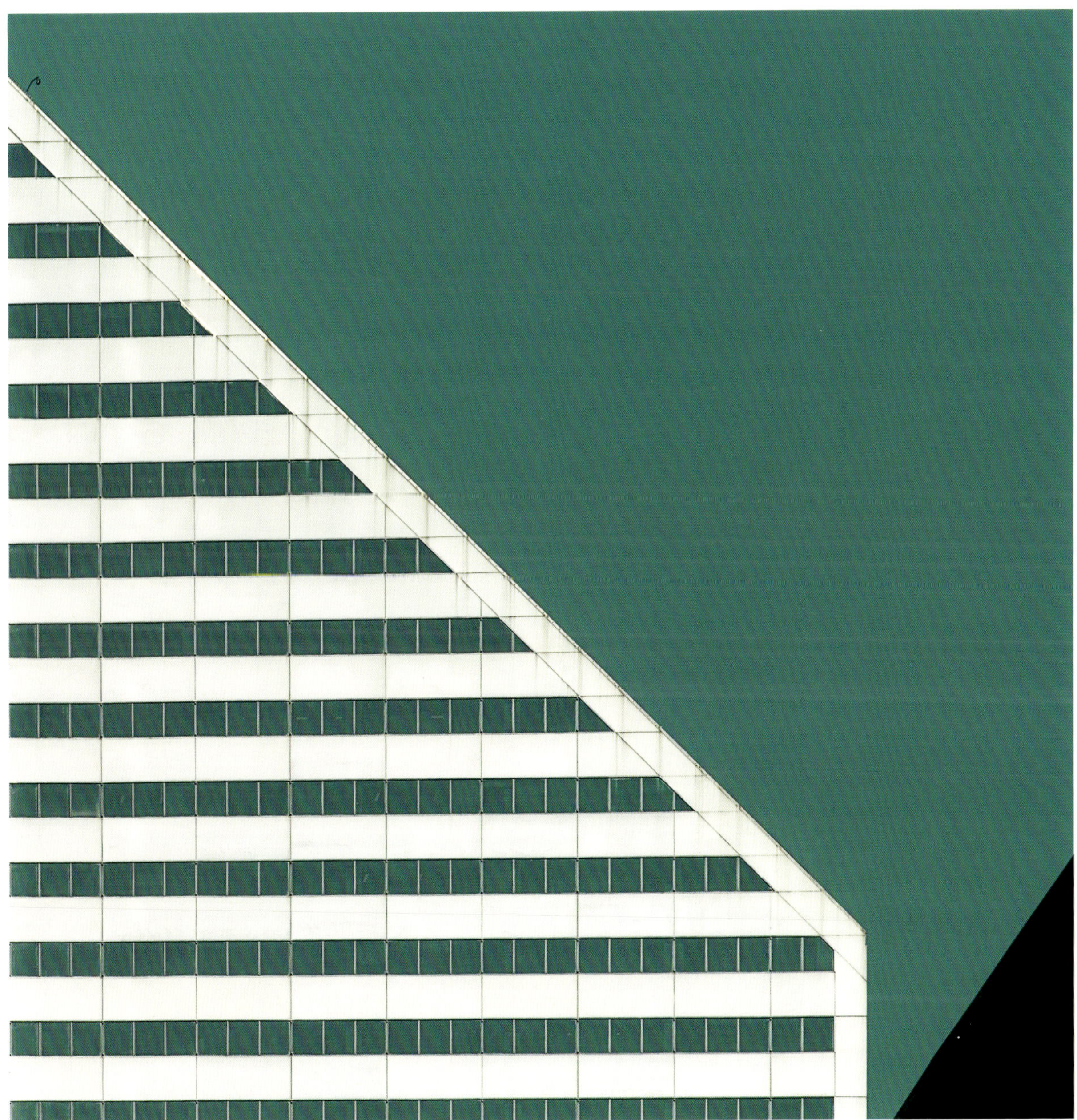

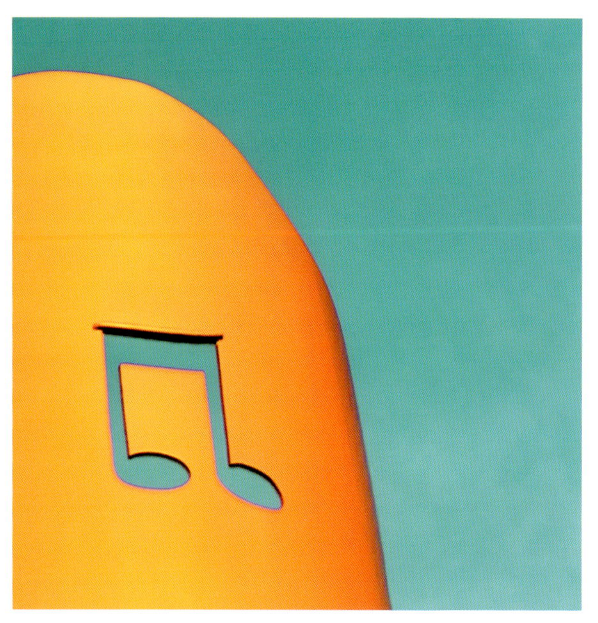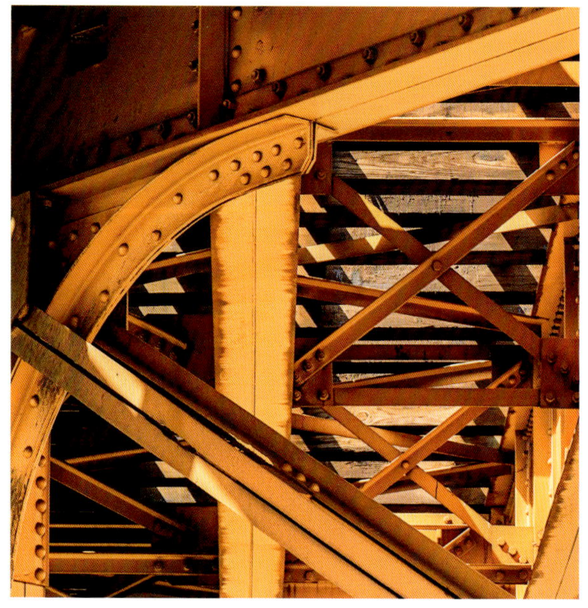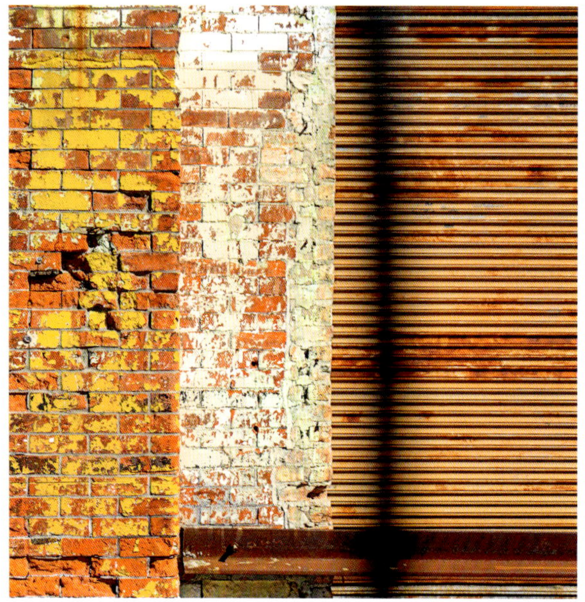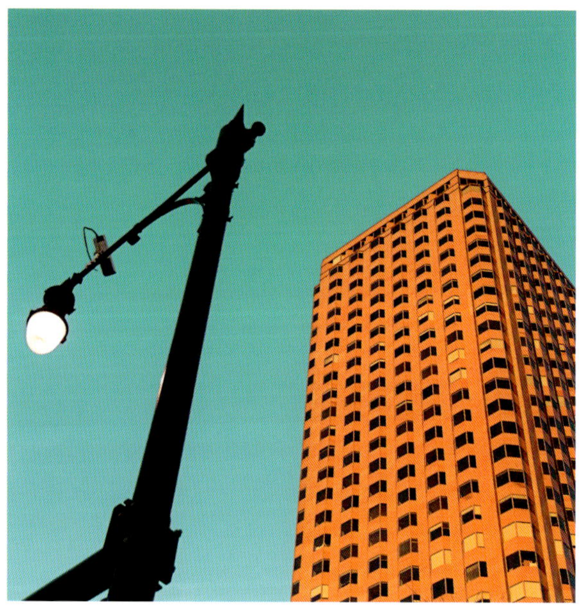

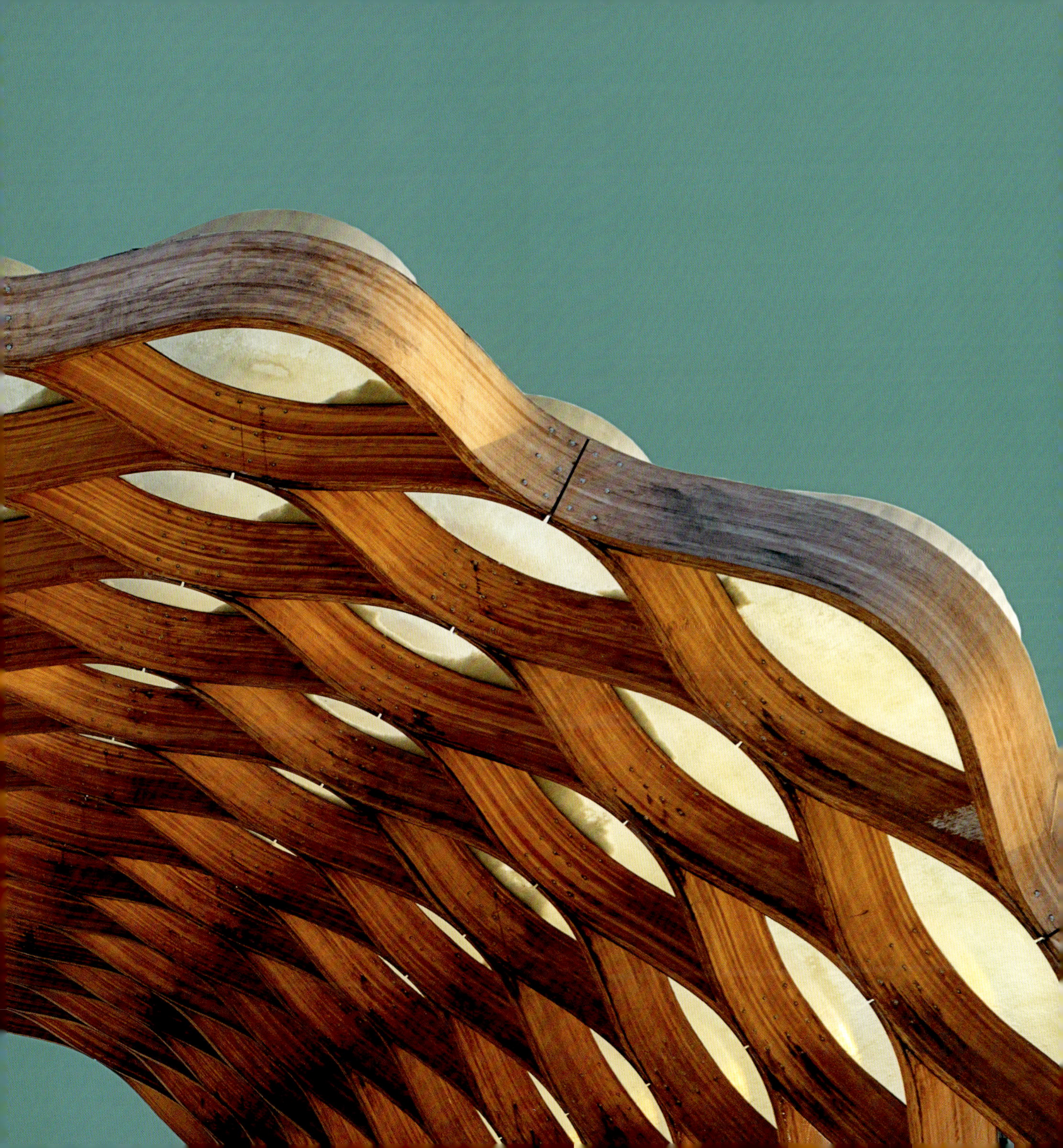

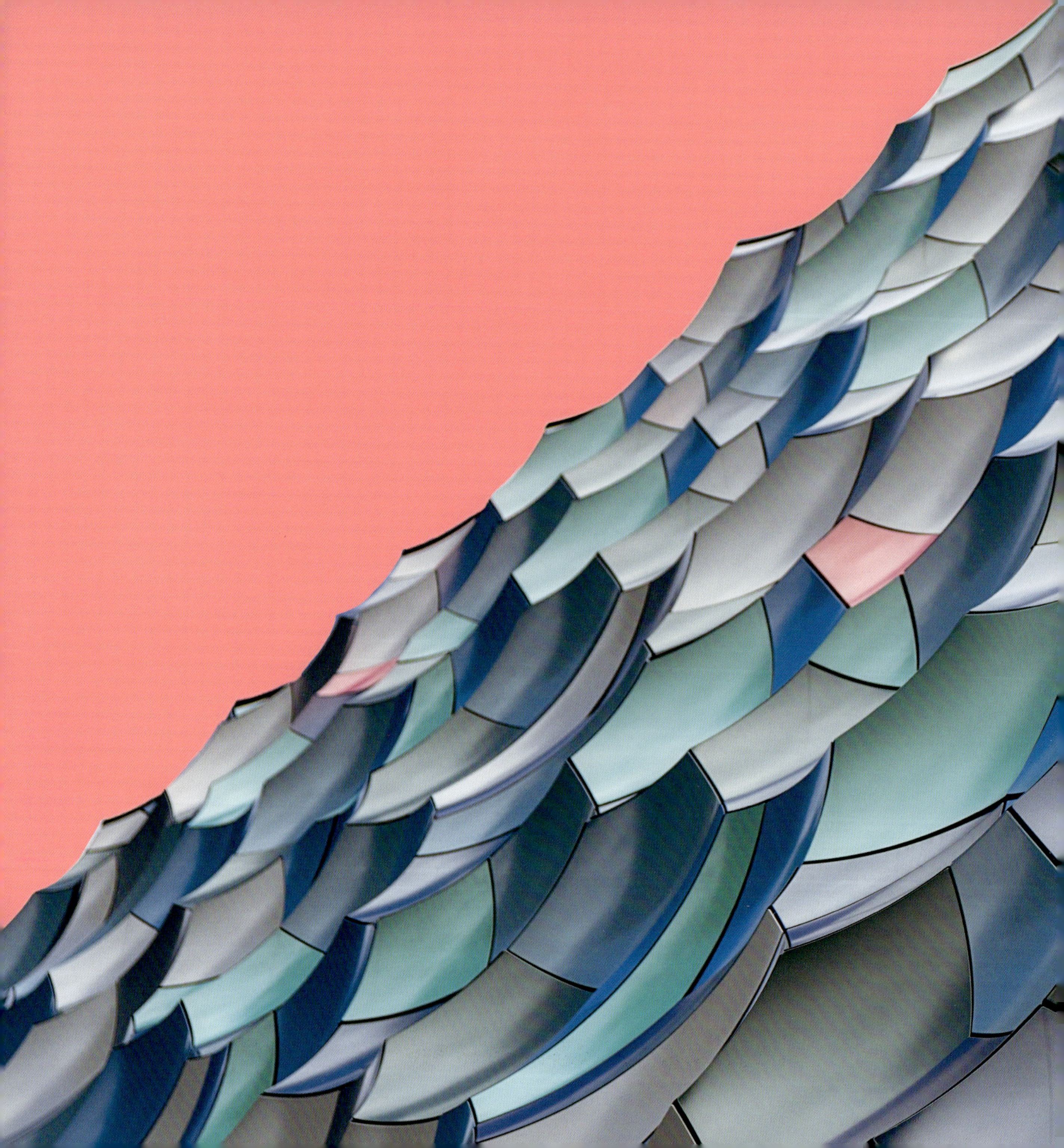

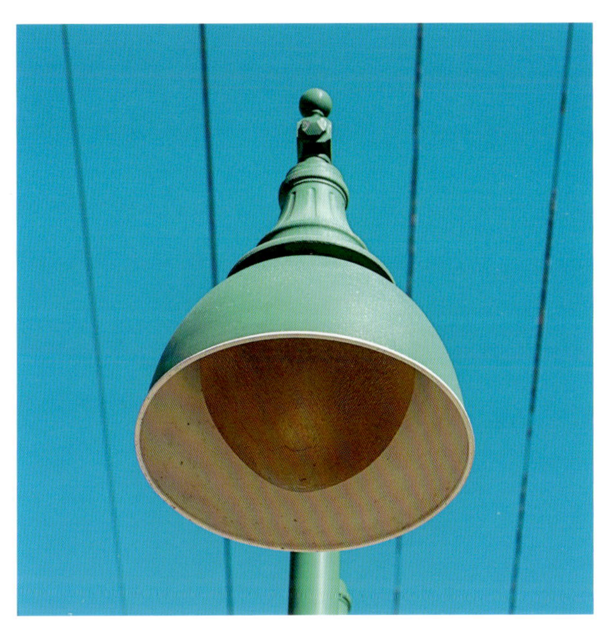
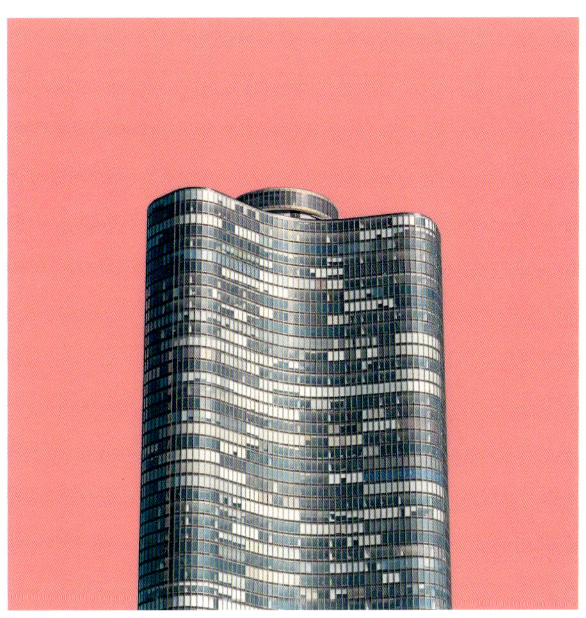
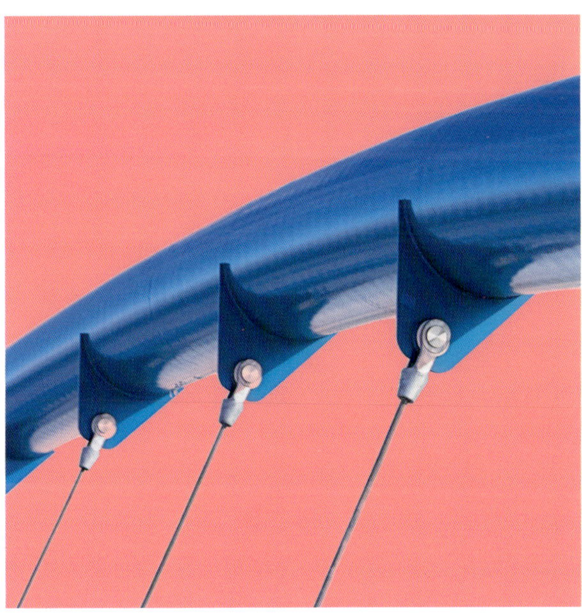
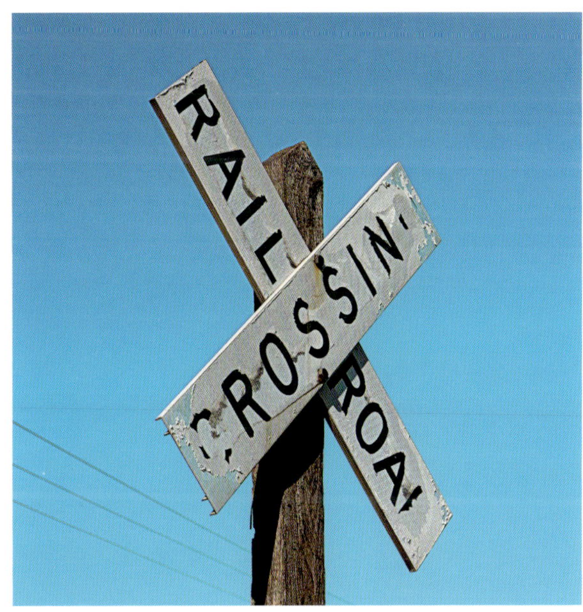

RAIL
CROSSIN
ROA

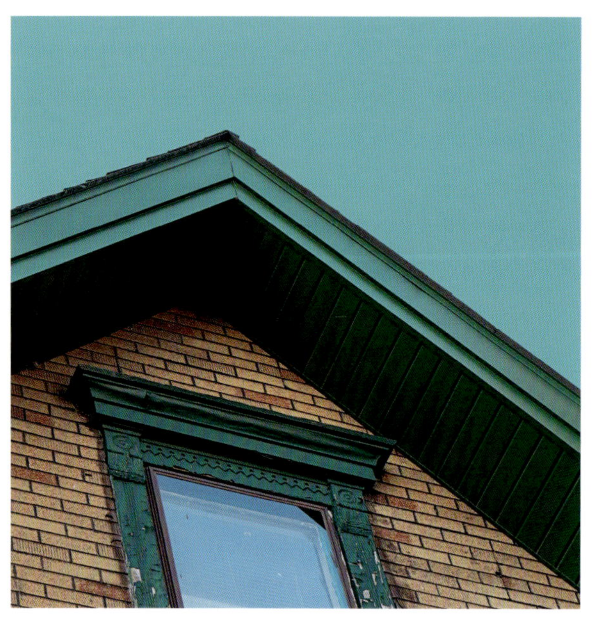

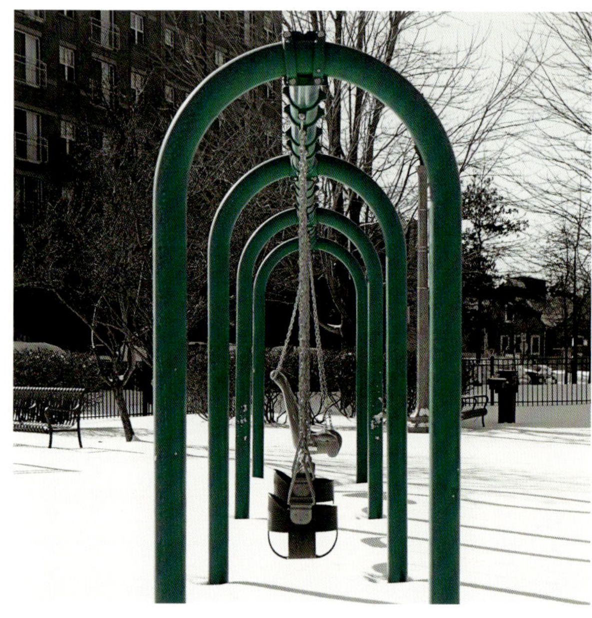

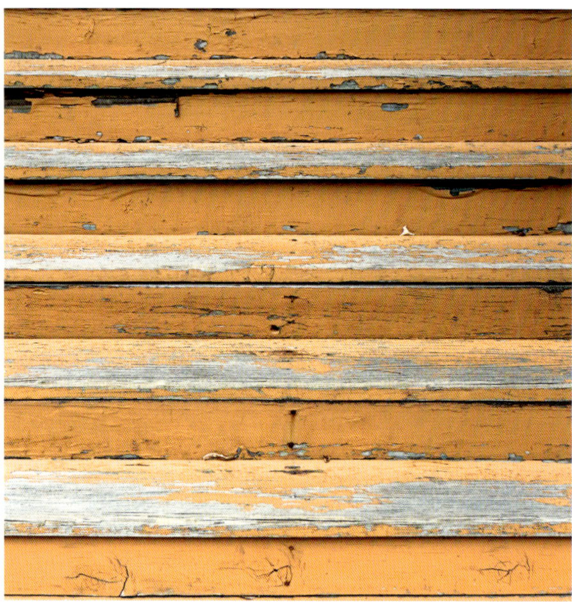

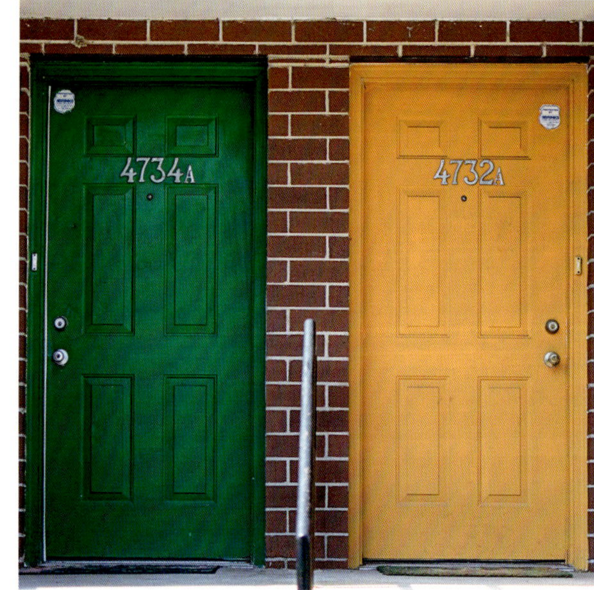
4734A
4732A

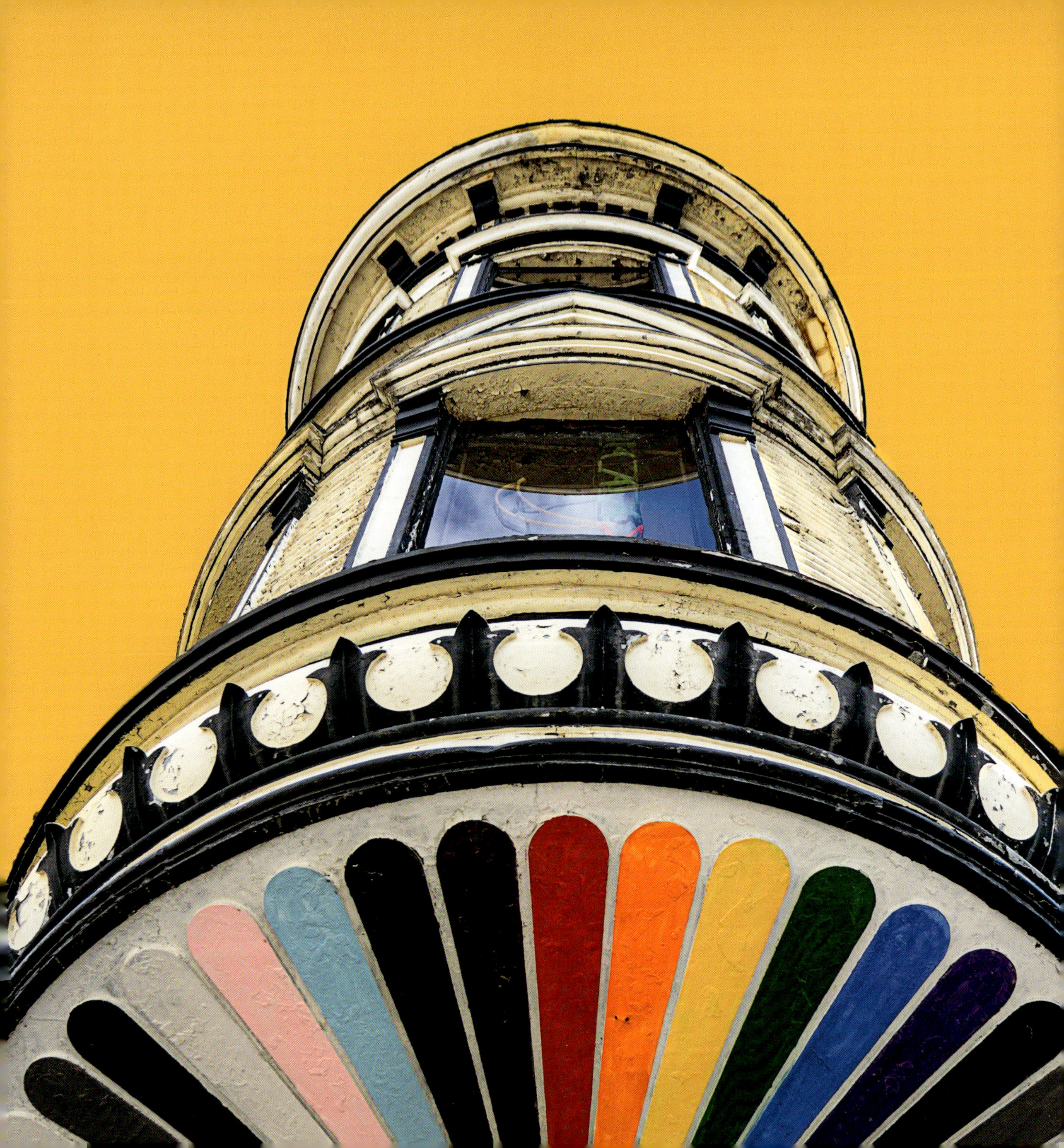

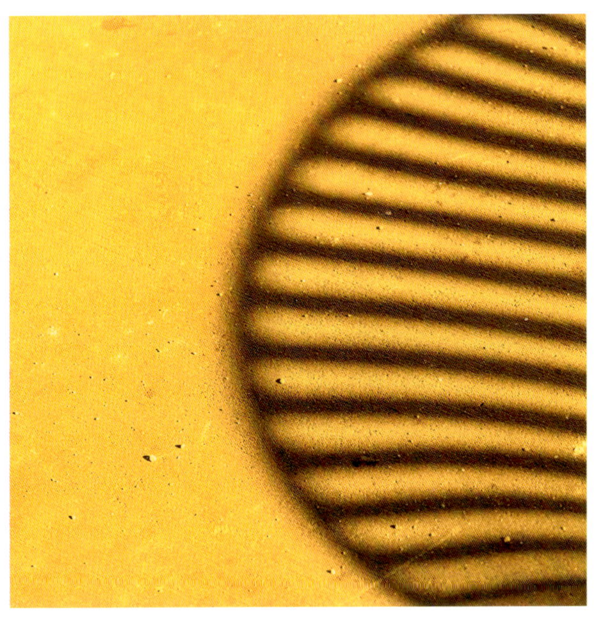

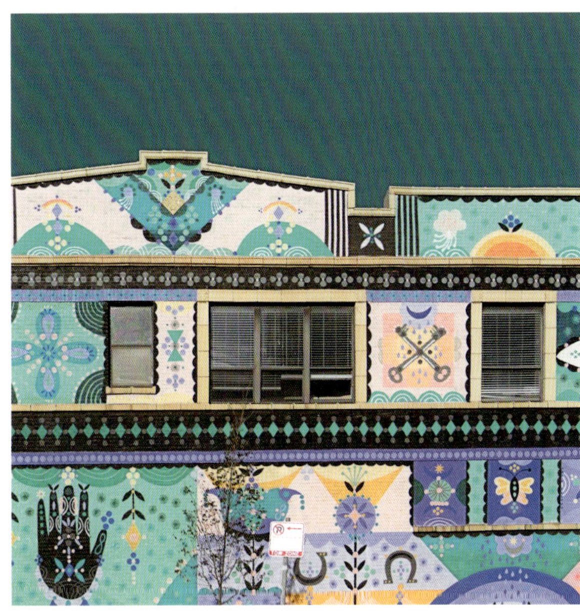

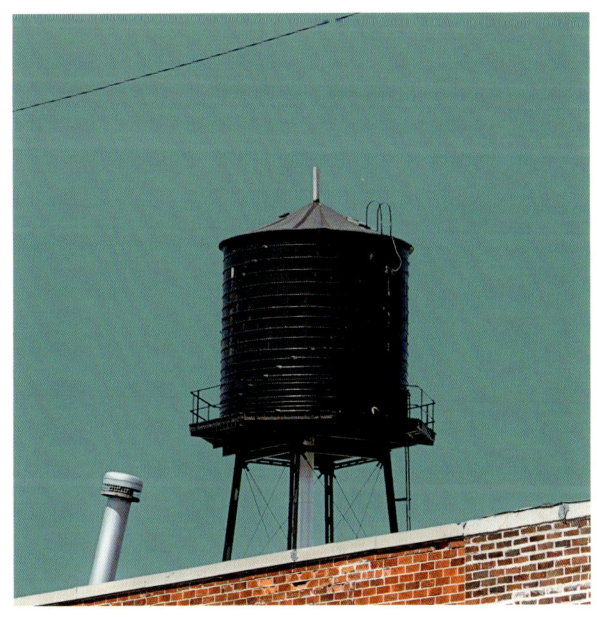

Color is always a motivation.

– Perle Fine

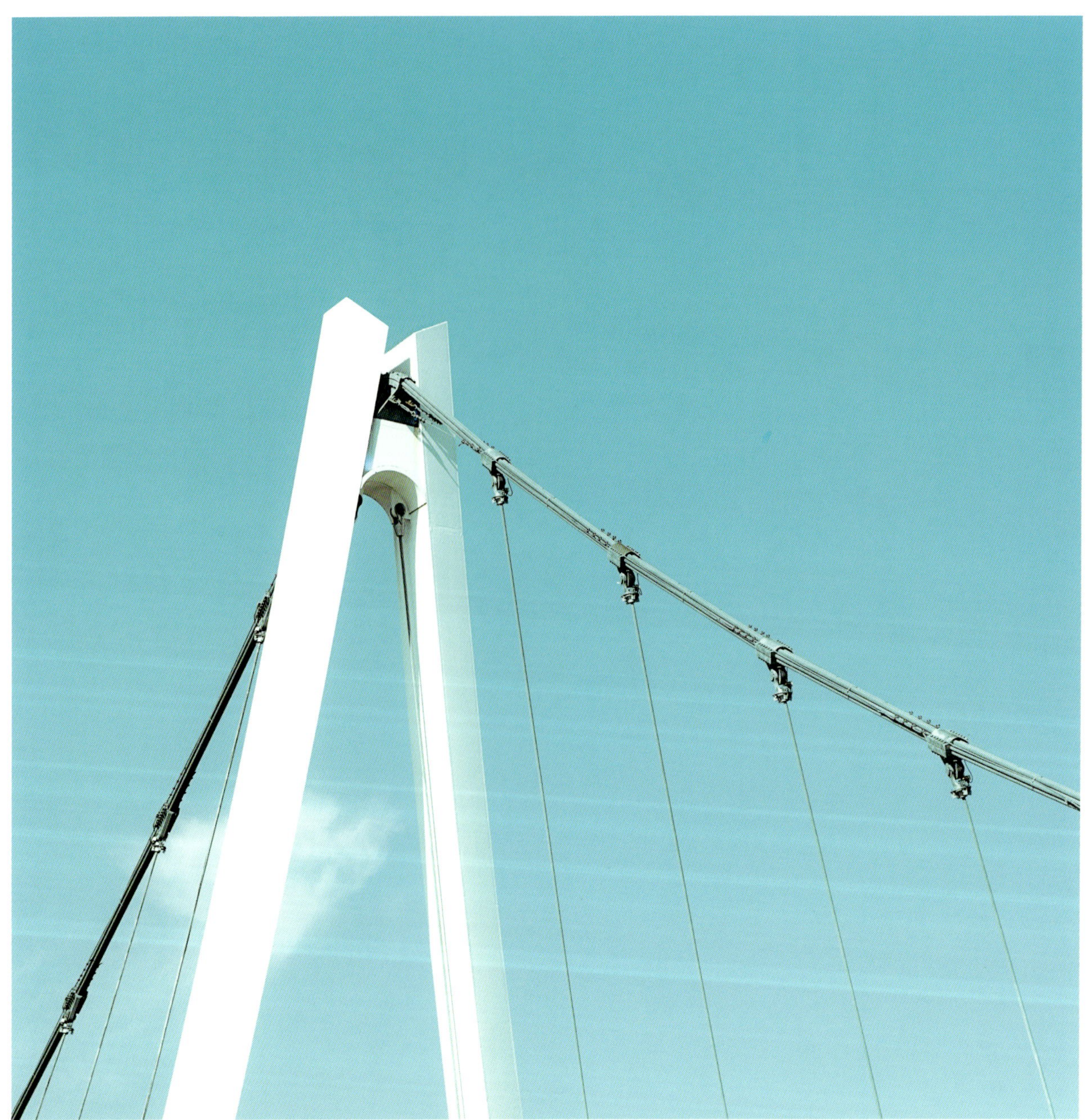

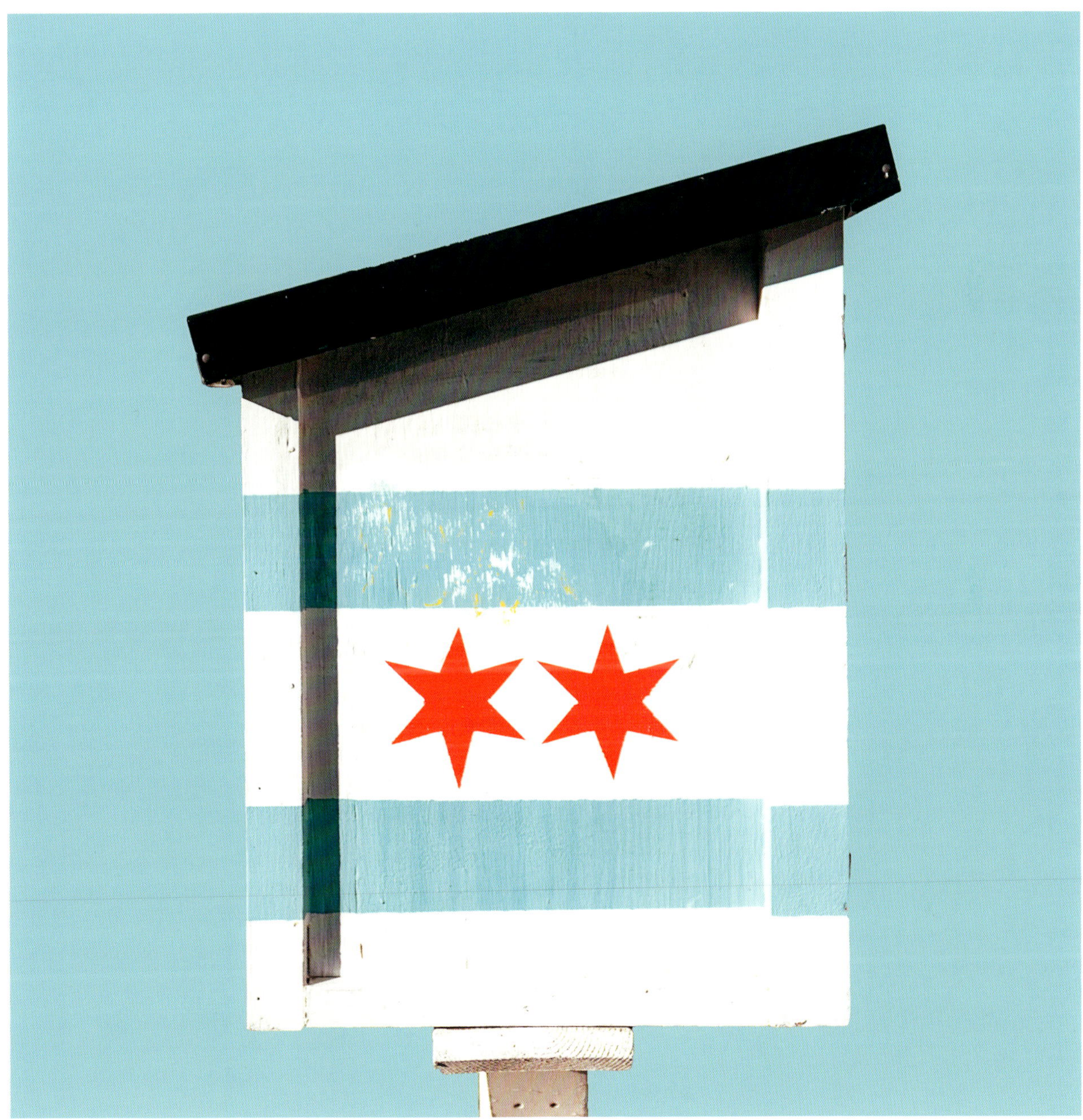

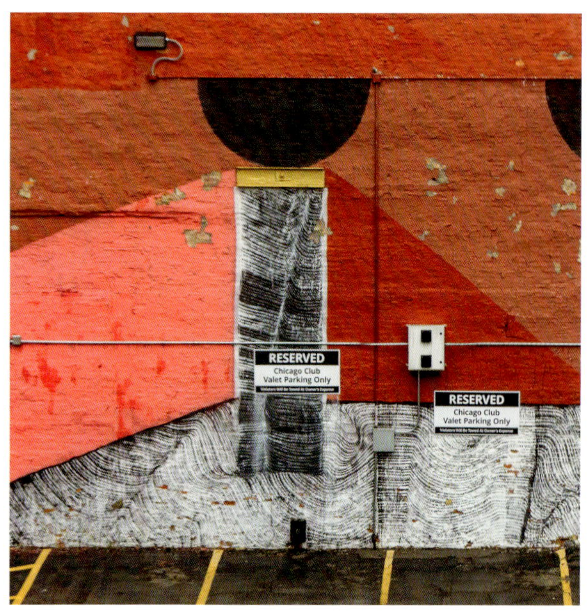
RESERVED
Chicago Club
Valet Parking Only
RESERVED
Chicago Club
Valet Parking Only

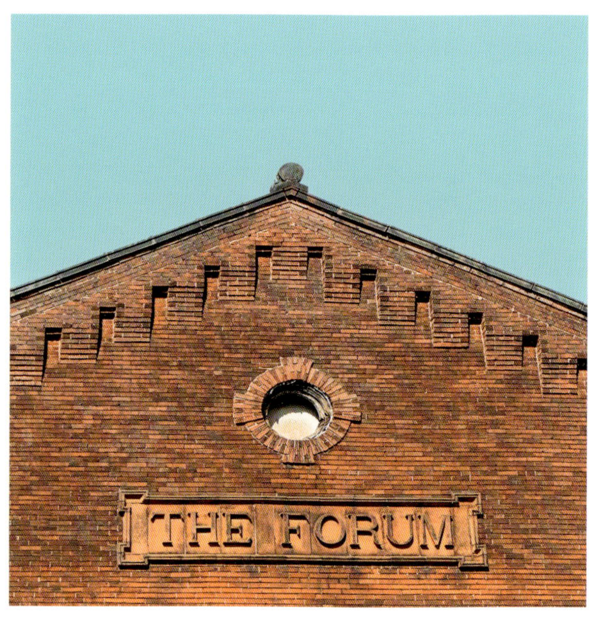
THE FORUM

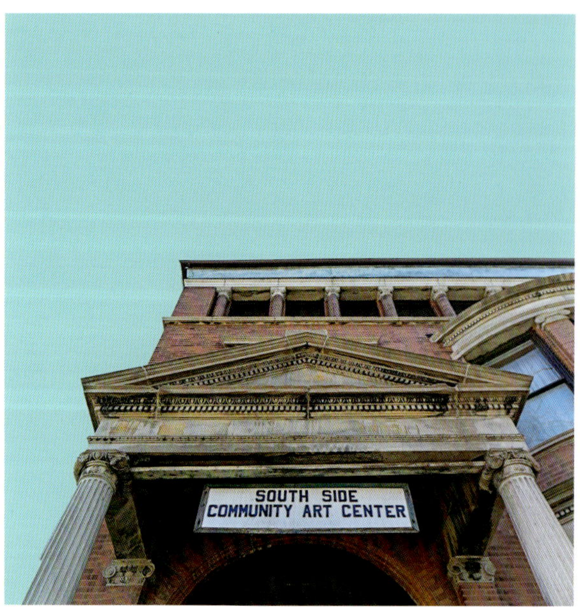
SOUTH SIDE
COMMUNITY ART CENTER

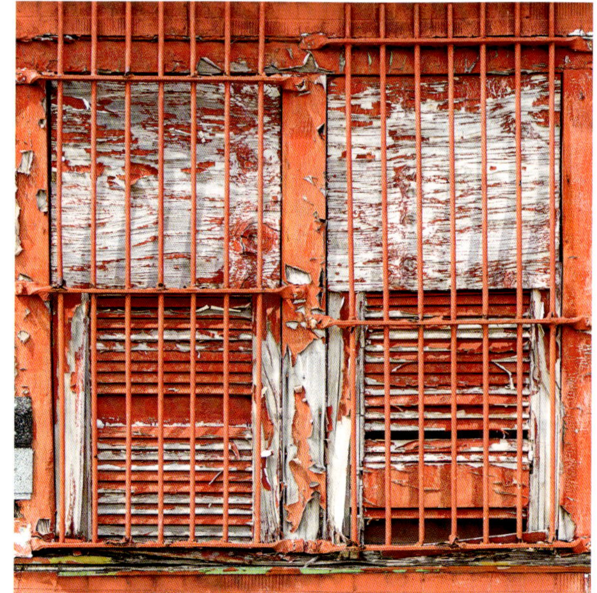

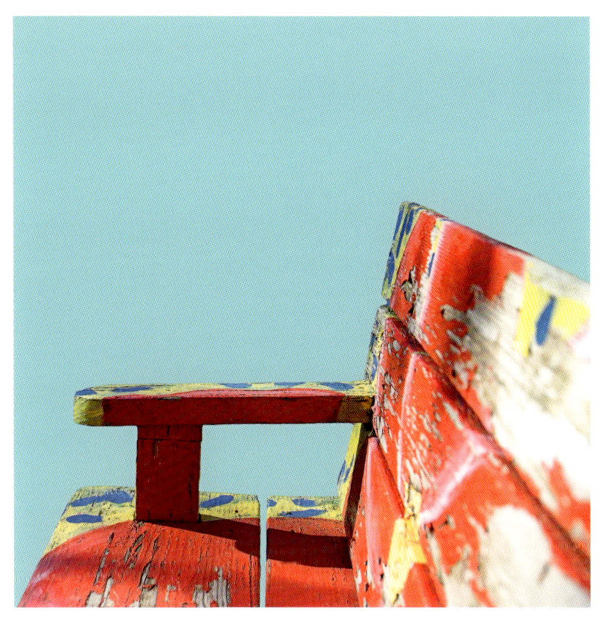
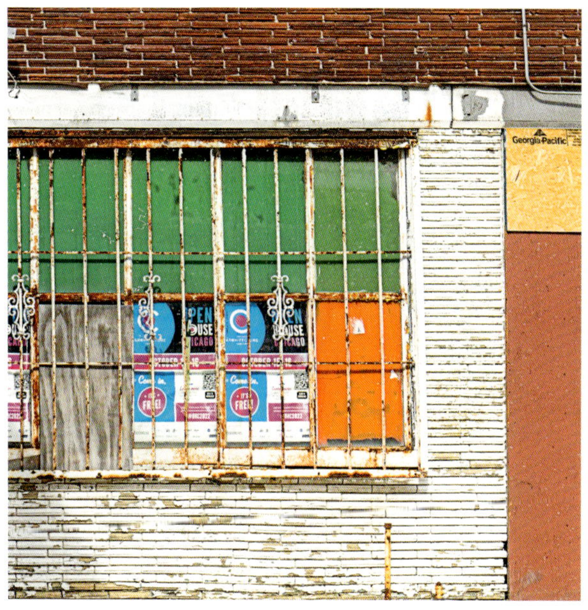
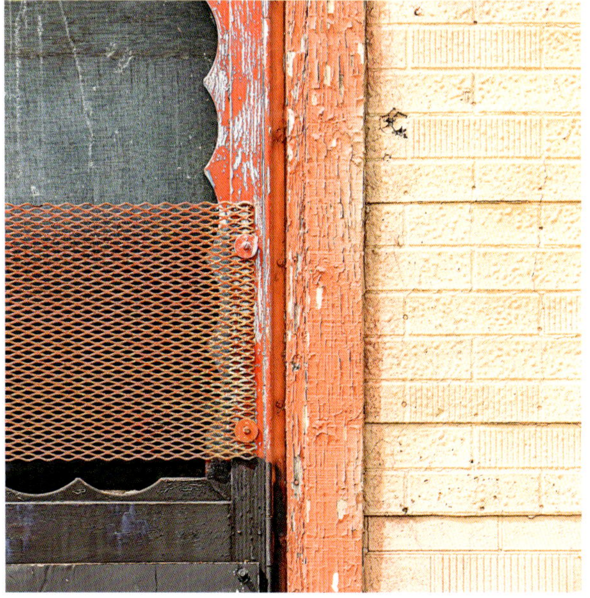
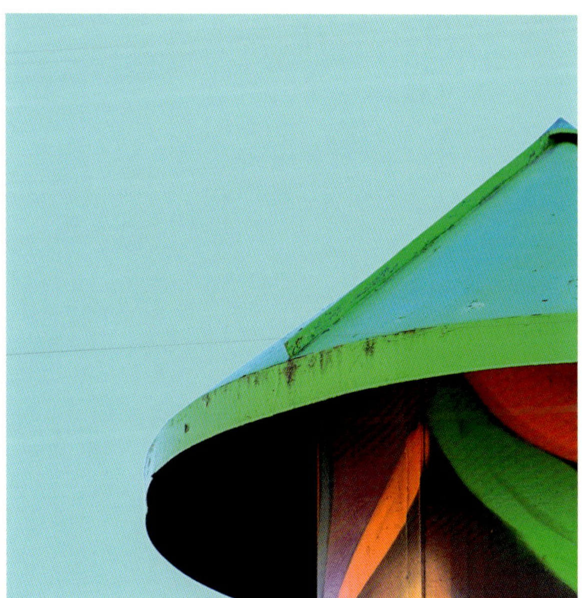

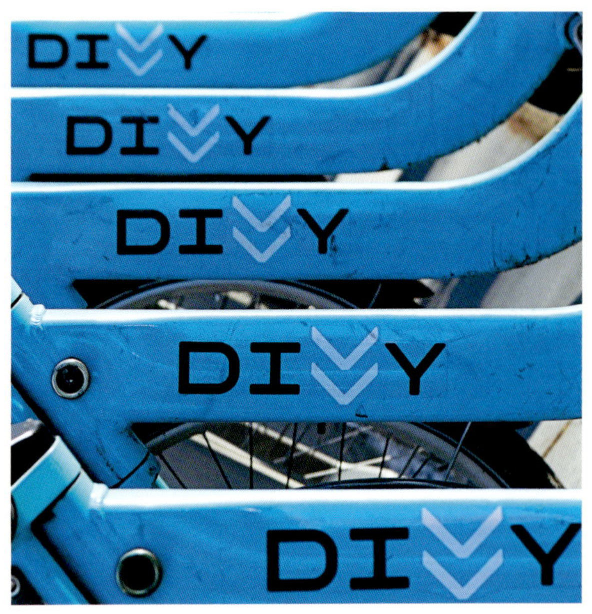

DIVVY
DIVVY
DIVVY
DIVVY
DIVVY

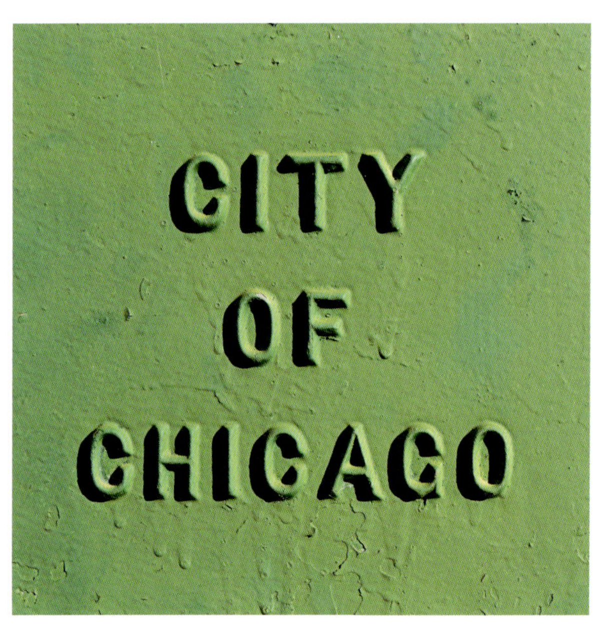

CITY
OF
CHICAGO

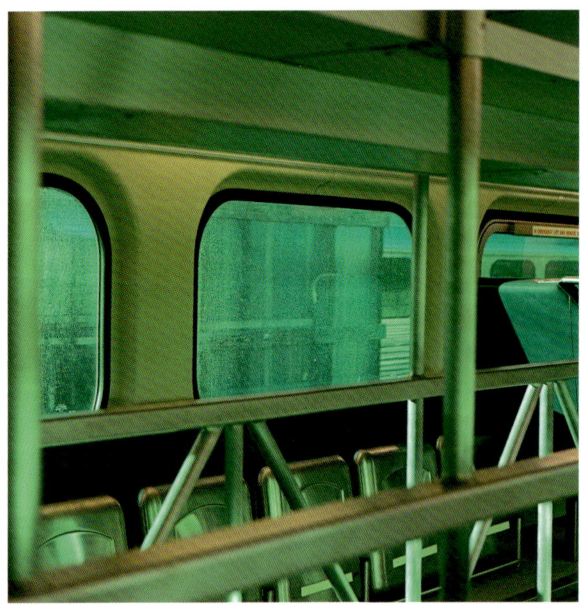

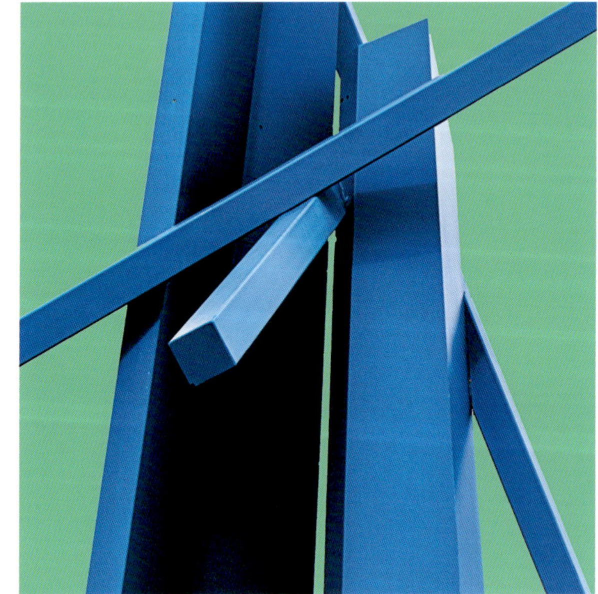

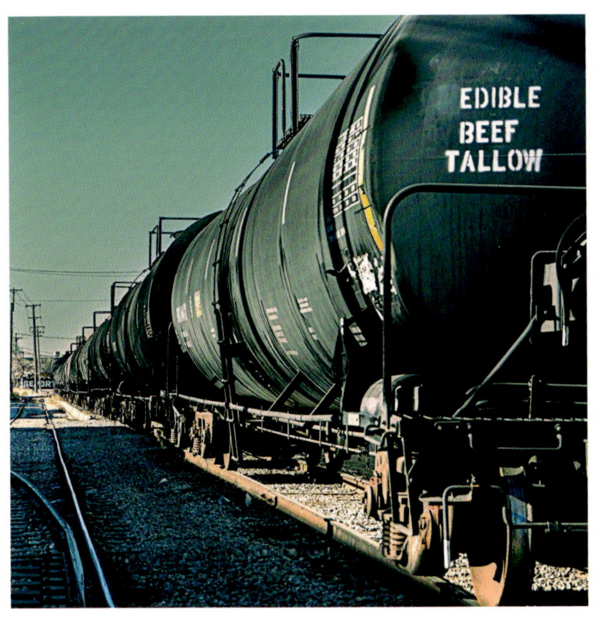

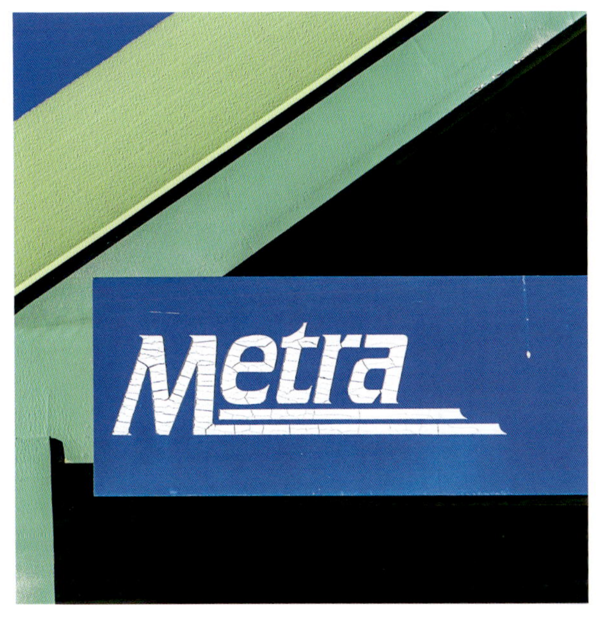

Metra

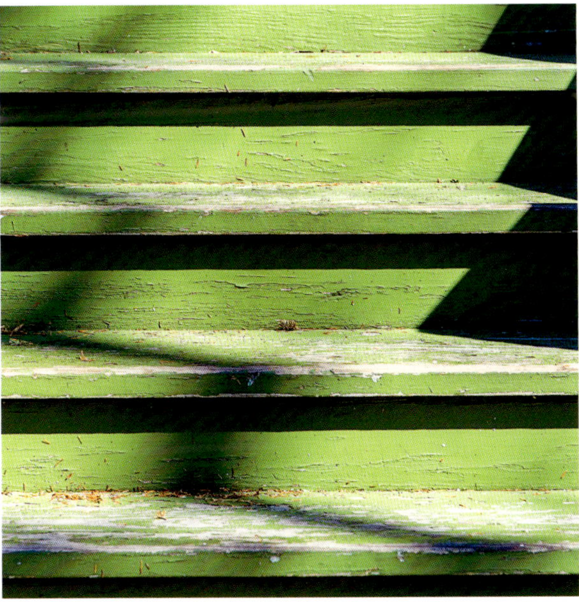

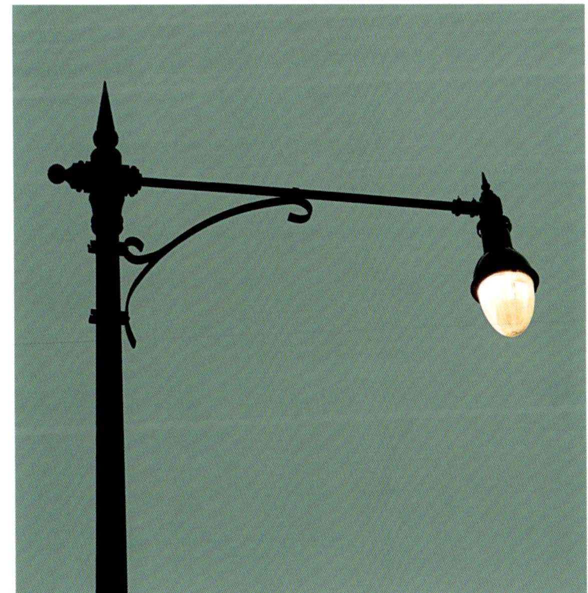

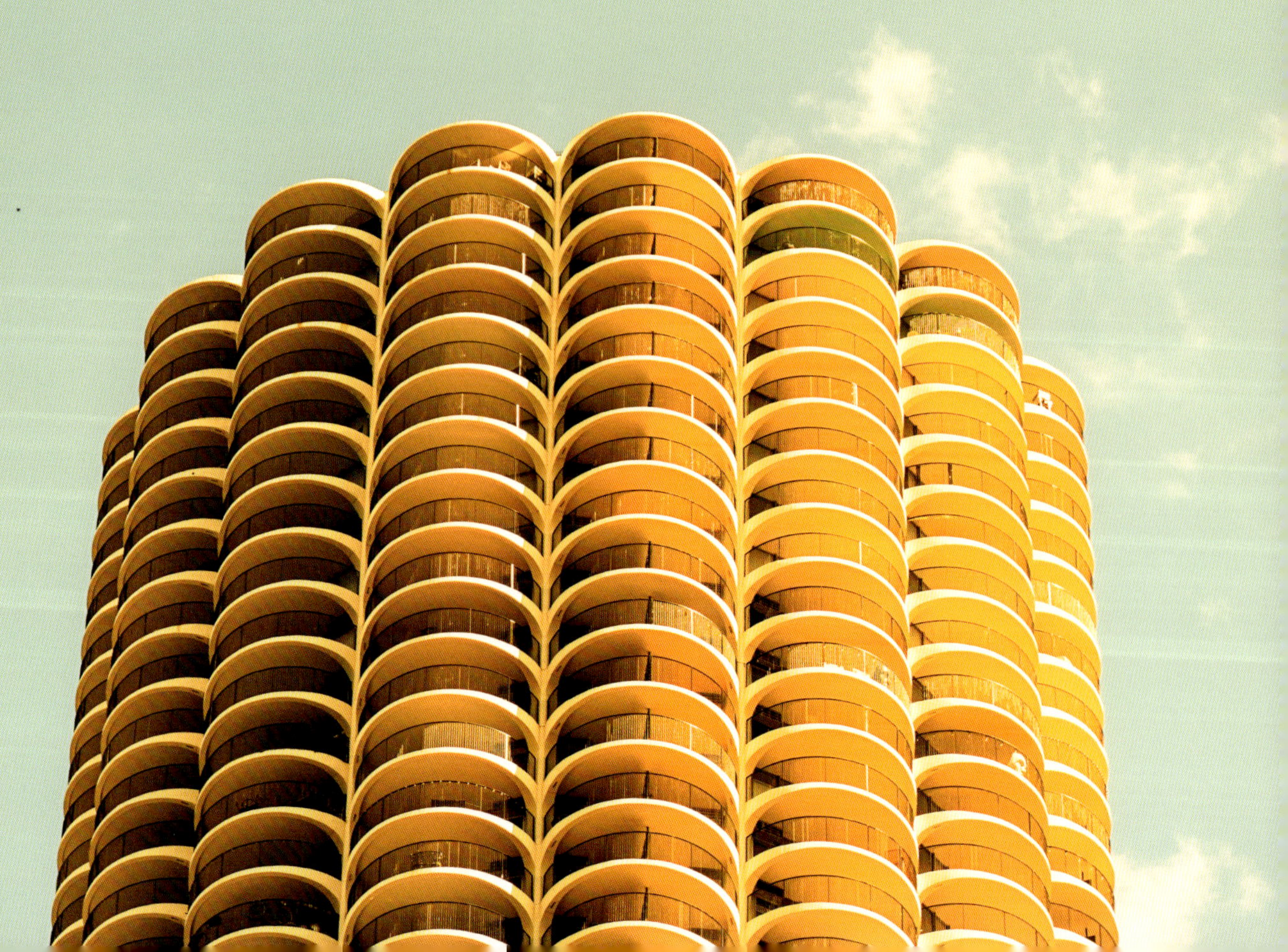

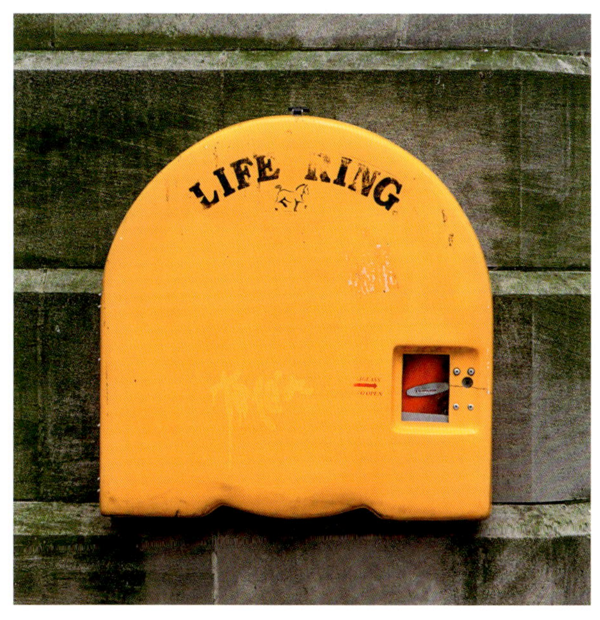
LIFE RING

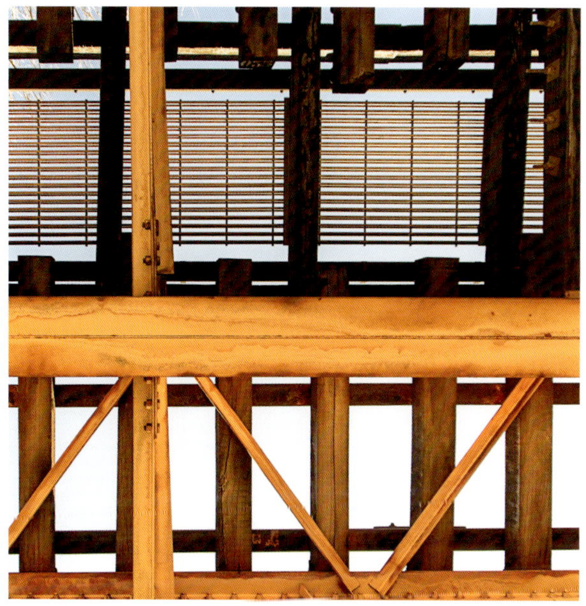

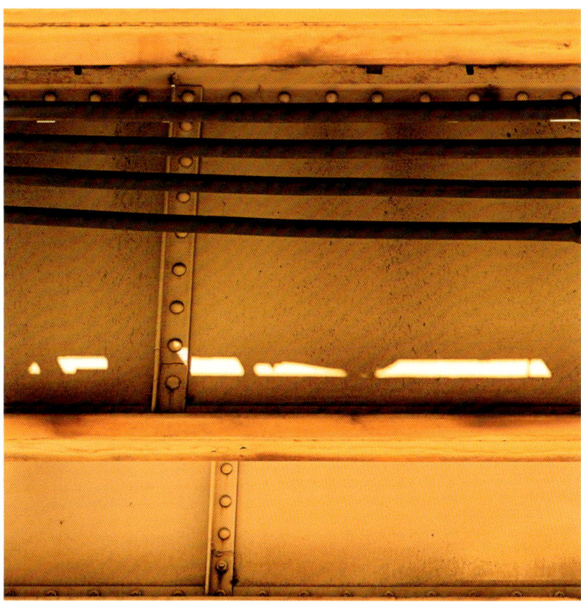

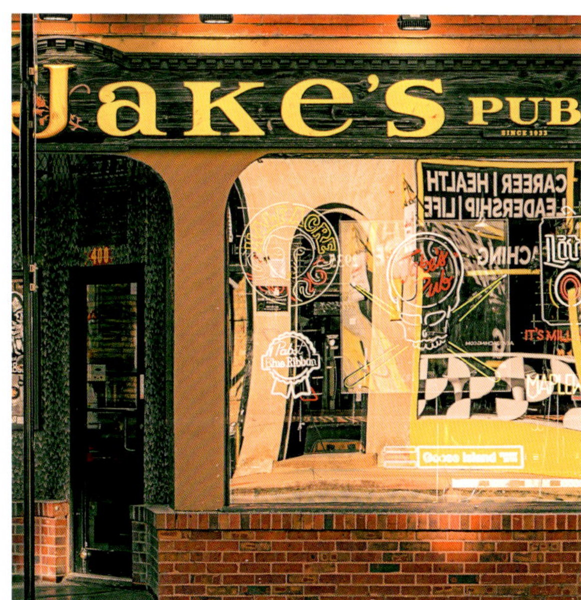
Jake's PUB
SINCE 1933
CAREER | HEALTH
LEADERSHIP | LIFE
Pabst
Blue Ribbon
IT'S MILL

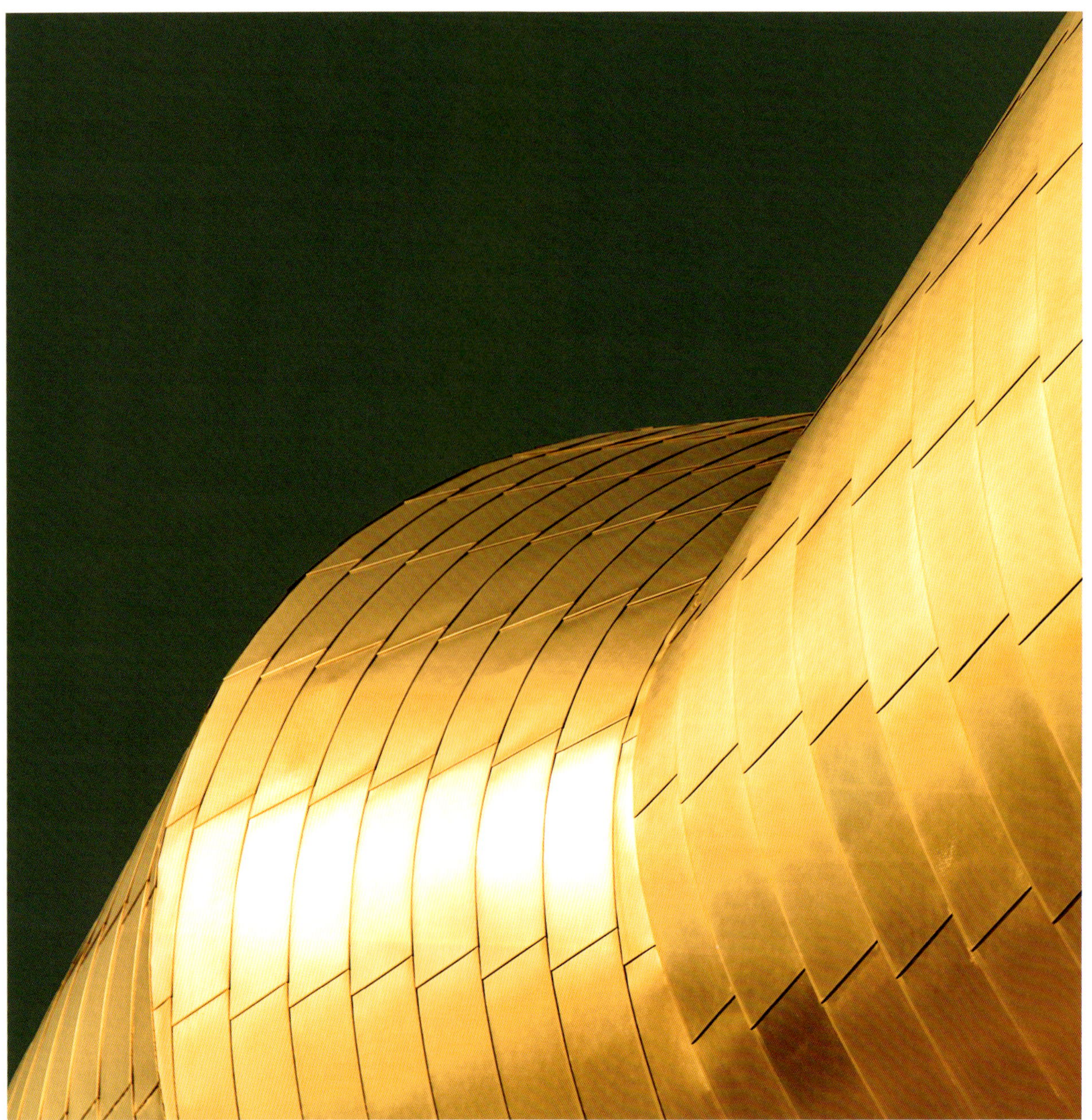

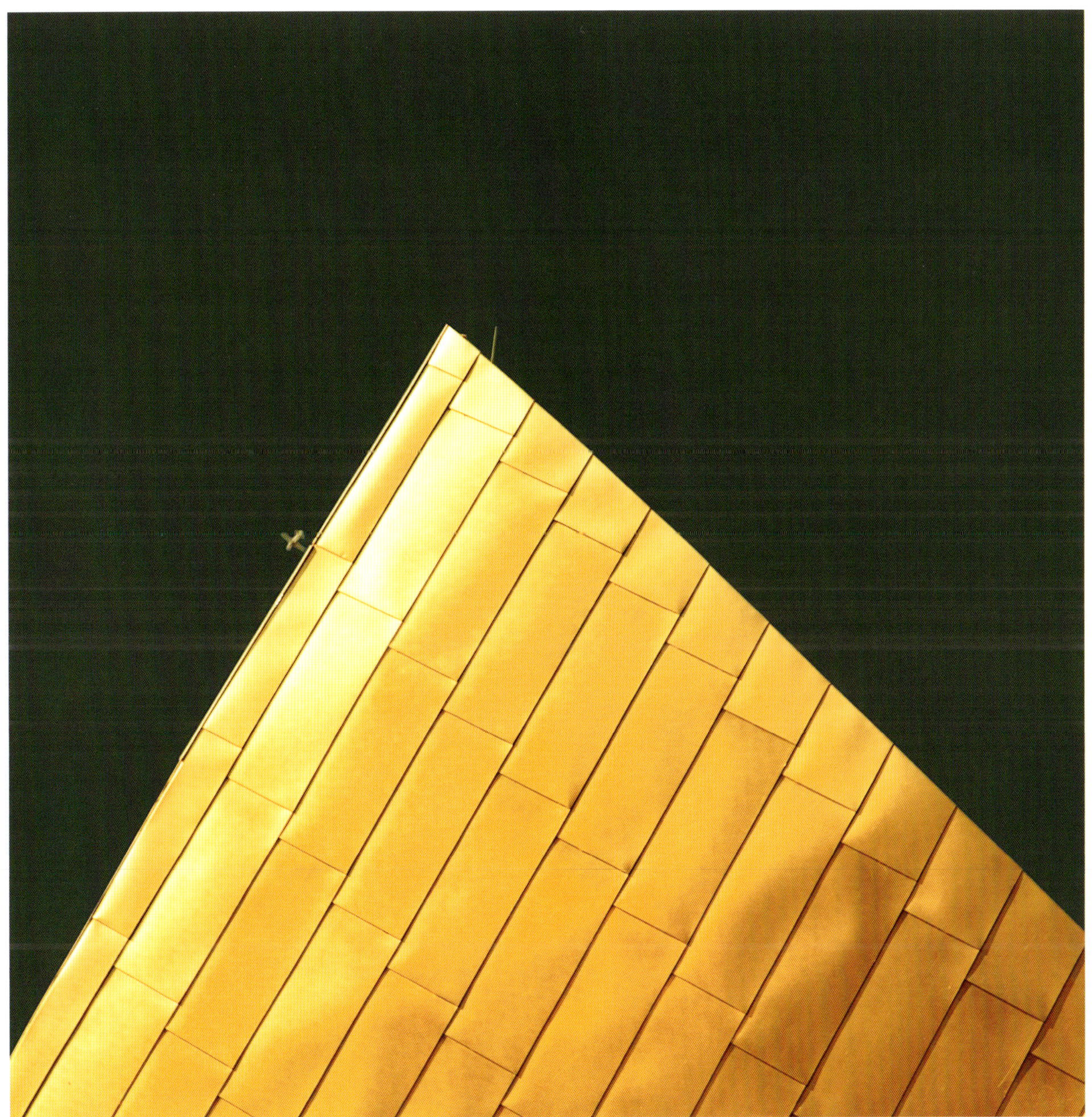

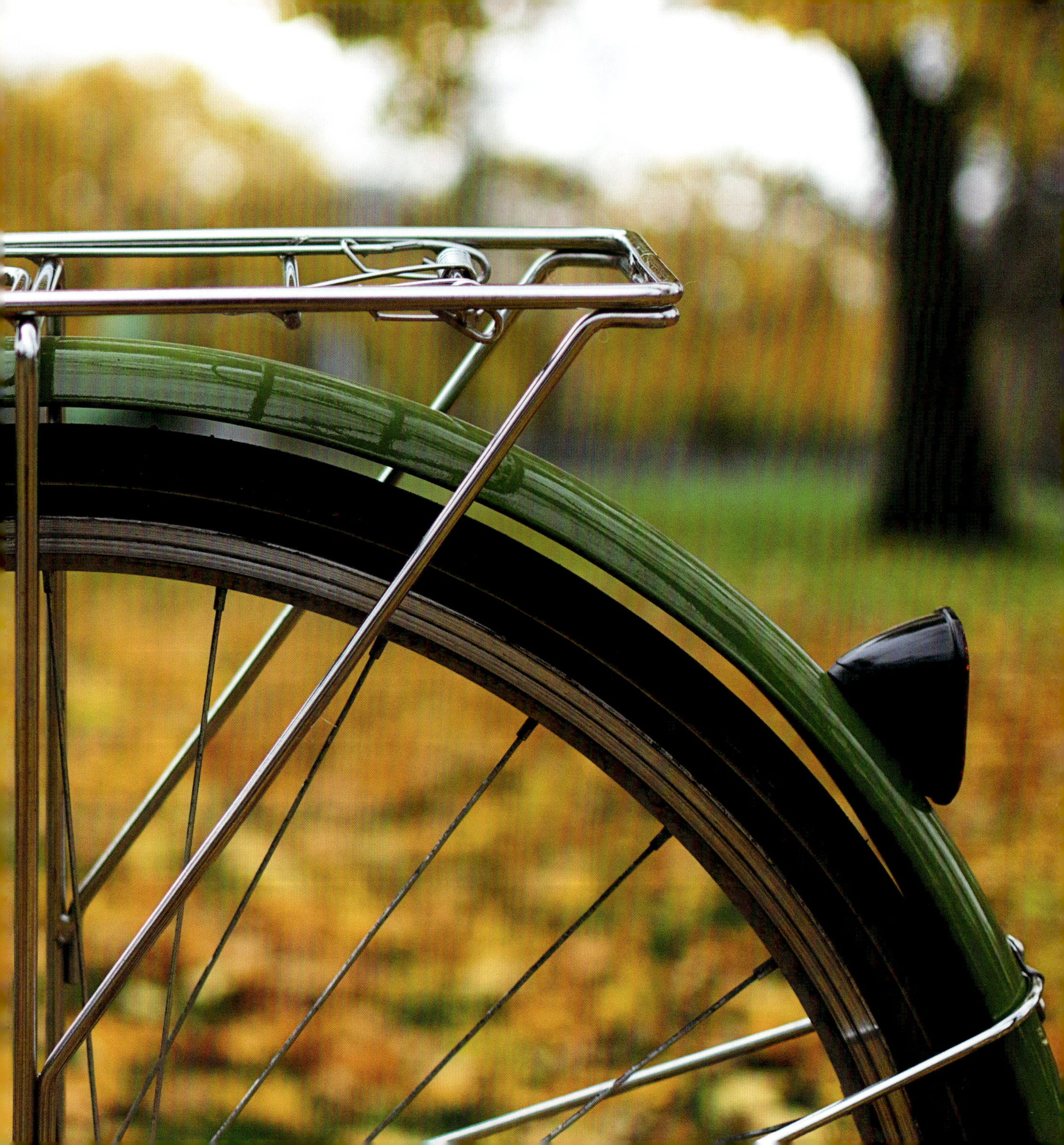

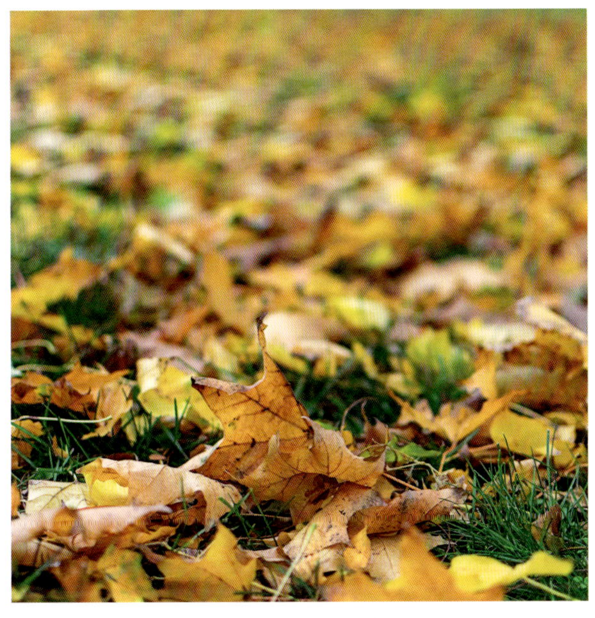
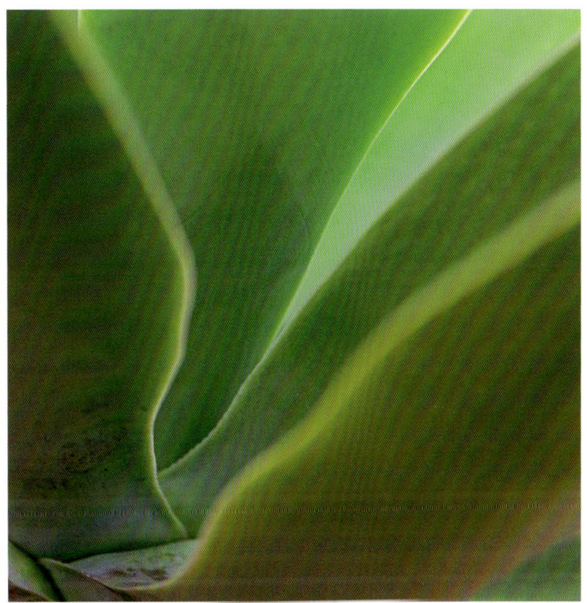
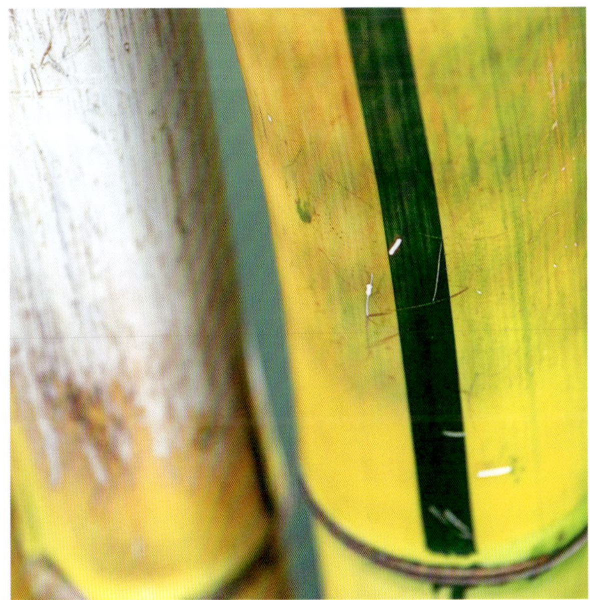
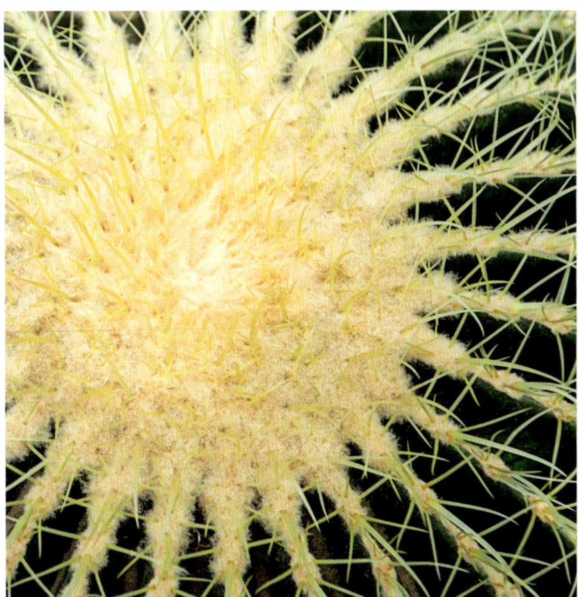

Color! What a deep and
mysterious language,
the language of dreams.

– Paul Gaughin

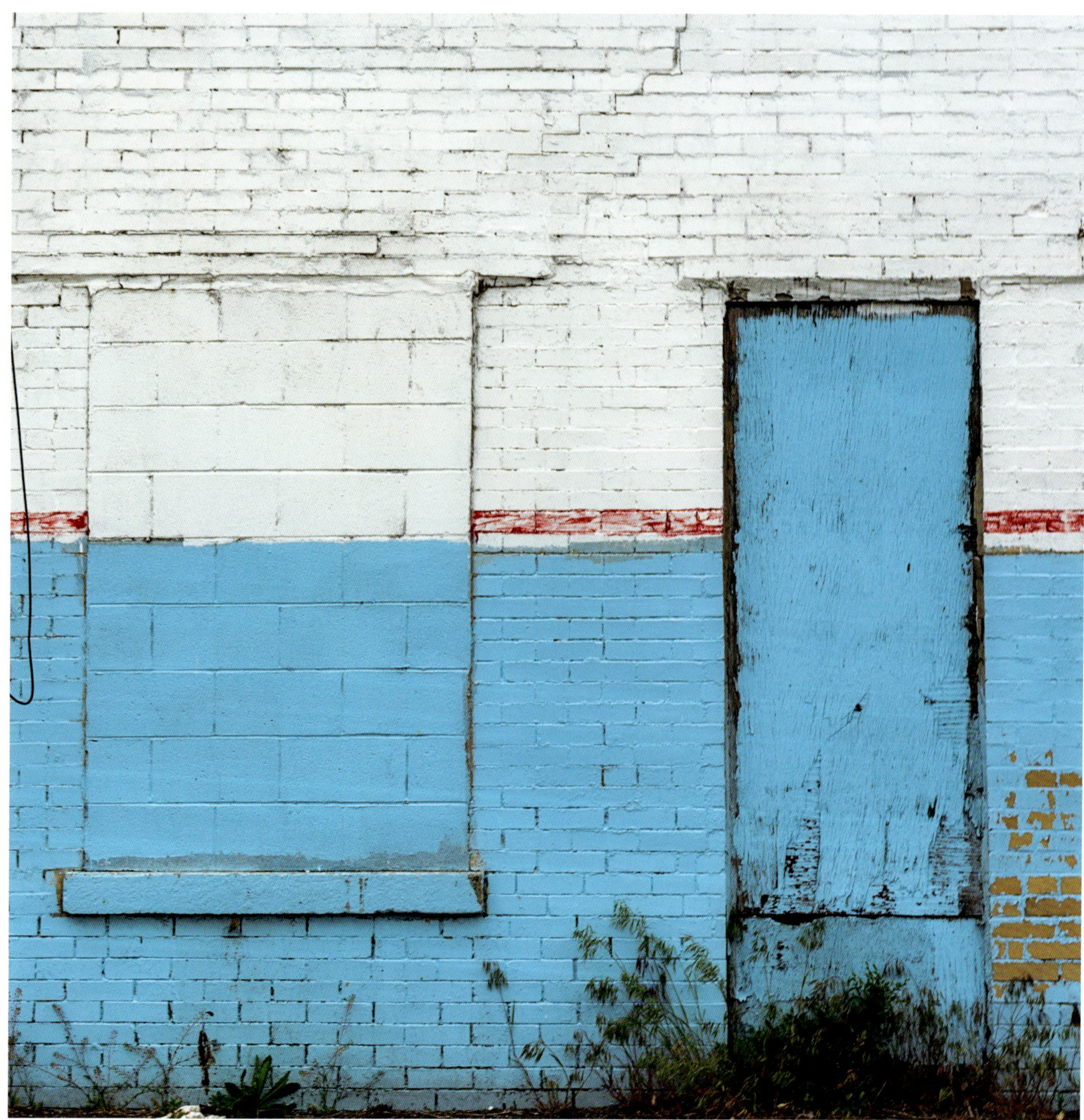

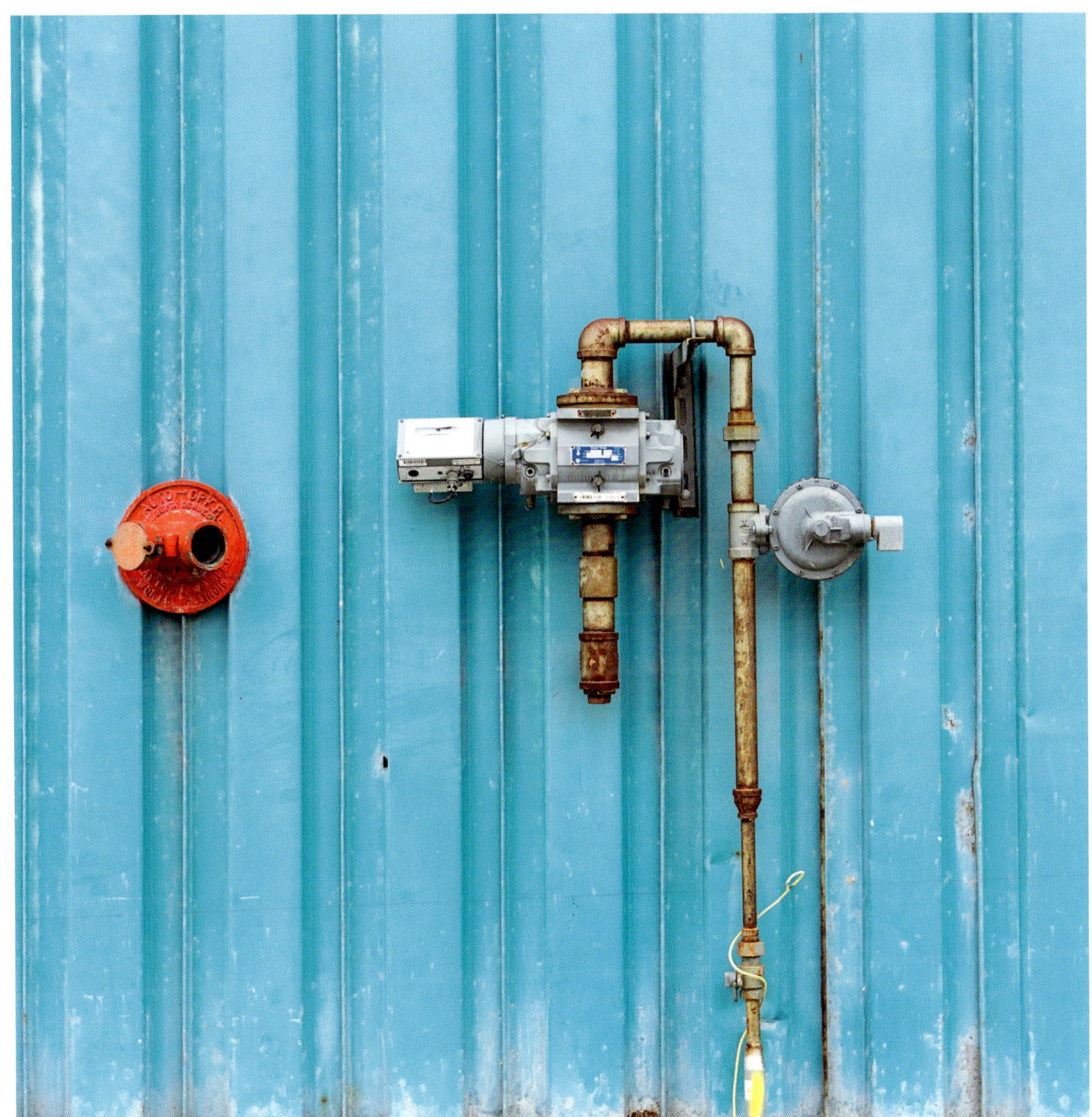

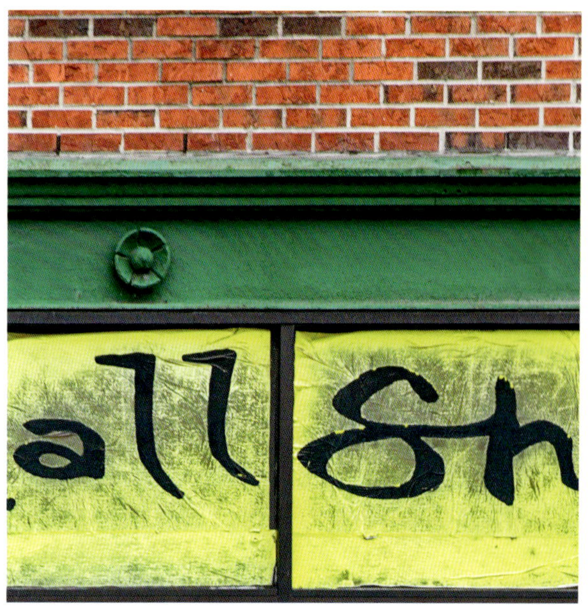
all Sh

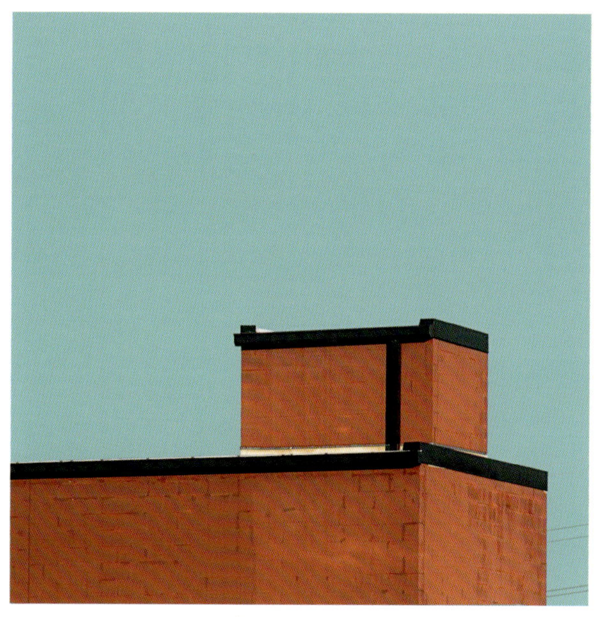

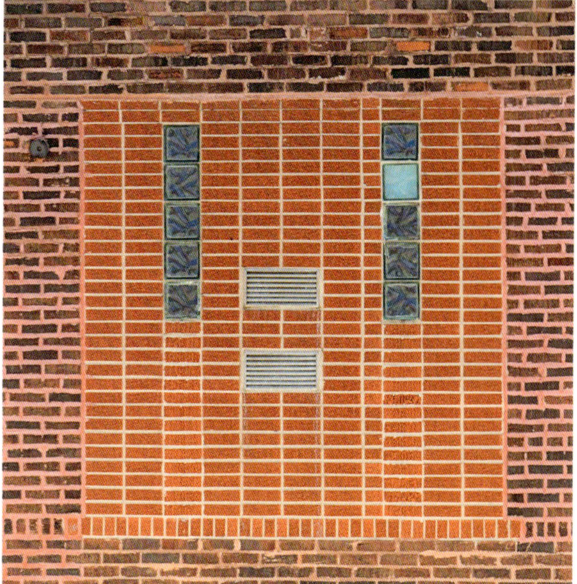

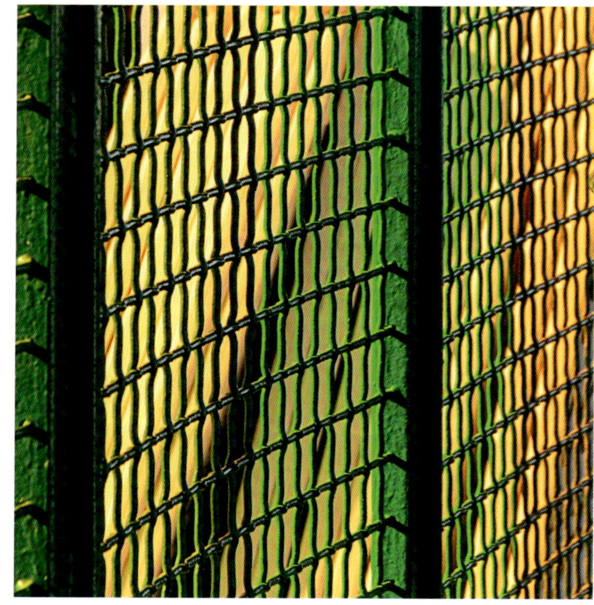

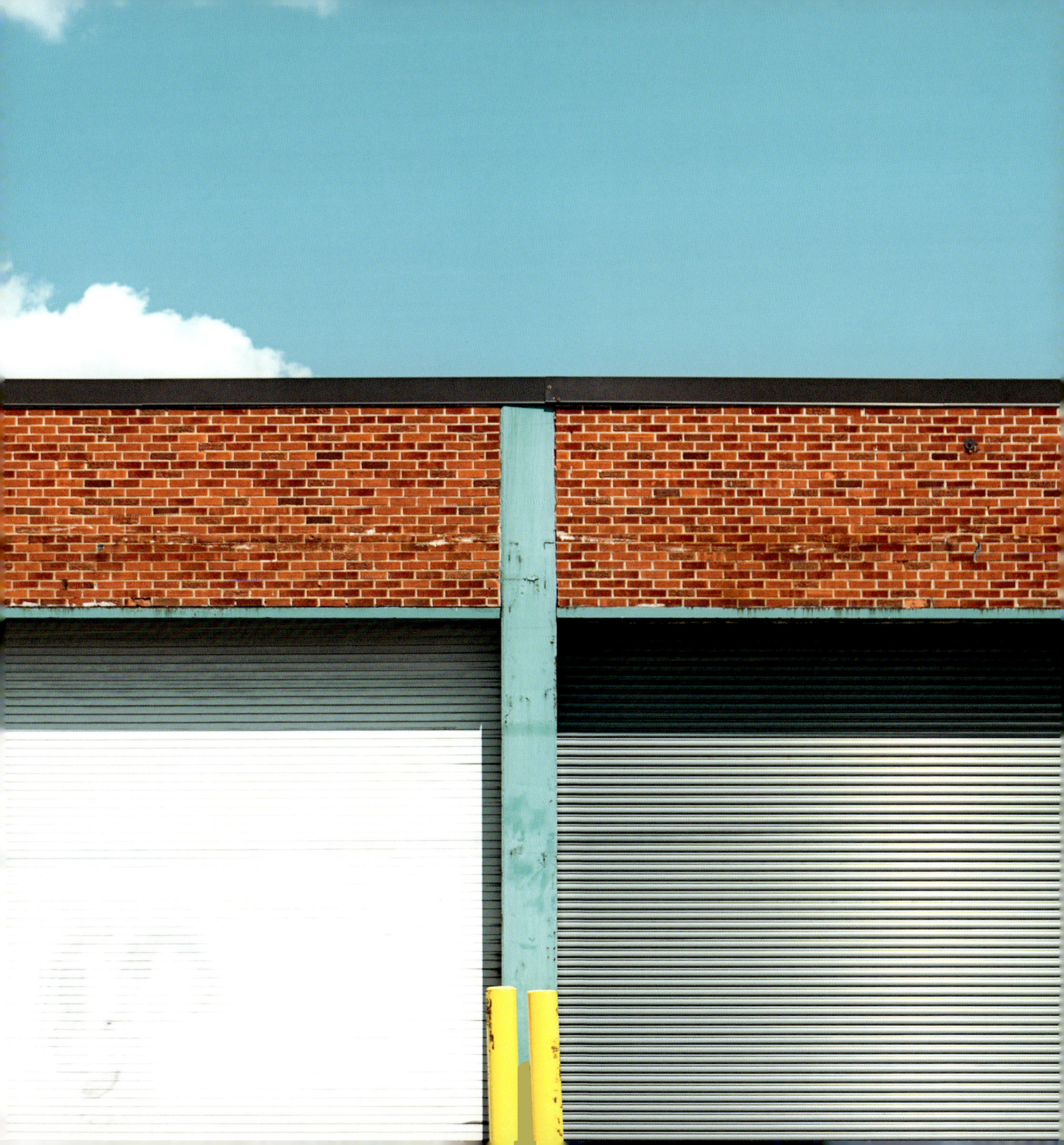

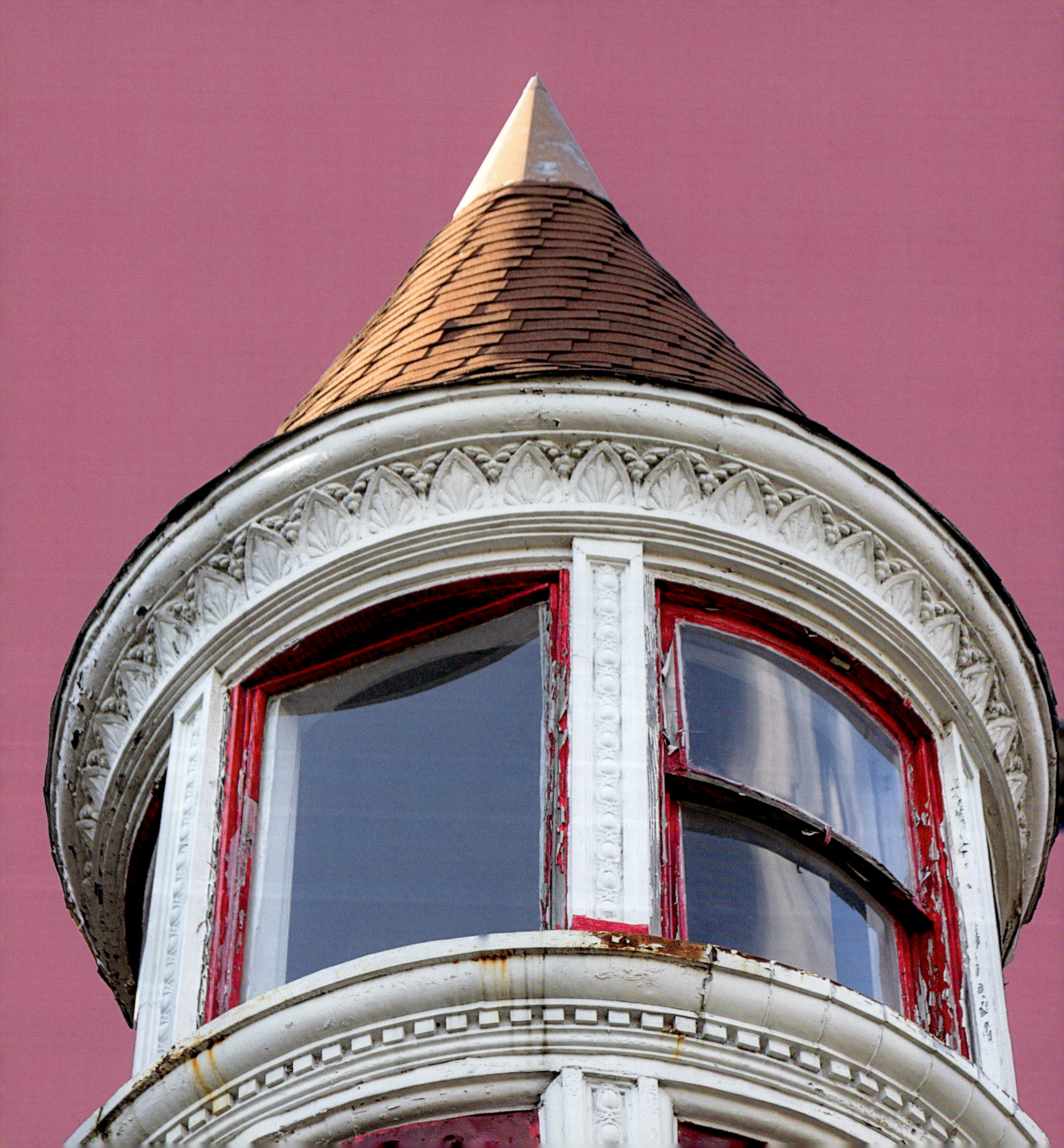

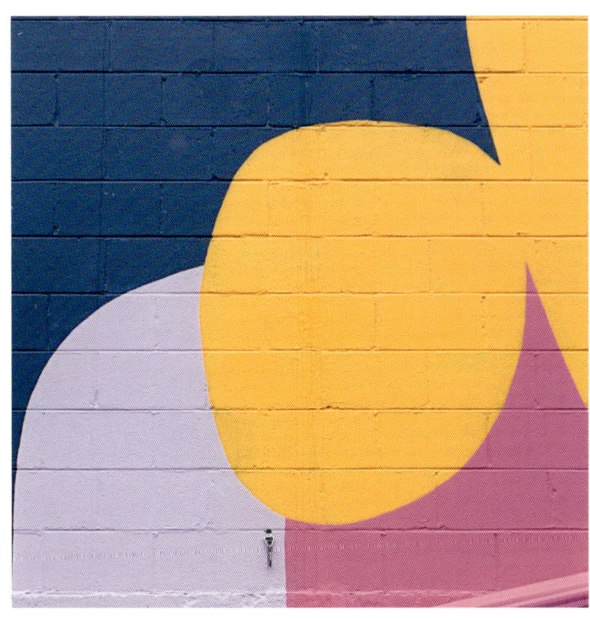
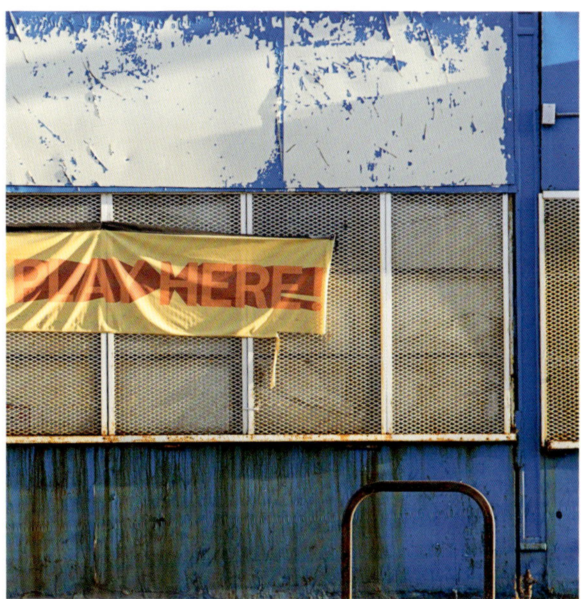
PLAY HERE
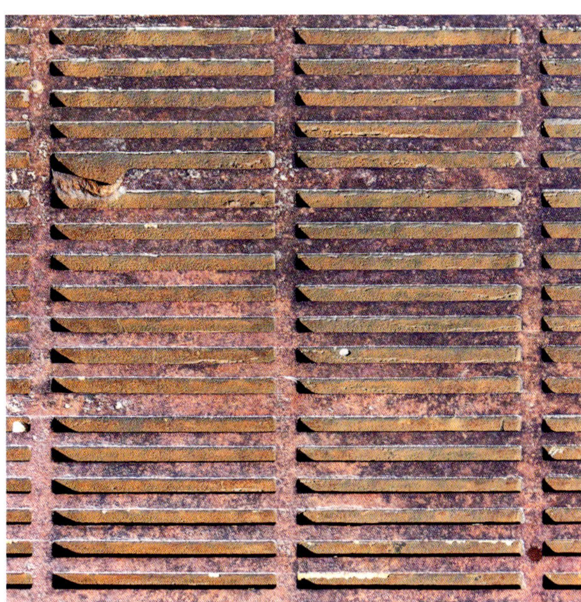
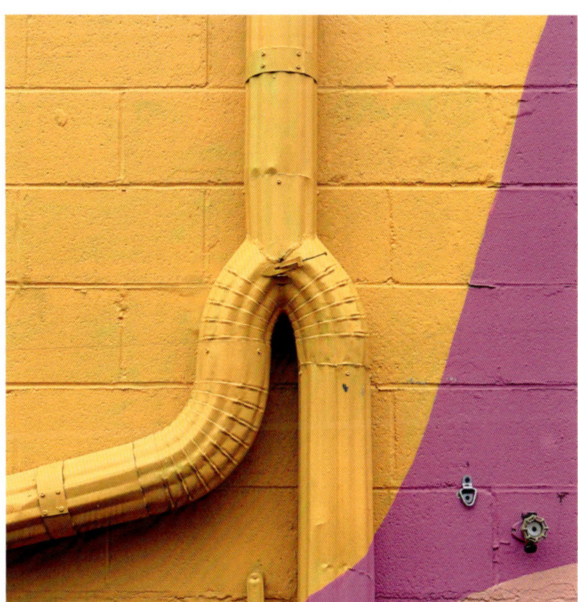

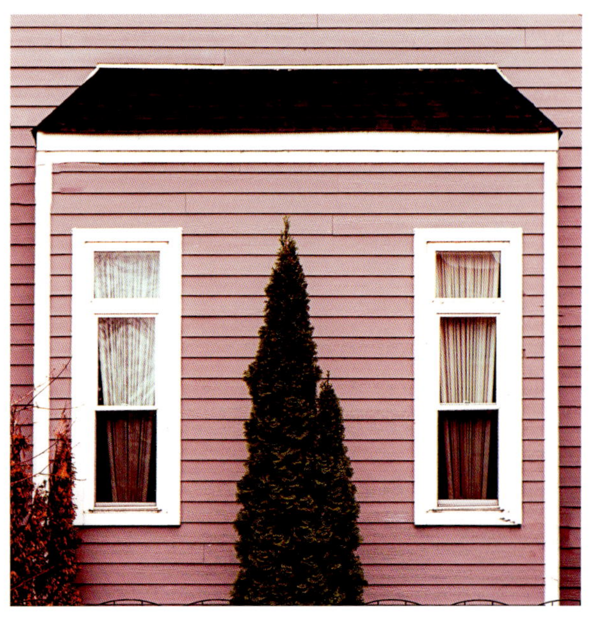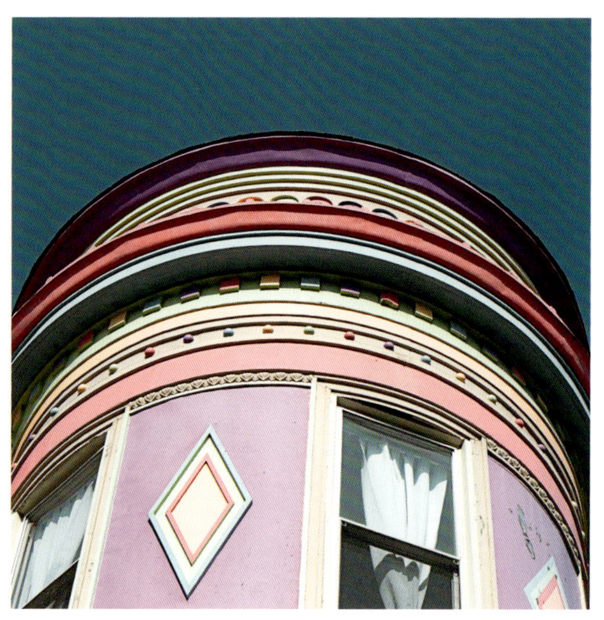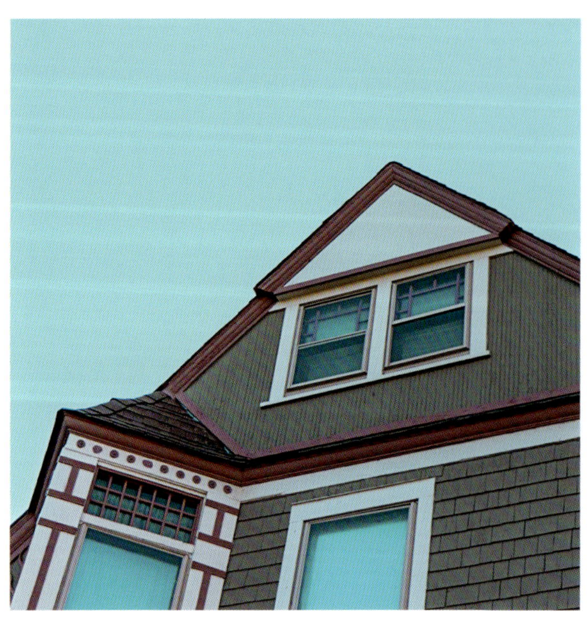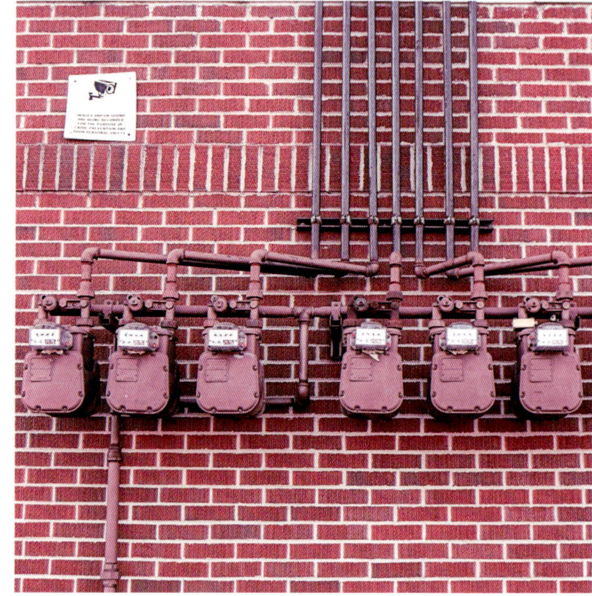

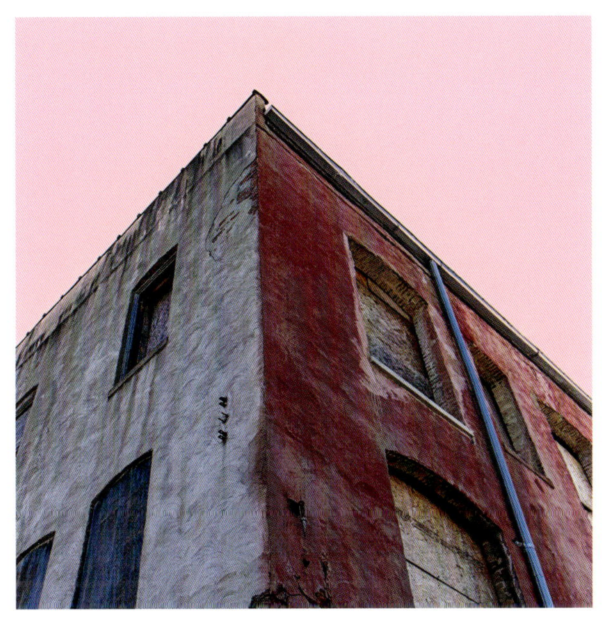
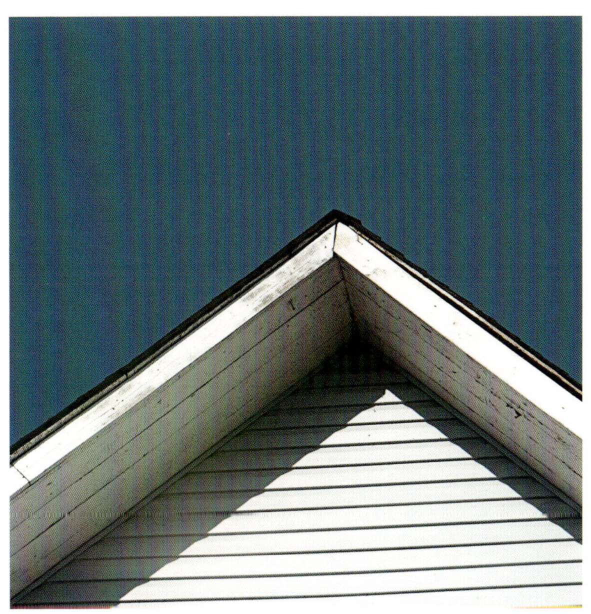
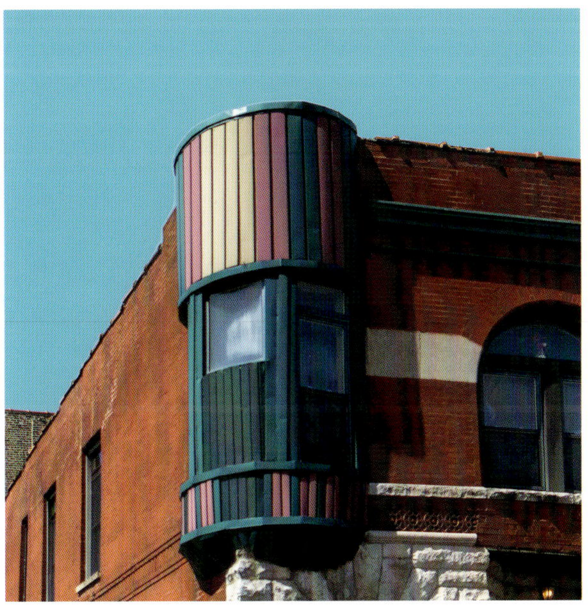
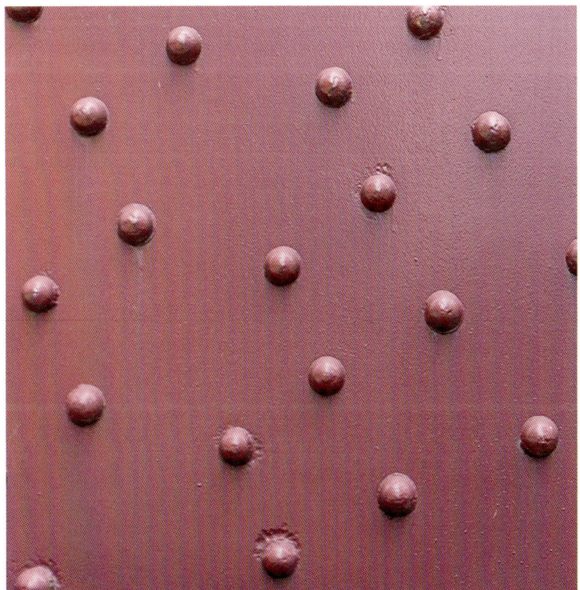

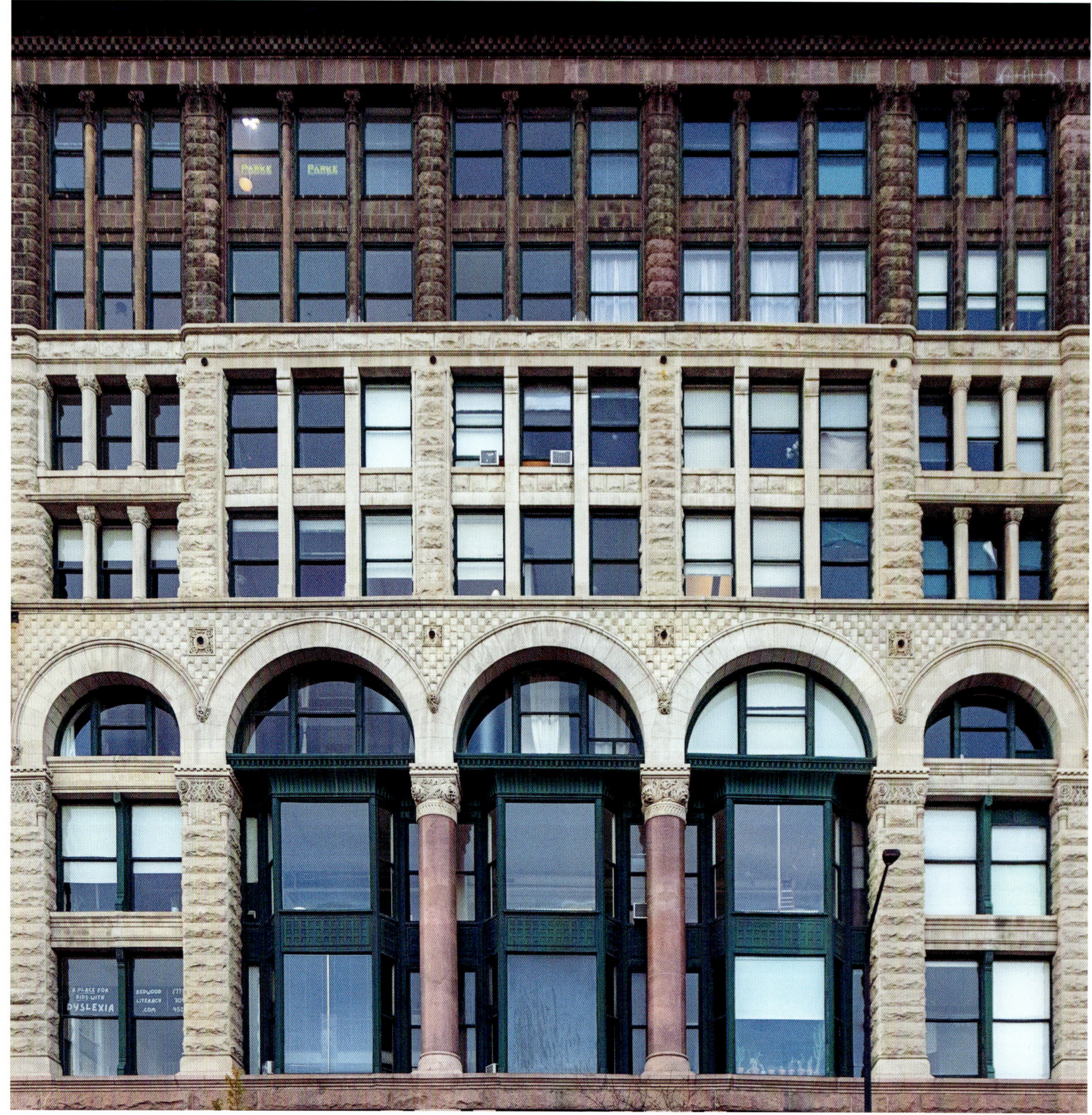
PARKE PARKE
A PLACE FOR
KIDS WITH
DYSLEXIA
REDWOOD
LITERACY
.COM

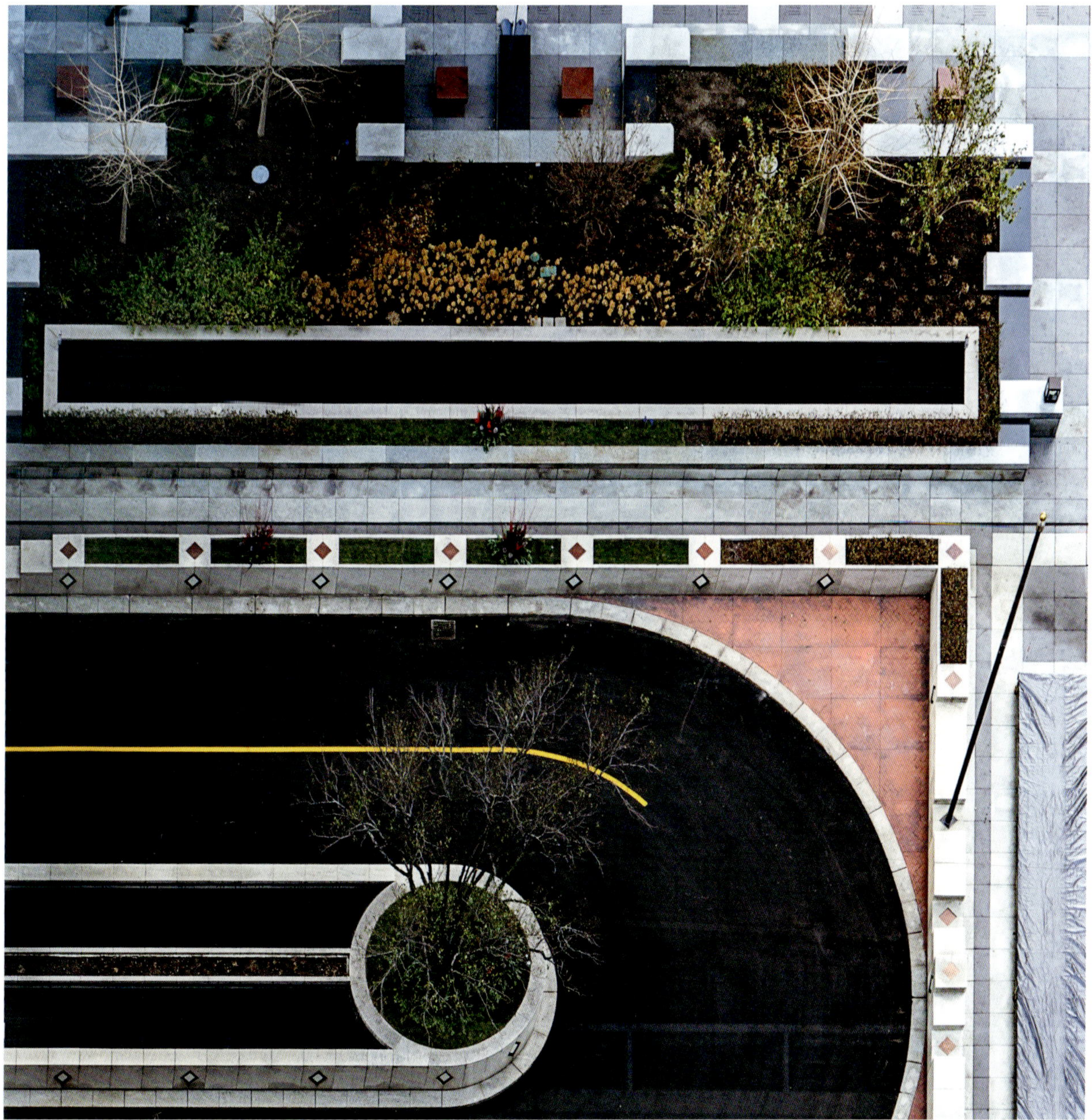

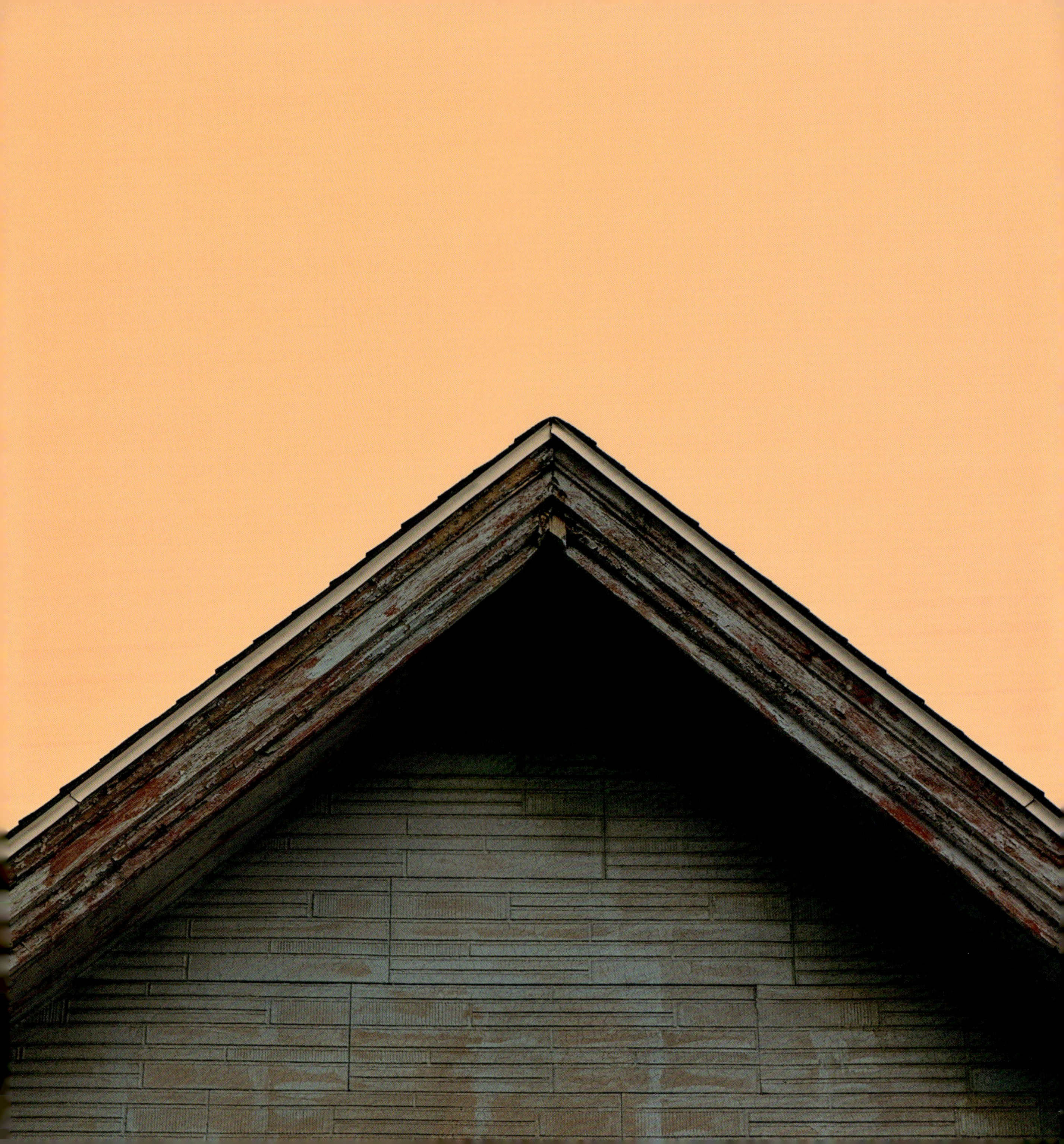

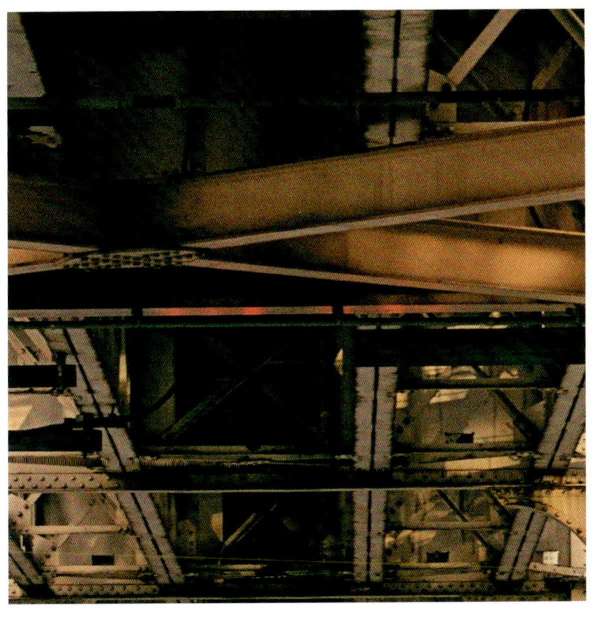

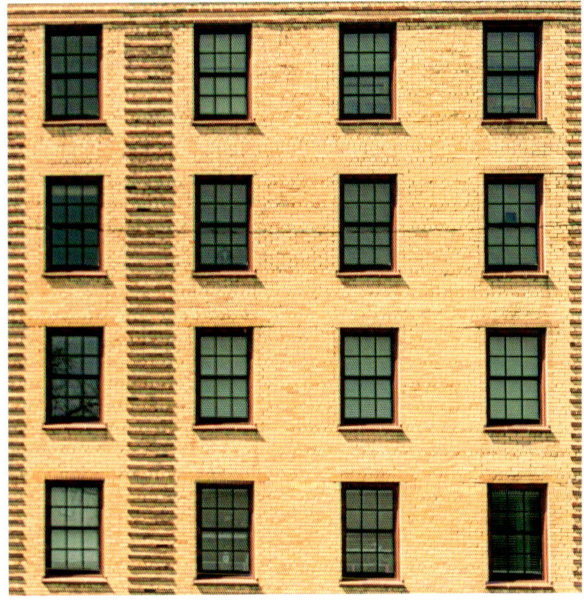

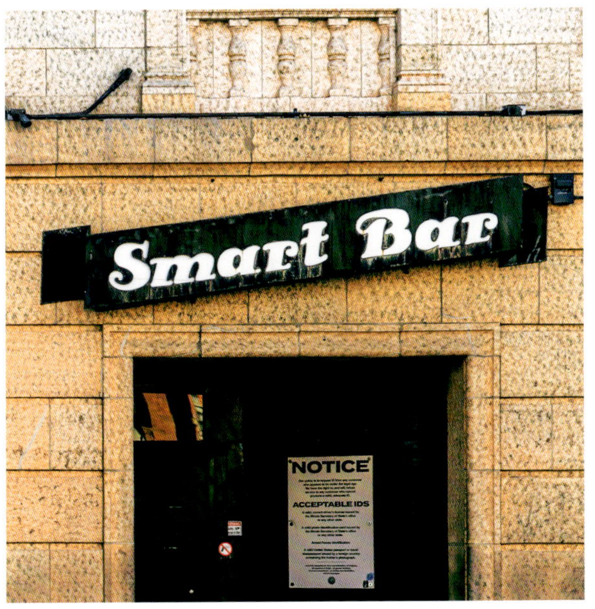
Smart Bar

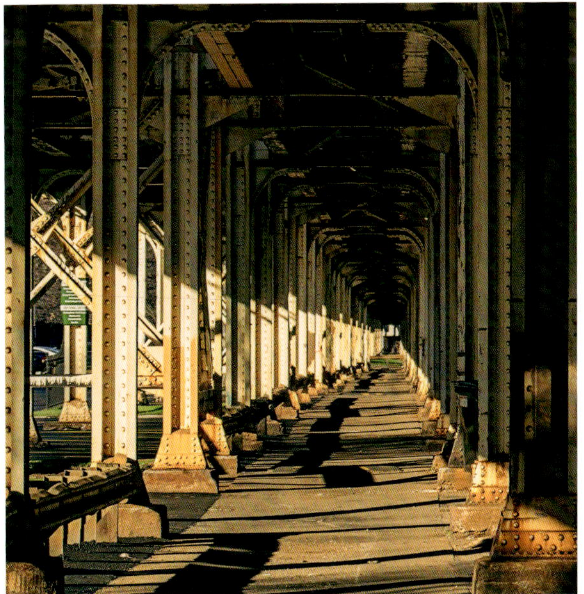

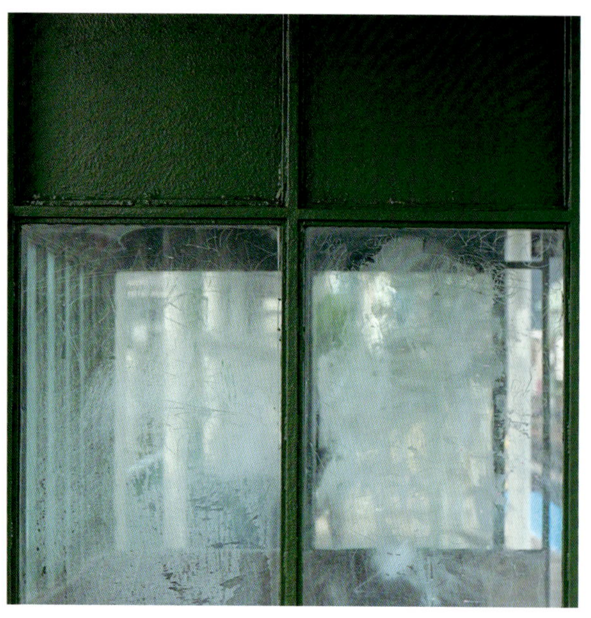
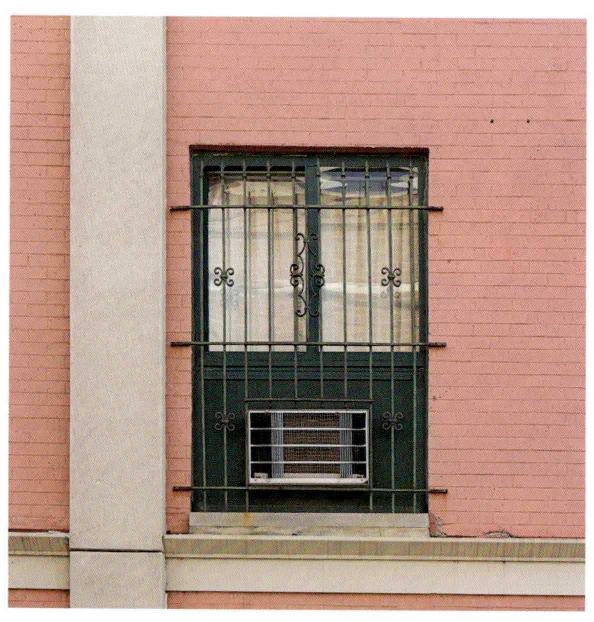
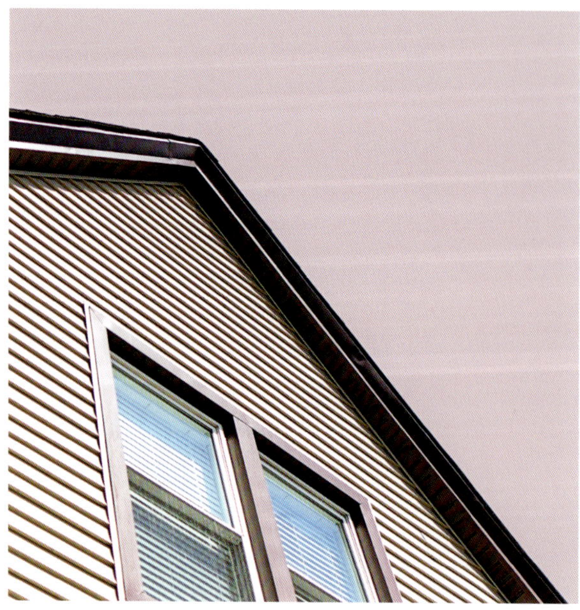
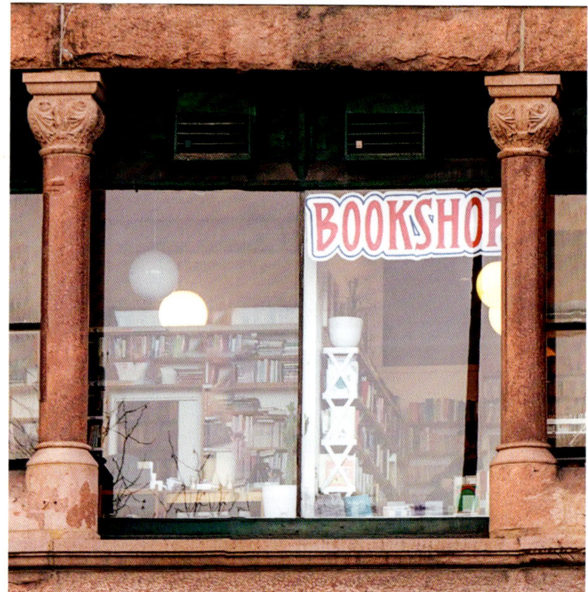
BOOKSHOP

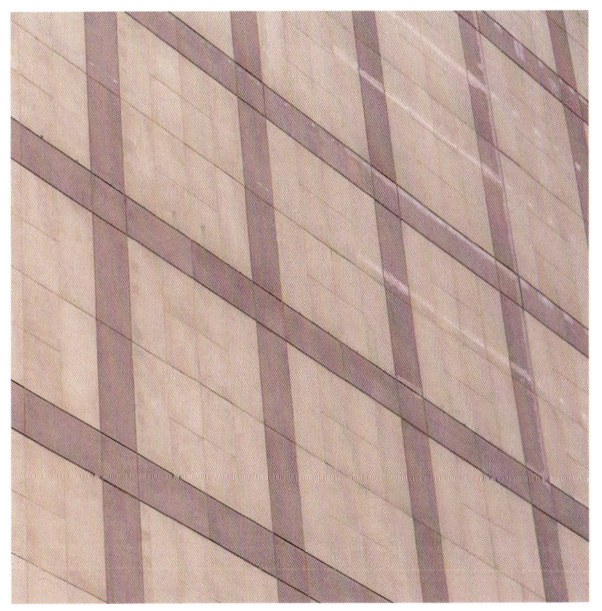
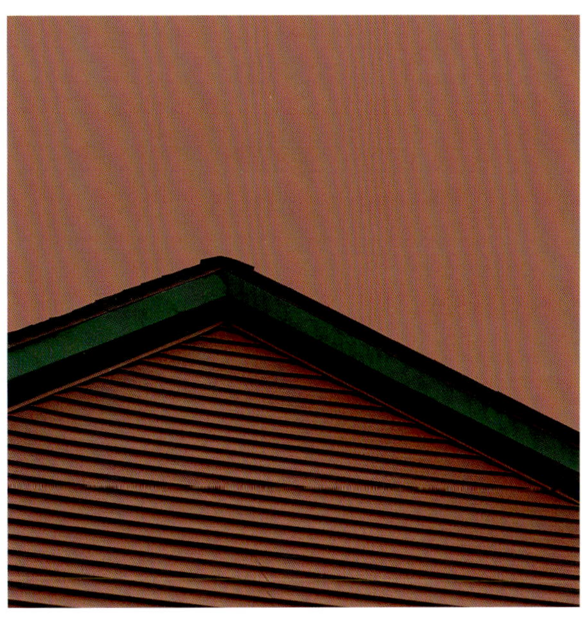
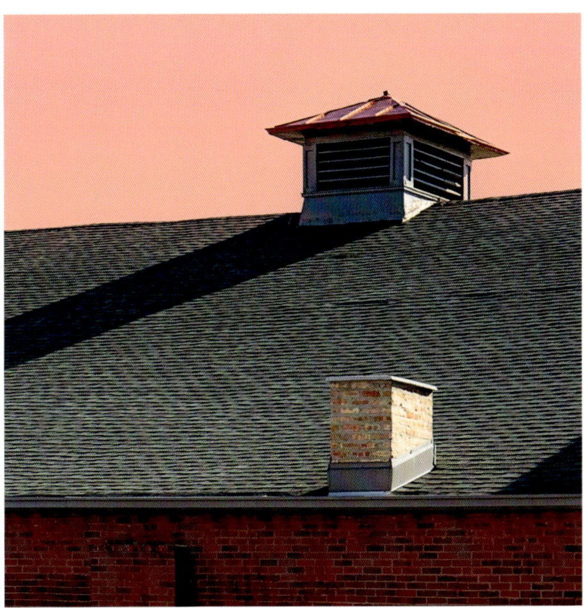
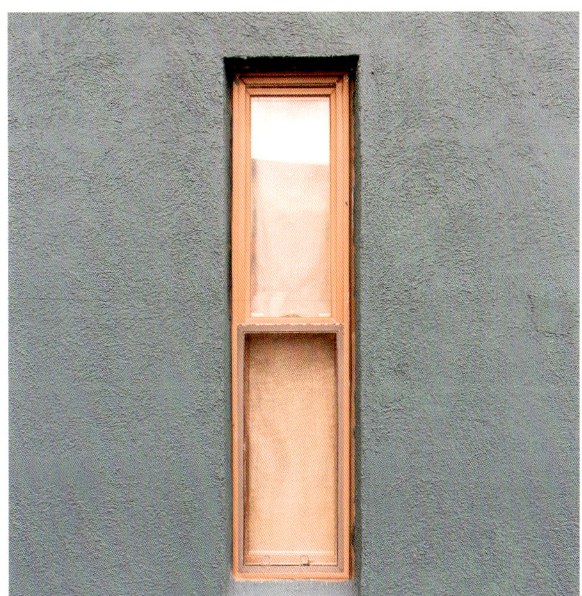

Color is a power which directly influences the soul.

– Wassily Kandinsky

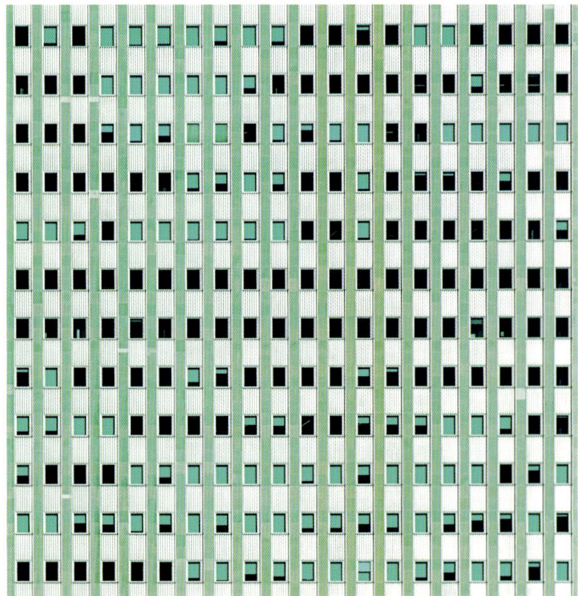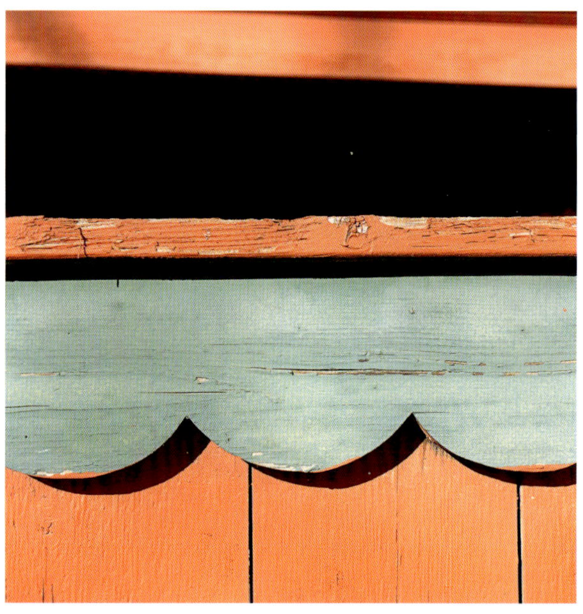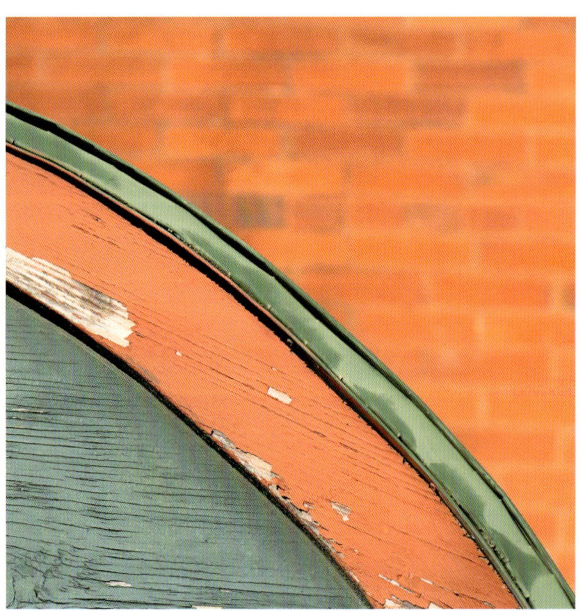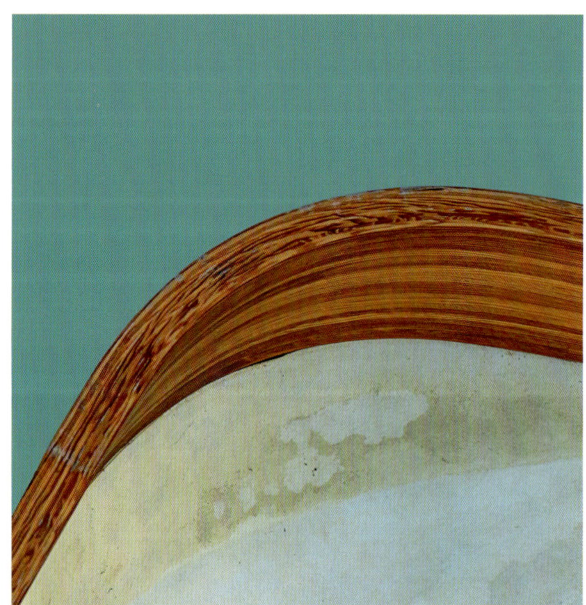

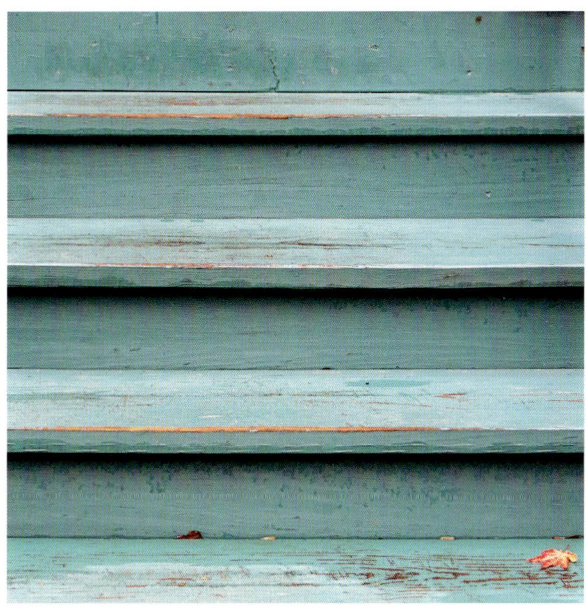

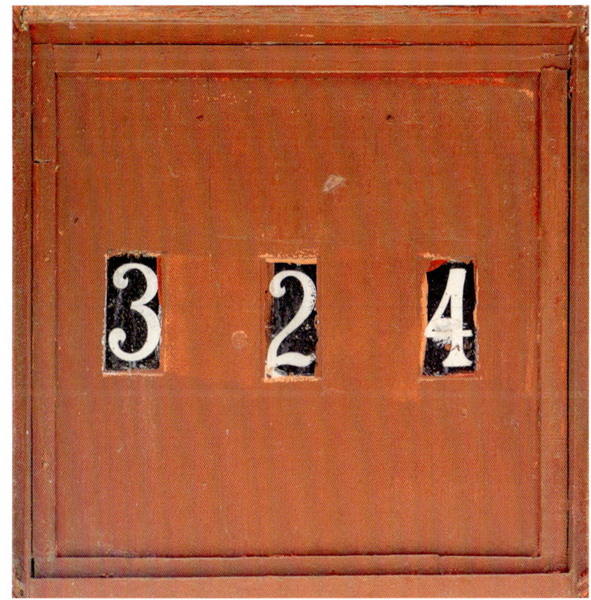

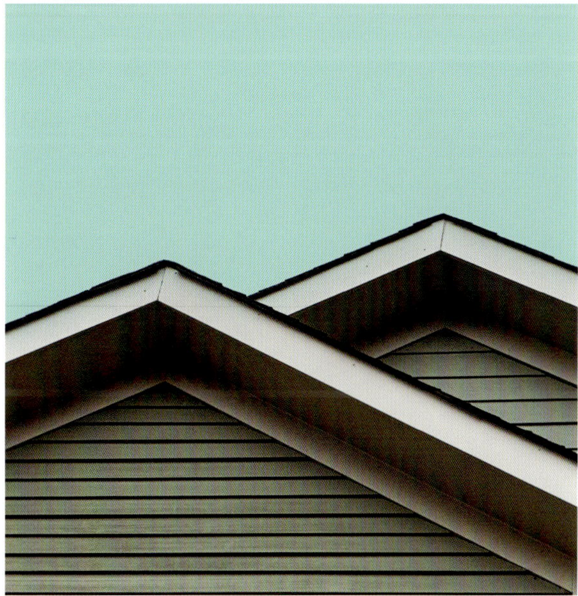

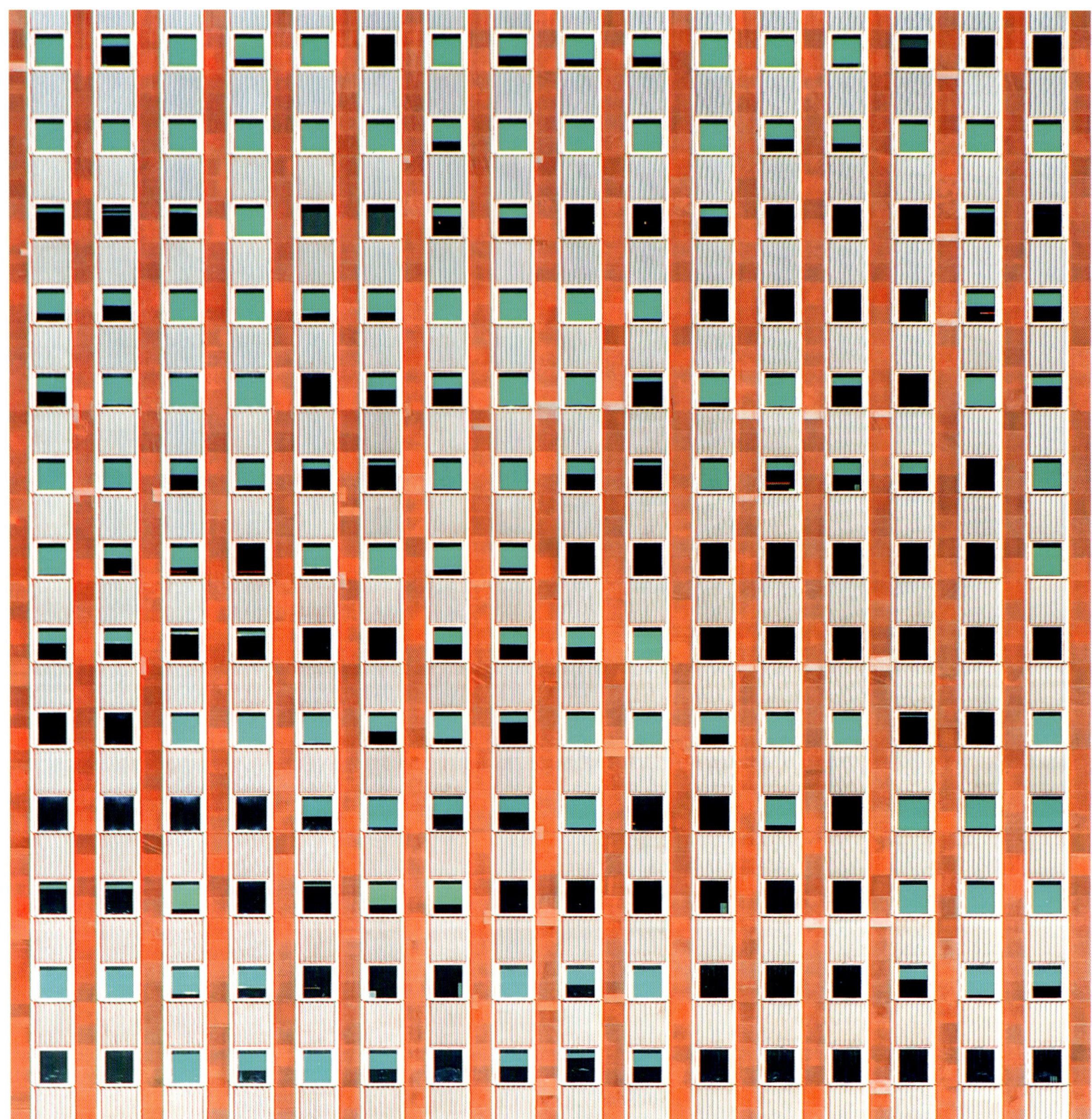

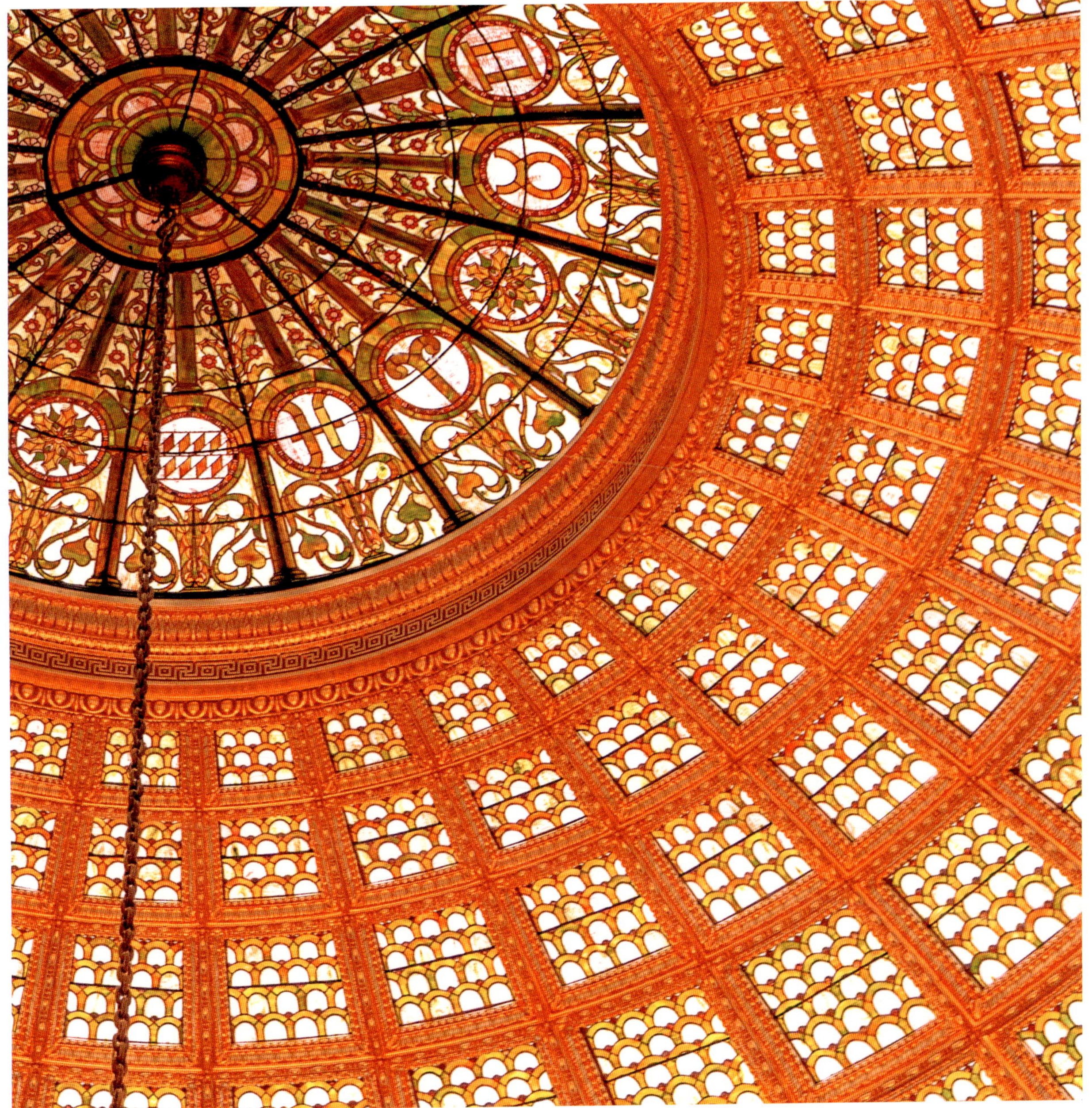

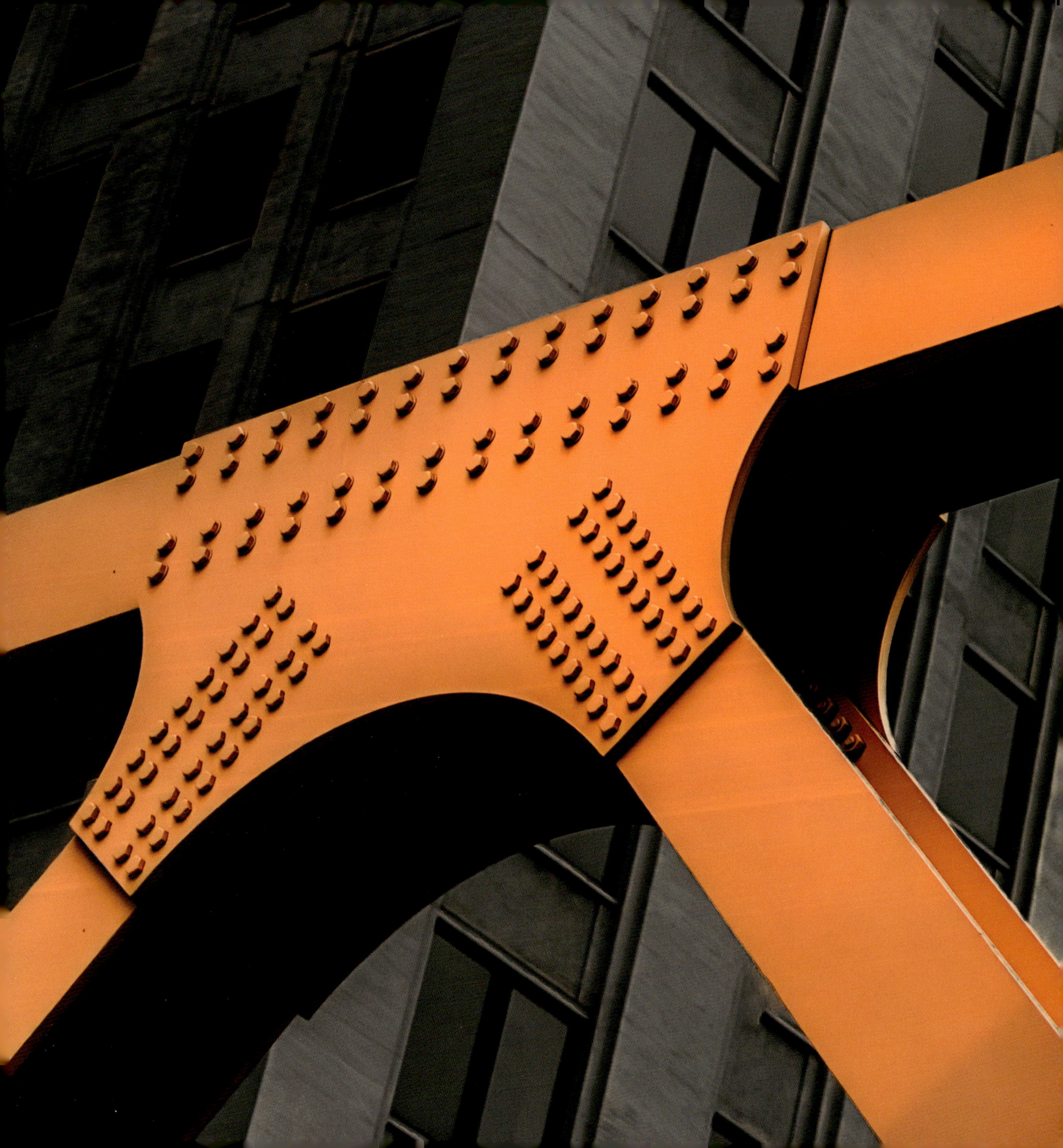

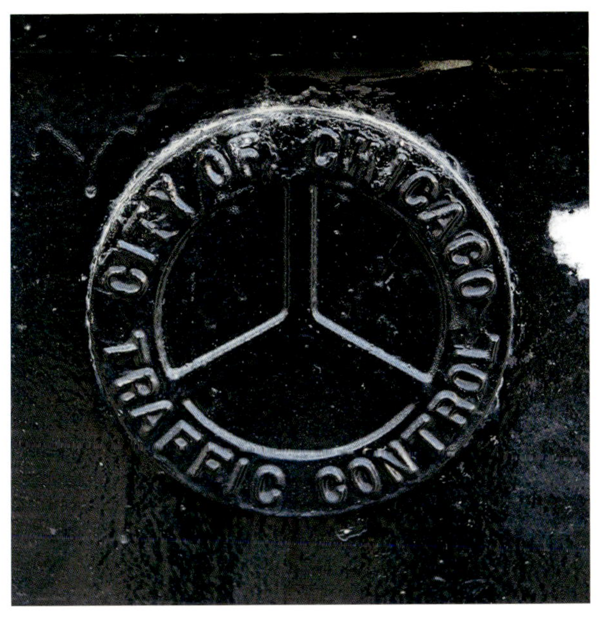
CITY OF CHICAGO
TRAFFIC CONTROL

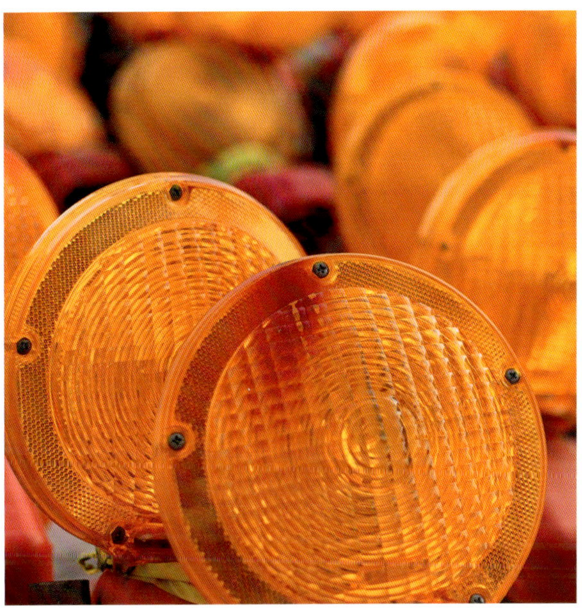

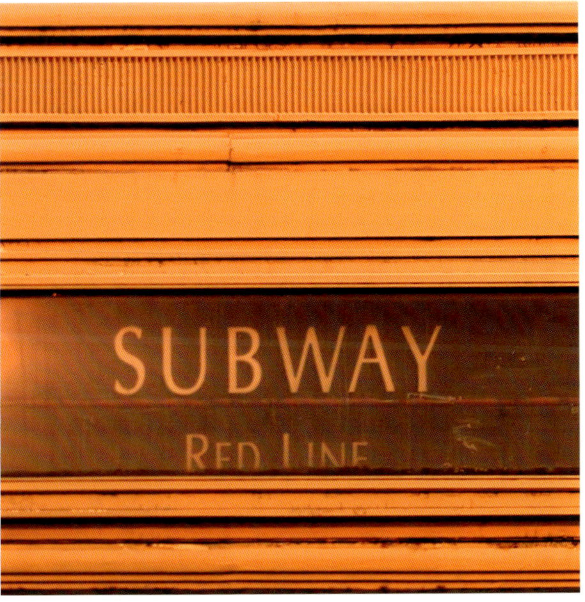
SUBWAY
RED LINE

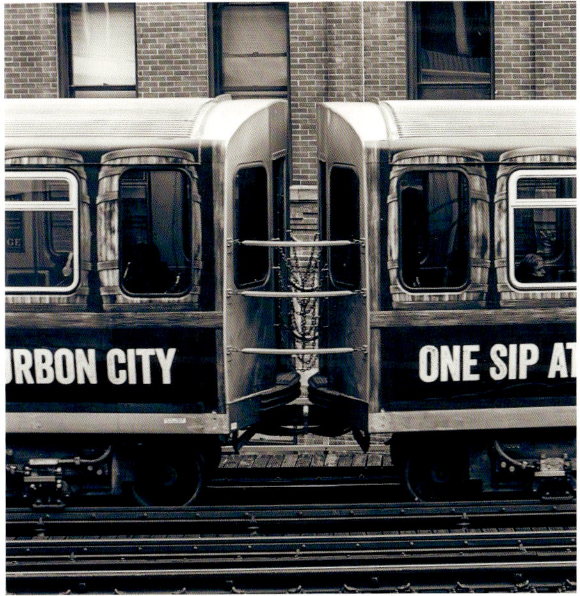
RBON CITY
ONE SIP AT

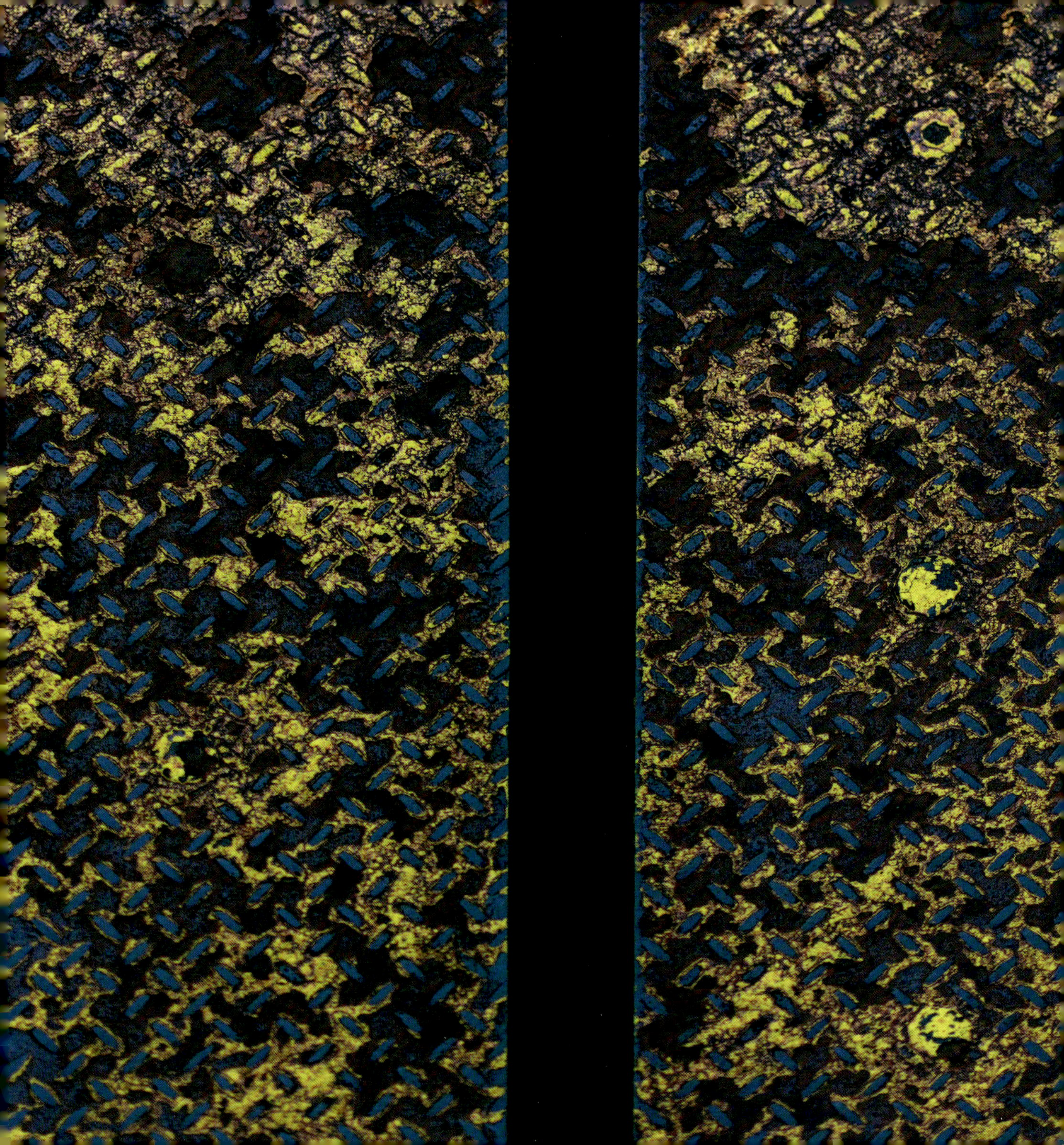

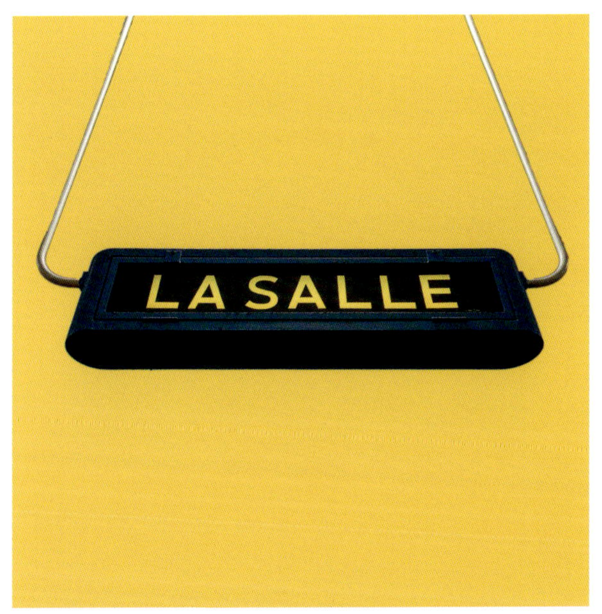
LA SALLE

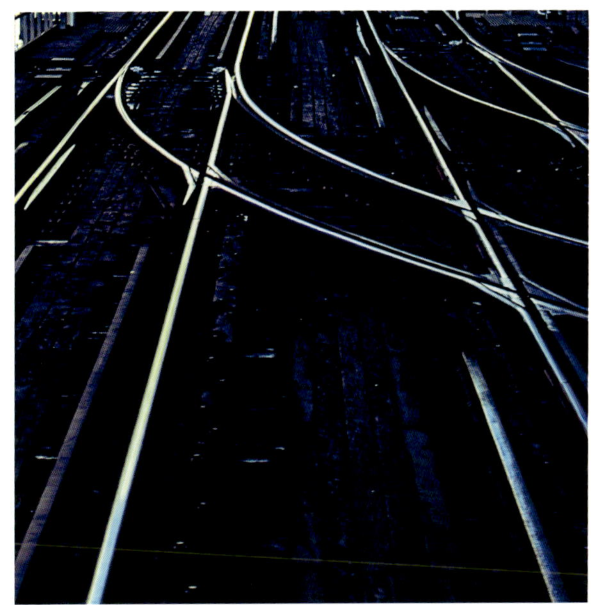

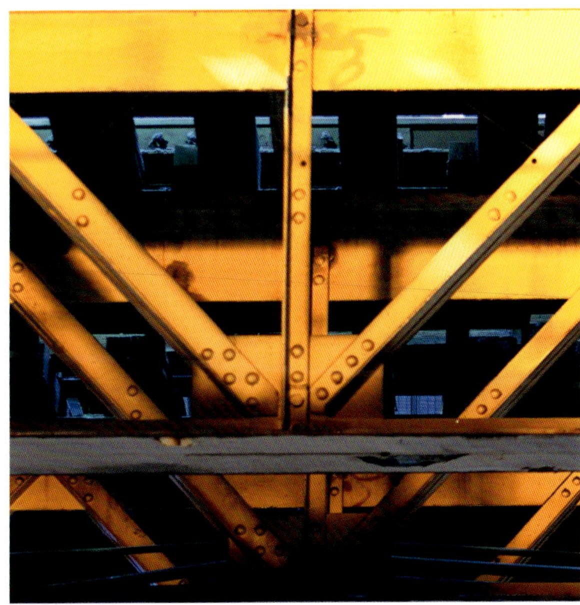

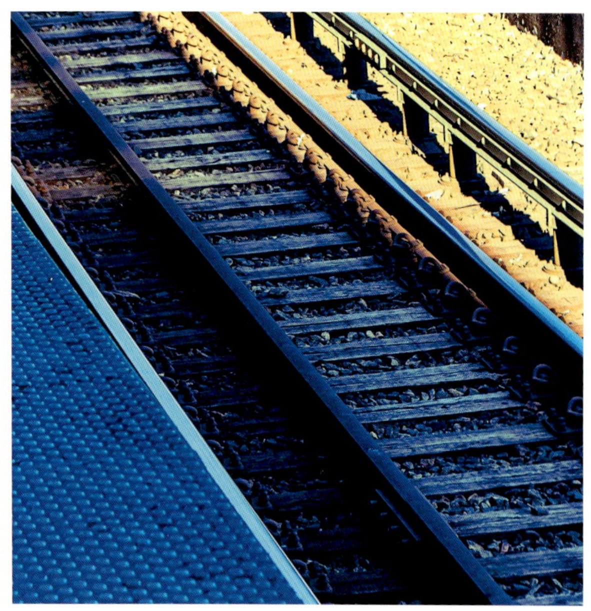
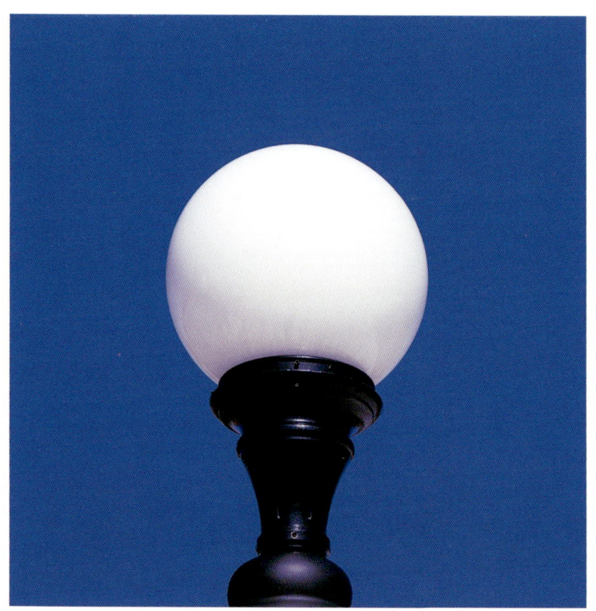
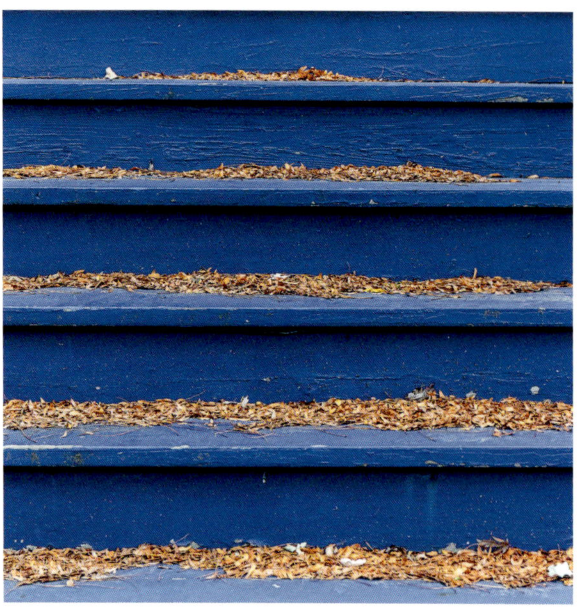
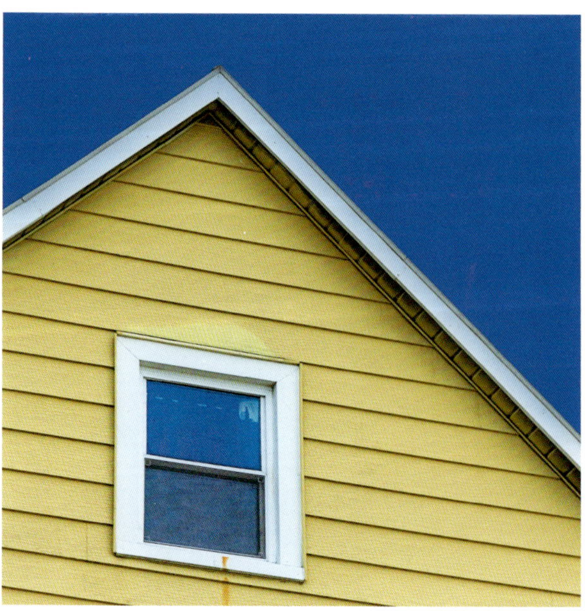

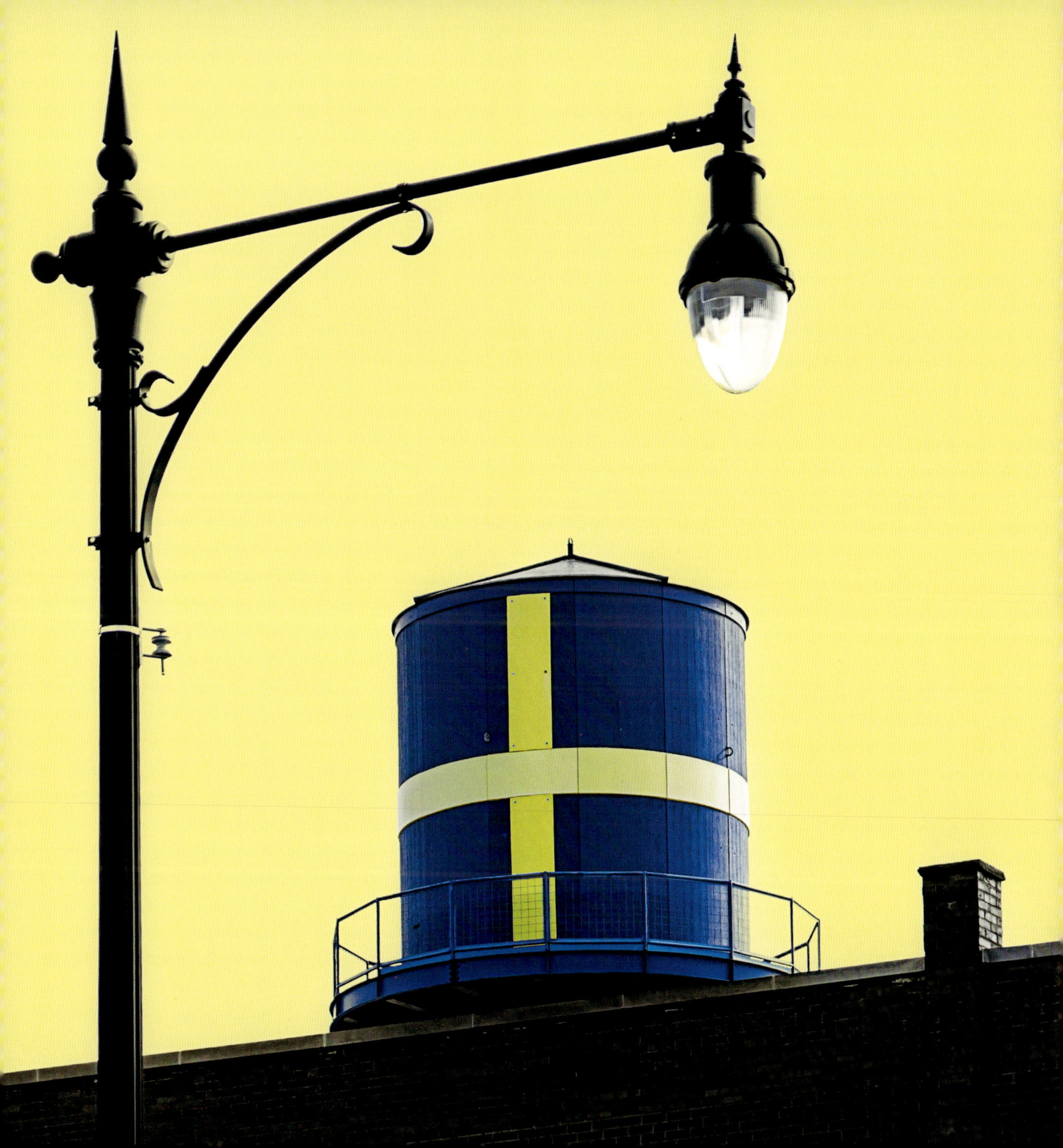

I found I could say things
with color and shapes that
I couldn't say any other way;
things I had no words for.

– Georgia O'Keeffe

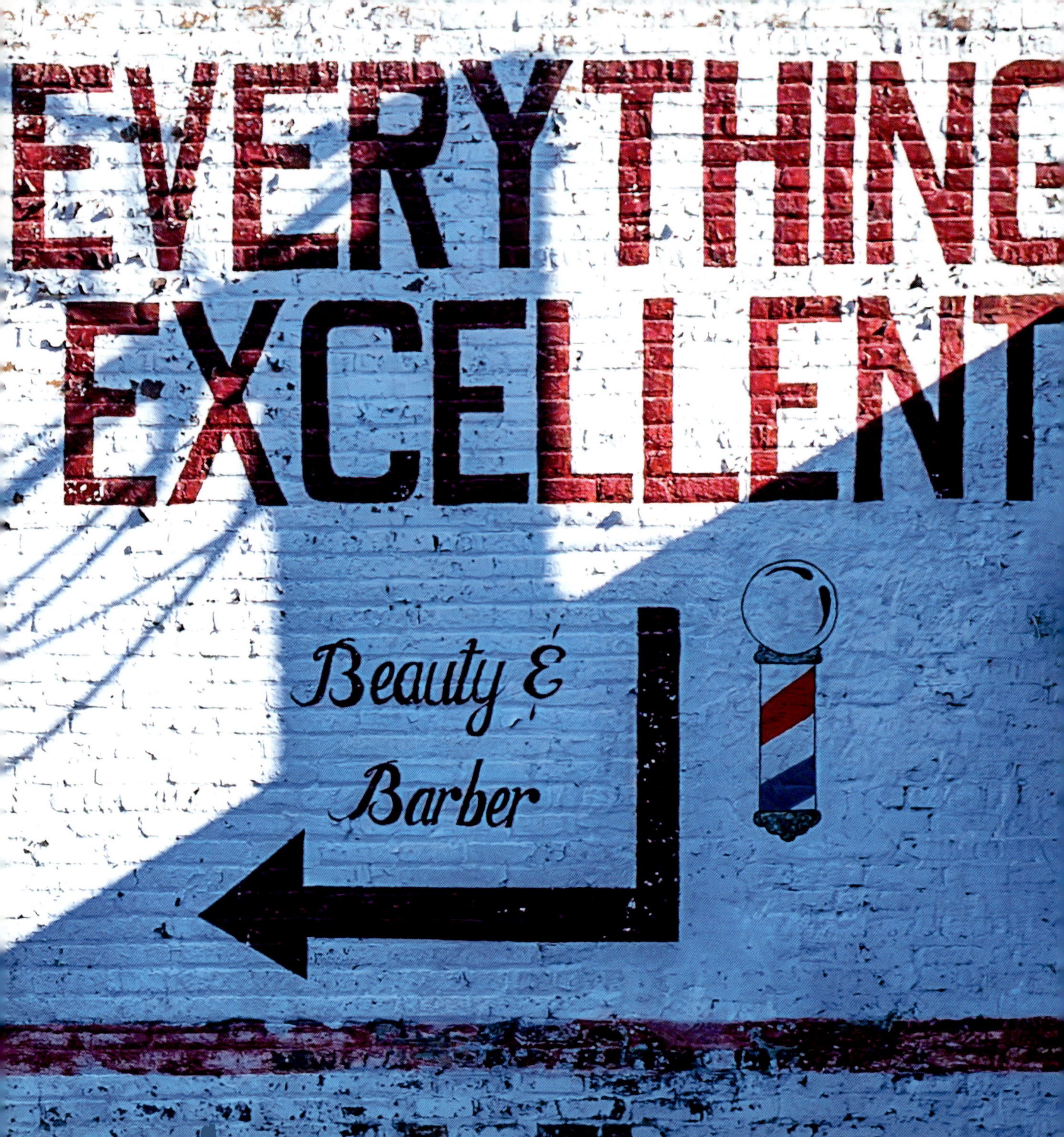

EVERYTHING
EXCELLENT
Beauty &
Barber

Acknowledgments

Thank you to everyone who encouraged me along the way—your support and positive feedback have been essential to keeping me going. I especially deeply want to thank my close friends and family who accompanied me and made this exploration so enjoyable. This book is yours.

I also want to thank Richard Stromberg's Chicago Photography Classes. This project would not have been possible without everything I learned there. I particularly want to thank all my teachers and classmates—you made this journey really fun and always made me feel so welcomed in Chicago.

I want to send a very special acknowledgment to the book *Tejiendo Imágenes* by Ana Paula Fuentes. I discovered *Tejiendo Imágenes* while visiting a friend in Oaxaca and I am so glad I did; it has been such an inspiration. *Chicago in Color* would probably not exist without it.

I also want to express gratitude for the supportive environment I found at the University of Chicago, and especially to Chihway, for fostering a culture of art within the department and for her kind mentorship.

Finally, I especially want to thank all the Chicagoans I encountered out there who made me feel so welcome. I think this is what makes Chicago so special—the city's particularly kind and open people. I met some of these wonderful people at various places and events that will always hold a special place in my heart for their role in building community and contributing to the city's charming vibe.

The amazing Jackalope Coffee & Tea House in Bridgeport, where I made a good portion of the book—it has been such a pleasure to spend my Sunday afternoons there. The Cove Lounge and its people. BFF Bikes in Bucktown, a shop that specializes in bikes for women, where I bought my bike, an essential companion on this journey. The Small Shop Cycles & Service in Bronzeville, my great local bike shop. The Sunday Service by the Rebuild Foundation for its incredible contagious energy. The Wednesday beer cans and the Nyctosaur crew for creating such a friendly and positive environment. The Bronzeville Summer Nights organizers, for making me feel included in my neighborhood. And so many more. Thank you, Chicago.

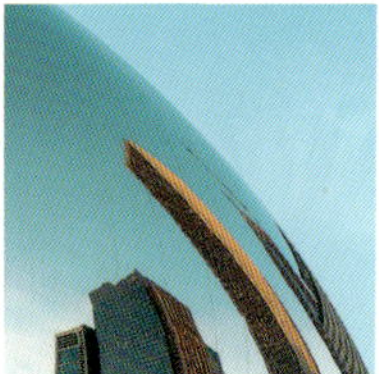

Cloud Gate,
Millennium Park

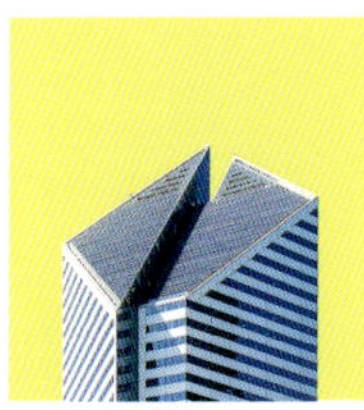

Crain Communications
Building, the Loop

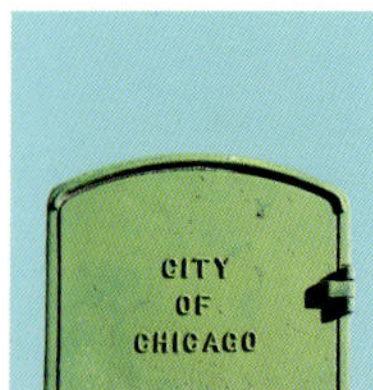

E. 47th Street &
S. Woodlawn Avenue,
Kenwood

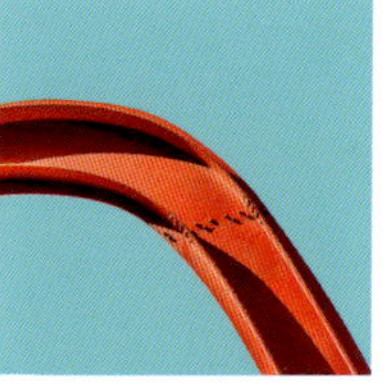

Flamingo sculpture,
the Loop

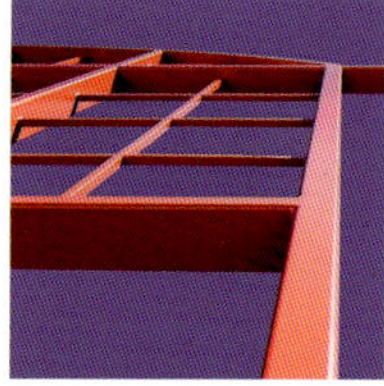

Pullman National
Historical Park, Pullman

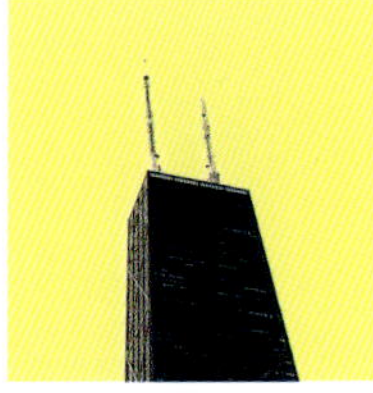

John Hancock Center,
Streeterville

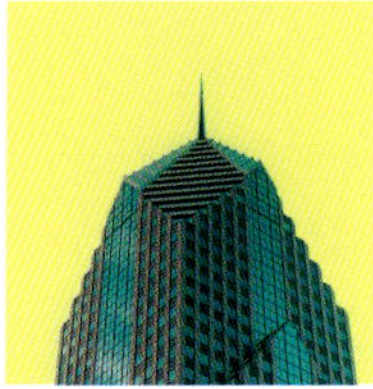

Two Prudential Plaza,
the Loop

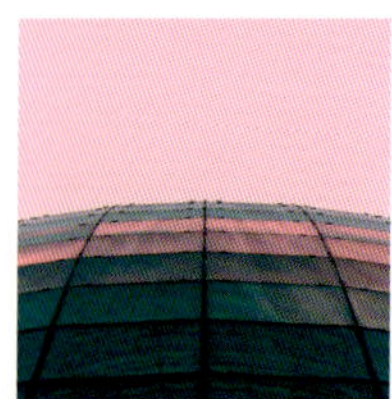

The Joe and Rika Mansueto
Library, Hyde Park

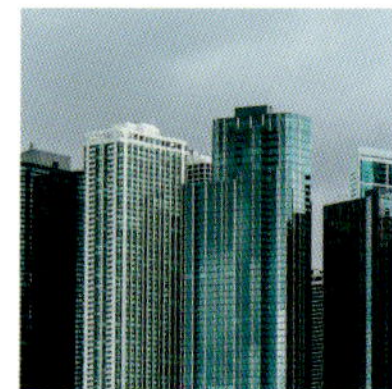

Skyline view, the Loop

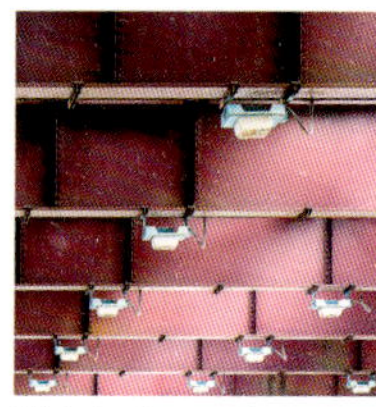

W. Lake Street &
W. Wacker Drive, the Loop

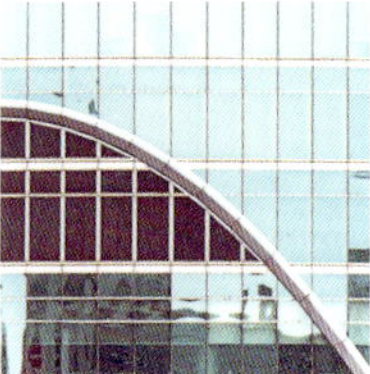

River Point, West Loop

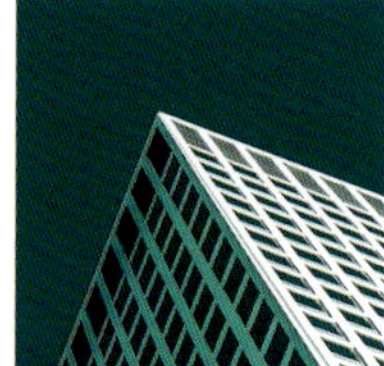

Fifth Third Center,
West Loop

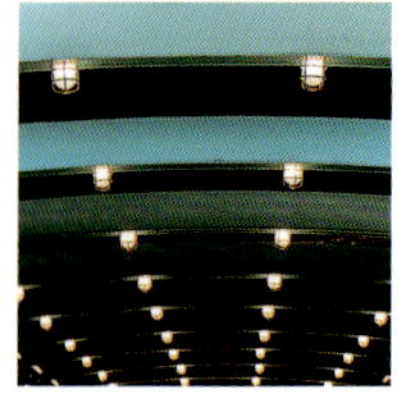

Chicago Riverwalk,
the Loop

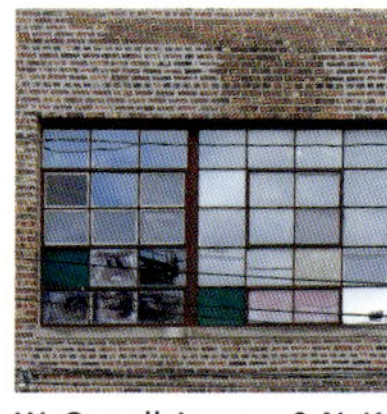

W. Carroll Avenue & N. Kedzie
Avenue, East Garfield Park

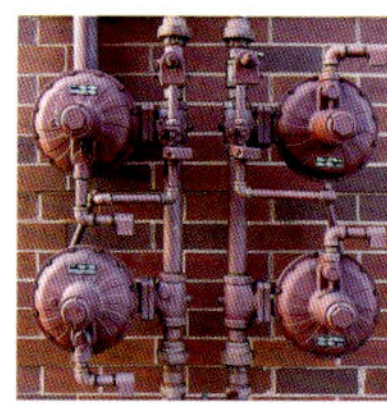

E. 45th Street & S. Cottage
Grove Avenue, Bronzeville

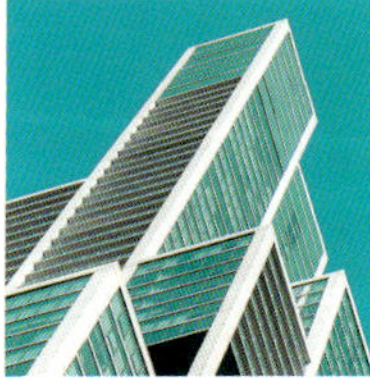

NEMA Chicago,
South Loop

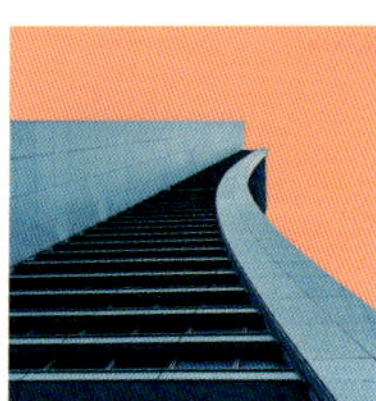

Chase Tower, the Loop

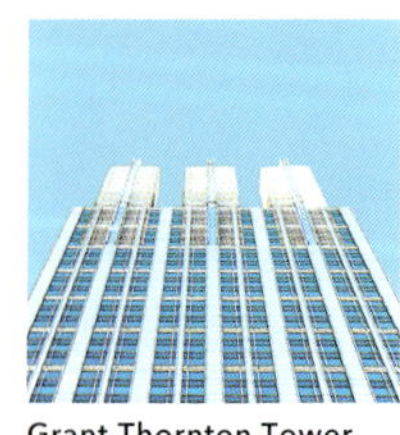

Grant Thornton Tower,
the Loop

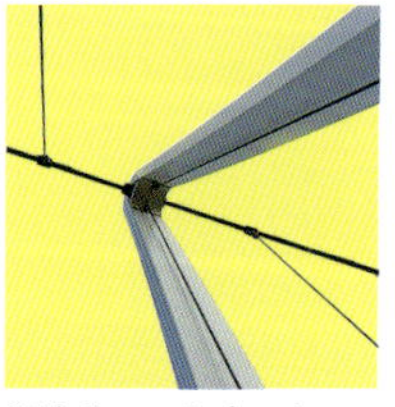

35th Street Pedestrian
Bridge, Bronzeville

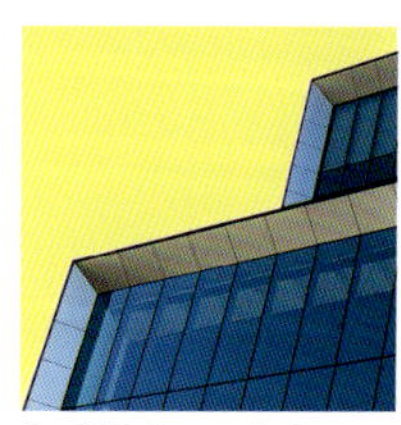

David Rubenstein Forum,
Woodlawn

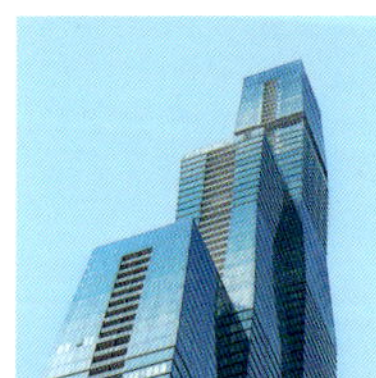

The St. Regis Chicago,
Lakeshore East

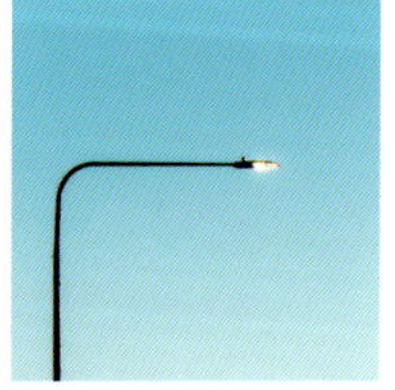

N. Damen Avenue &
N. Elston Avenue, Bucktown

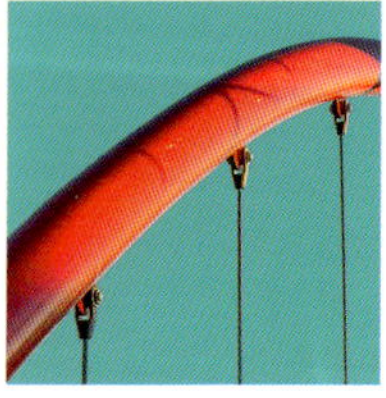

Damen Avenue Bridge,
Bucktown

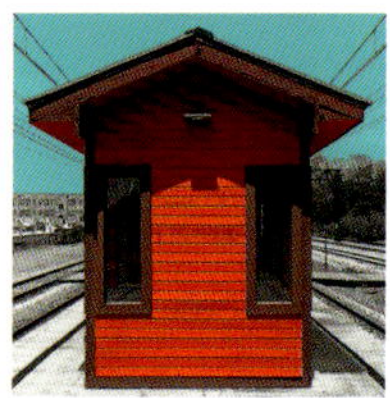

47th Street Metra station,
Kenwood

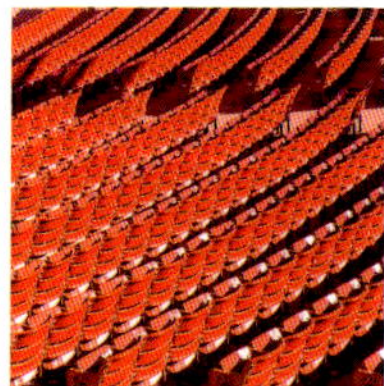

Jay Pritzker Pavilion,
Millennium Park

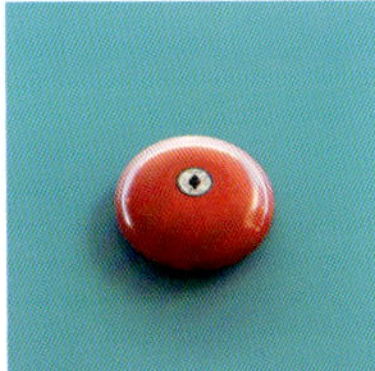

E. Washington Street &
N. State Street, the Loop

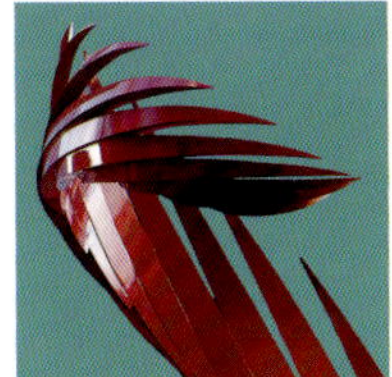

Constellation sculpture,
West Loop

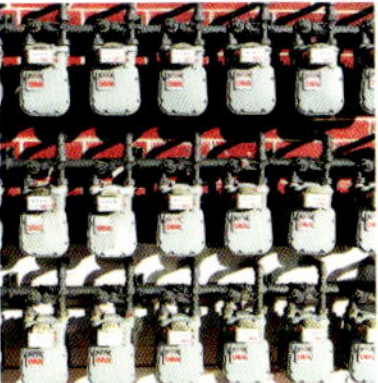

N. Ravenswood Avenue
& W. Wilson Avenue,
Ravenswood

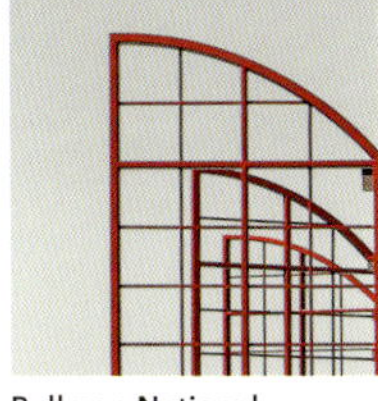

Pullman National
Historical Park, Pullman

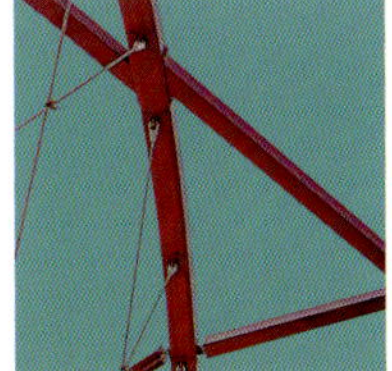

Clybourn Place Bridge,
Lincoln Park

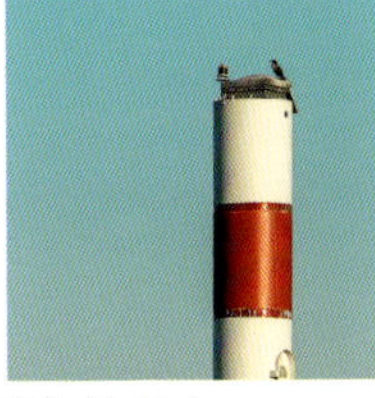

DuSable Harbor,
New Eastside

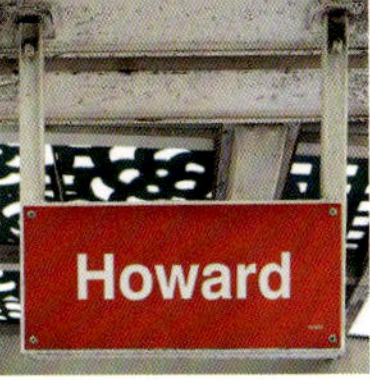

47th Street CTA station,
Bronzeville

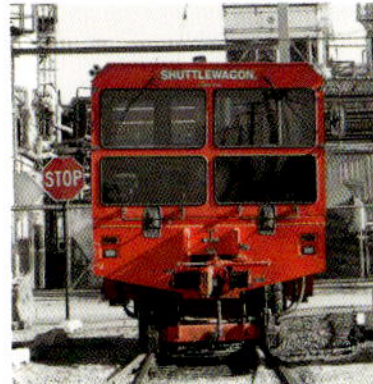

S. Morgan Street &
W. 38th Street, Bridgeport

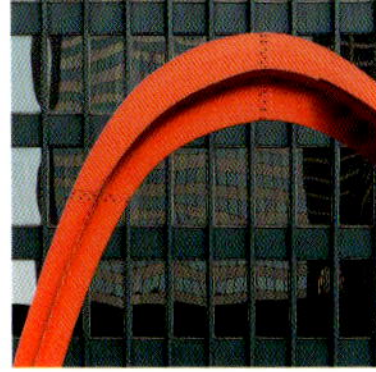

Flamingo sculpture,
the Loop

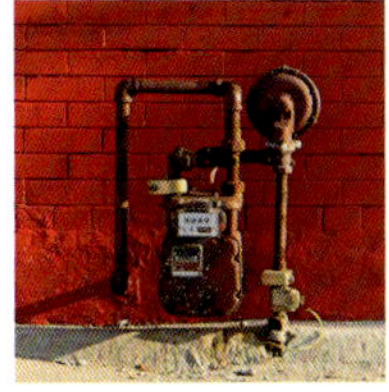

E. Pershing Road & S. Giles
Avenue, Bronzeville

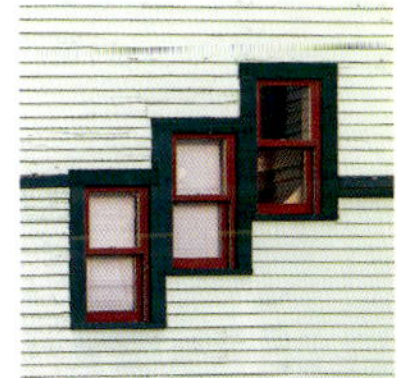

E. 45th Street & S. Ellis
Avenue, Kenwood

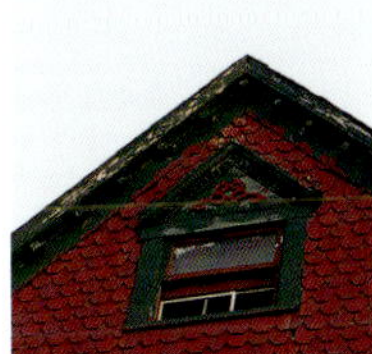

E. 45th Street & S. Ellis
Avenue, Kenwood

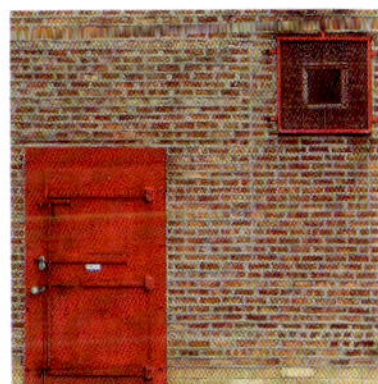

W. 37th Place & S. Halsted
Street, Bridgeport

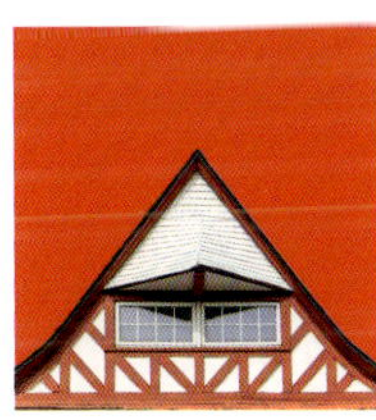

S. Oakenwald Avenue,
Bronzeville

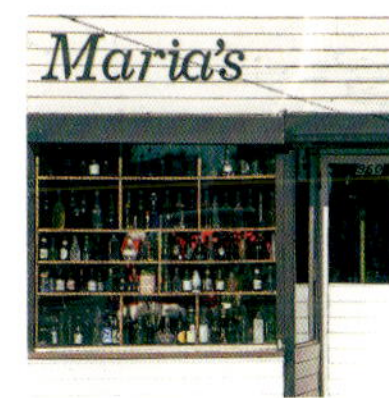

Maria's Community Bar,
Bridgeport

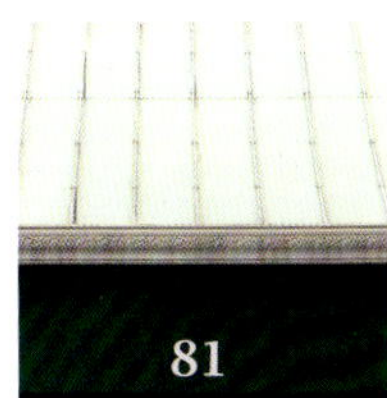

E. Van Buren Street &
S. Michigan Avenue,
the Loop

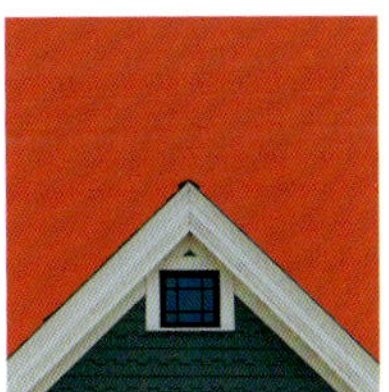

E. 54th Street &
S. Greenwood Avenue,
Hyde Park

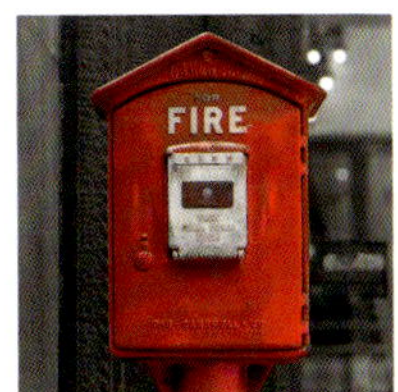

CIBC Theater, the Loop

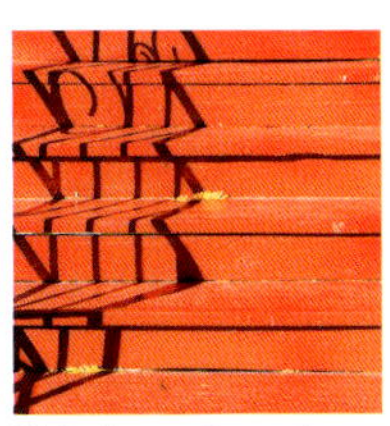

W. Cullerton Street &
S. Wood Street, Pilsen

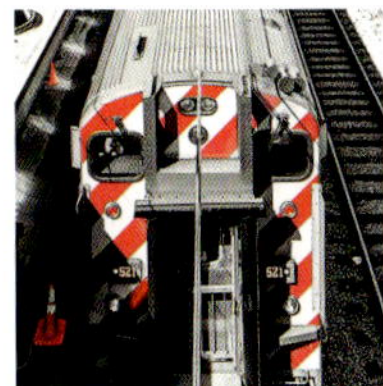

Van Buren Metra station,
the Loop

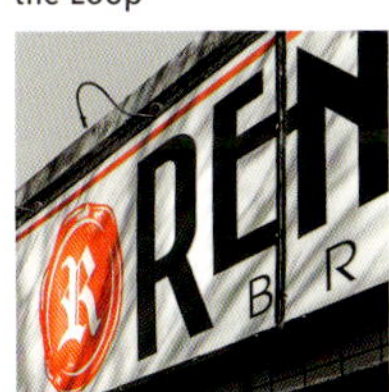

The Renaissance
Bronzeville

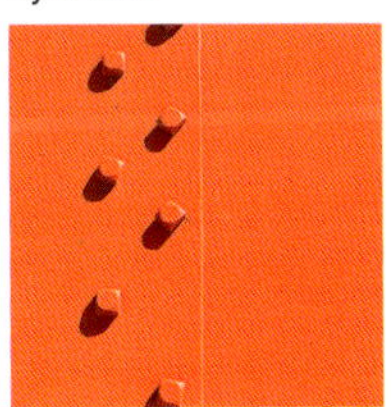

Flamingo sculpture,
the Loop

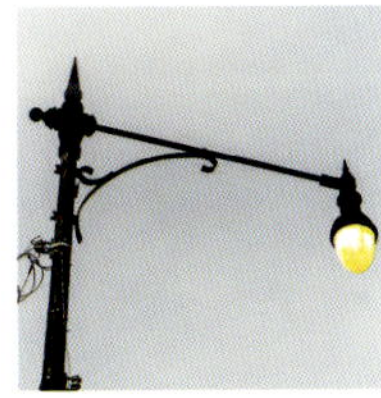

W. Irving Park Road &
N. Ravenswood Avenue,
North Center

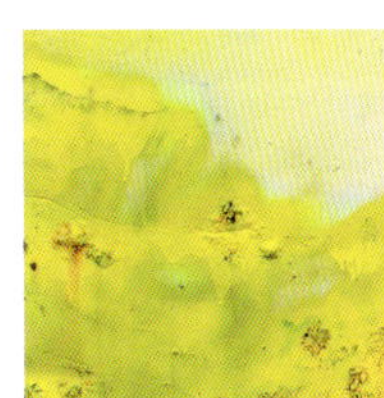

Hyde Park

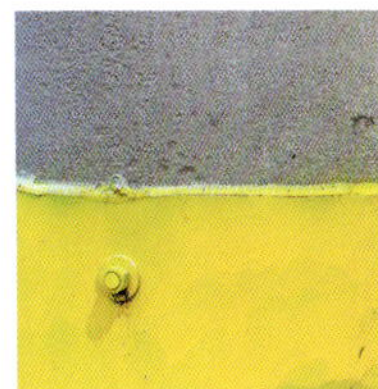

Hyde Park

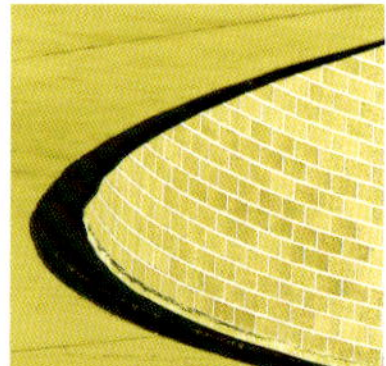

Navy Pier

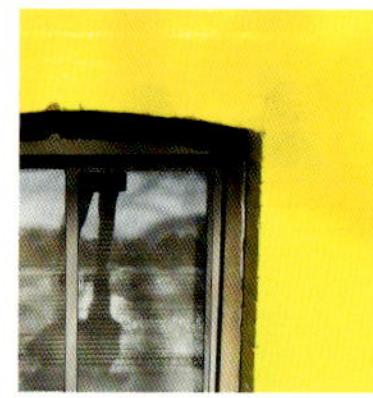

E. 48th Street &
S. Dorchester Avenue,
Kenwood

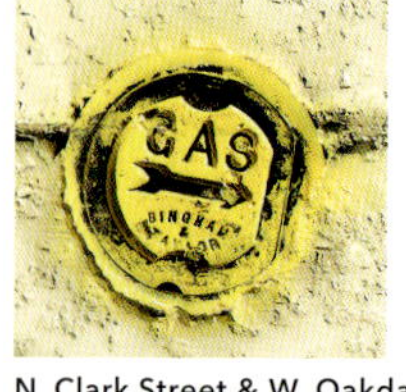

N. Clark Street & W. Oakdale
Avenue, Lakeview

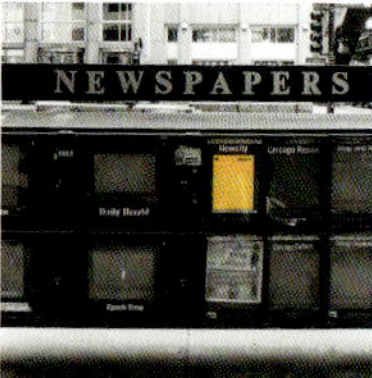

N. LaSalle Street &
W. Madison Street,
the Loop

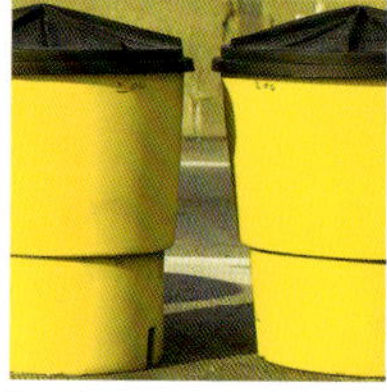

Dan Ryan Expressway,
Armour Square

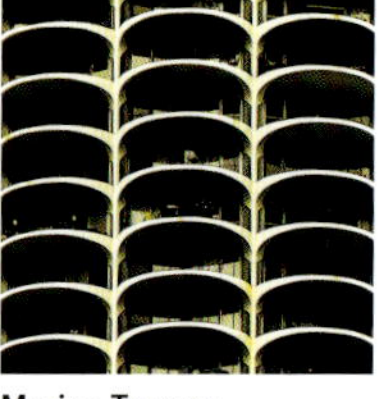

Marina Towers,
River North

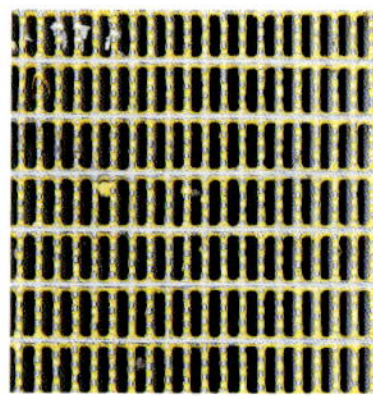

S. Wells Street & W. Van
Buren Street, the Loop

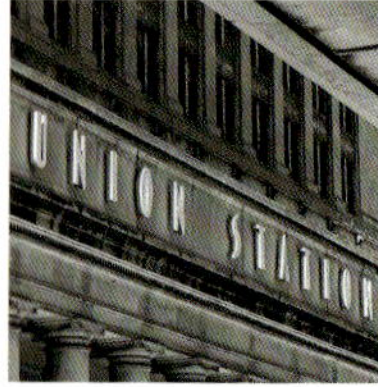

Union Station, West Loop

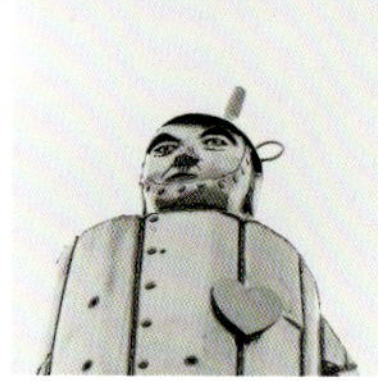

Oz Park, Lincoln Park

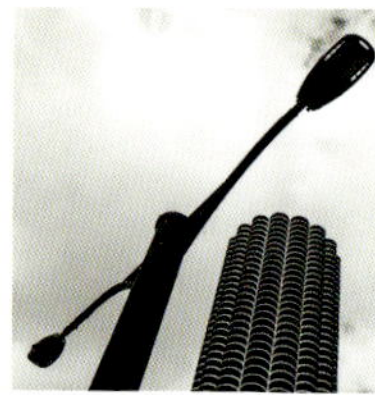

Marina Towers,
River North

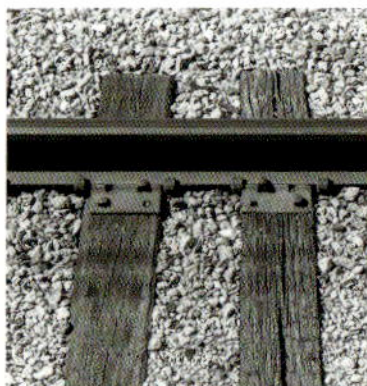

51st/53rd Street Metra
station, Hyde Park

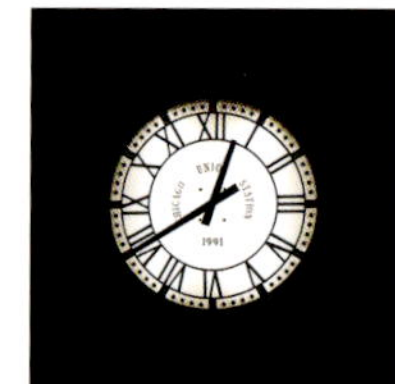

Union Station, West Loop

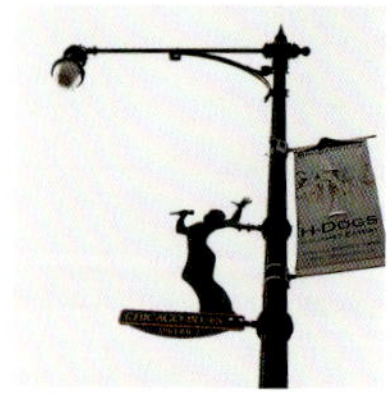

E. 47th Street &
S. Martin Luther King Drive,
Bronzeville

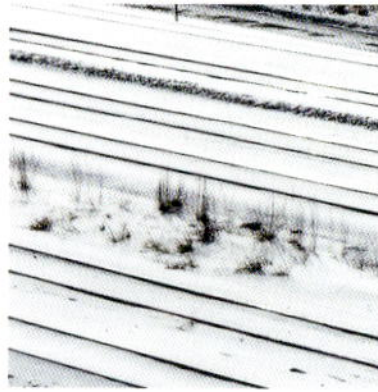

Metra tracks, Oakland

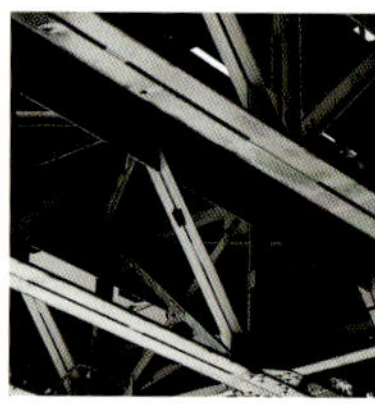

CTA tracks, the Loop

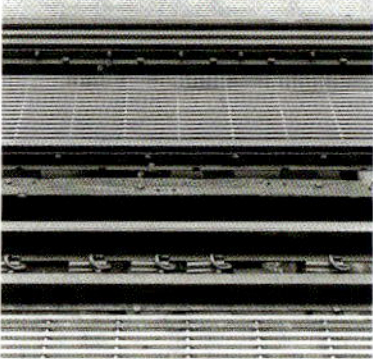

43rd Street CTA station,
Bronzeville

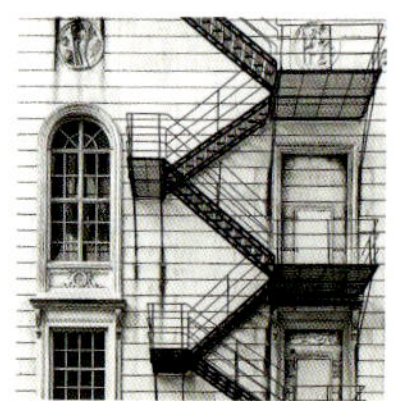

The Palmer House,
the Loop

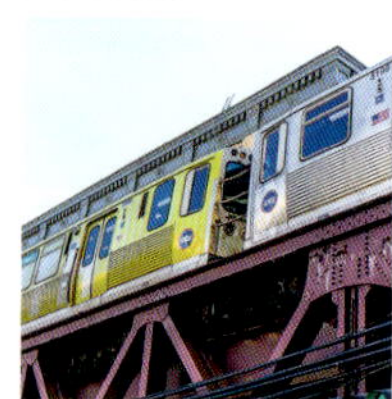

CTA train, the Loop

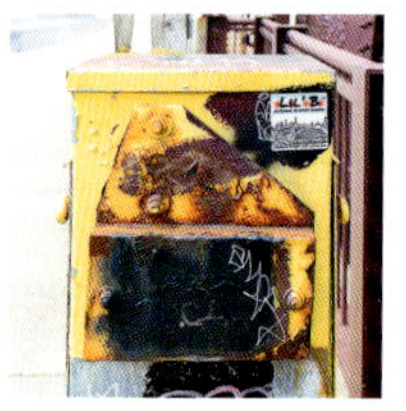

W. Lake Street & W. Wacker
Drive, the Loop

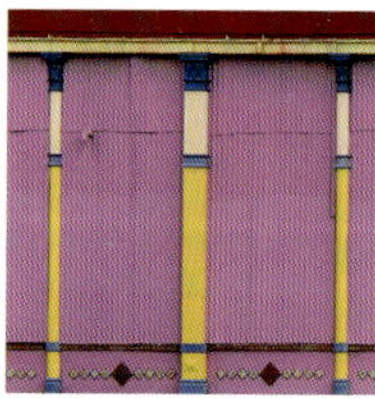

W. Cullerton Street &
S. Laflin Street, Pilsen

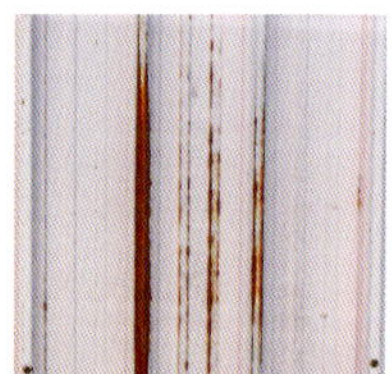

N. Wood Street & W. Carroll
Avenue, West Town

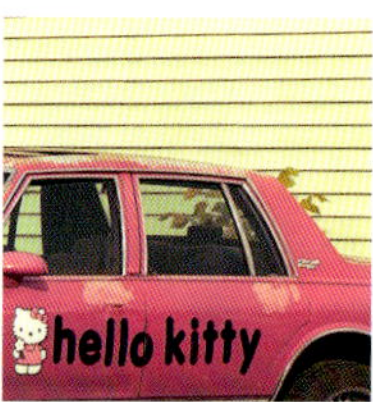

S. Commercial Avenue
& S. Baltimore Avenue,
South Chicago

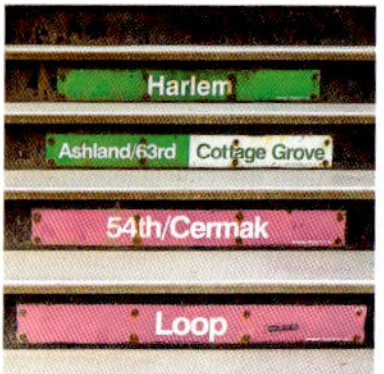

Clinton CTA station,
West Loop

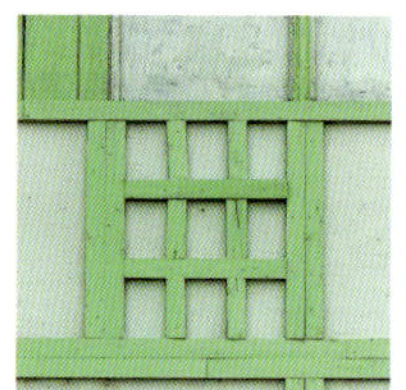

E. 43rd Street & S. Wabash
Avenue, Bronzeville

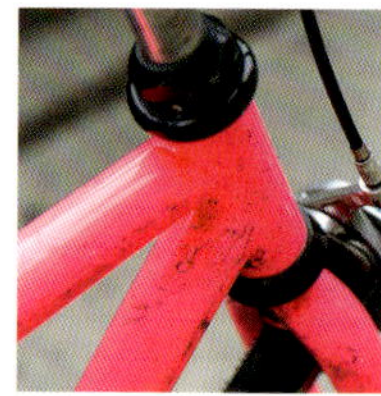

Bike, Logan Square

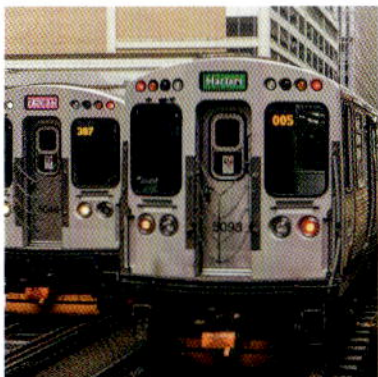

State/Lake CTA station,
the Loop

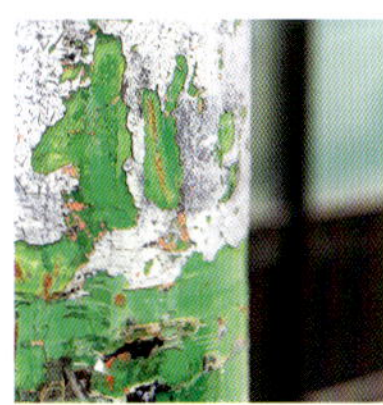

N. Clark Street,
Ravenswood

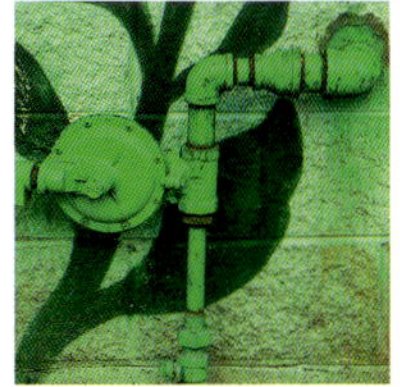

N. Clark Street & W. Oakdale
Avenue, Lakeview

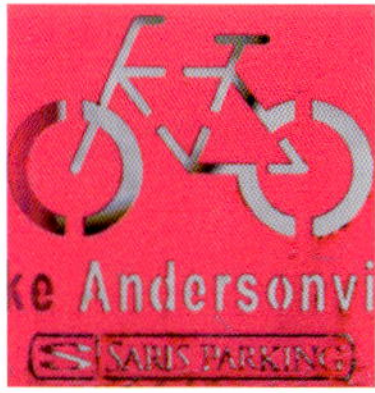

W. Argyle Street & N. Clark
Street, Andersonville

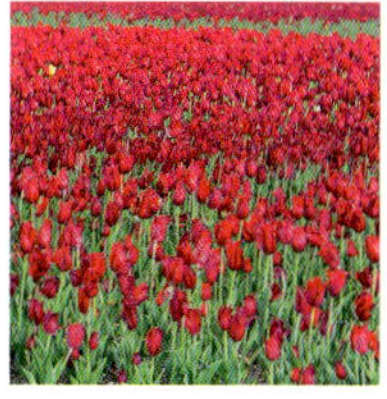

S. Prairie Avenue & E. 53rd
Street, Washington Park

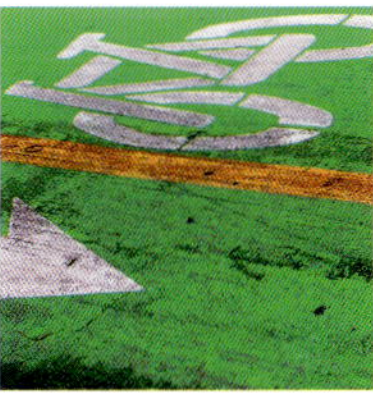

S. Dearborn Street &
W. Madison Street,
the Loop

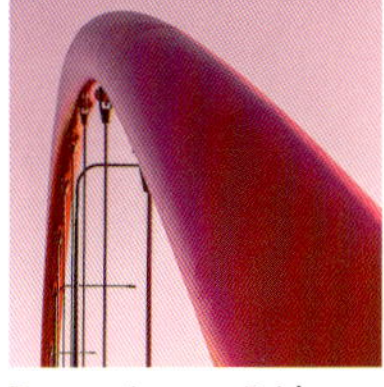

Damen Avenue Bridge,
Bucktown

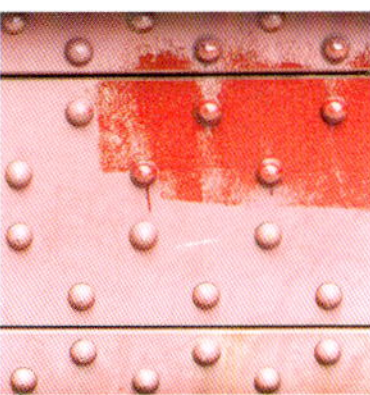

State Street Bridge,
the Loop

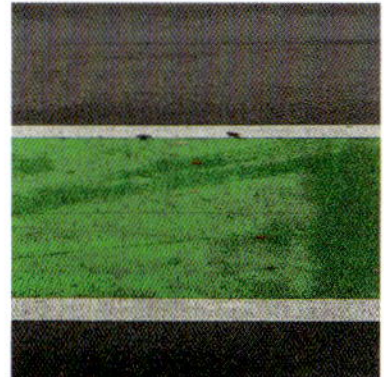

W. Kinzie Street & N. Wells
Street, River North

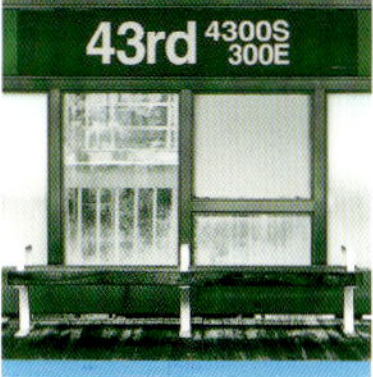

43rd Street CTA station,
Bronzeville

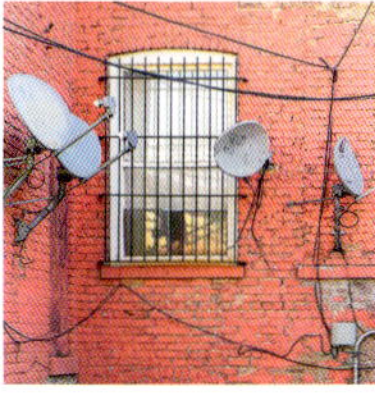

S. Calumet Avenue,
Bronzeville

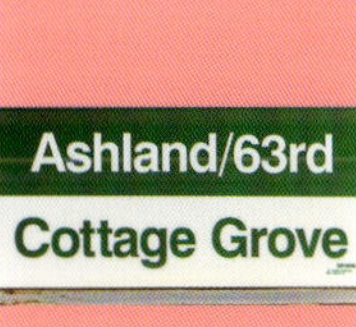

Kedzie CTA station,
Kedzie

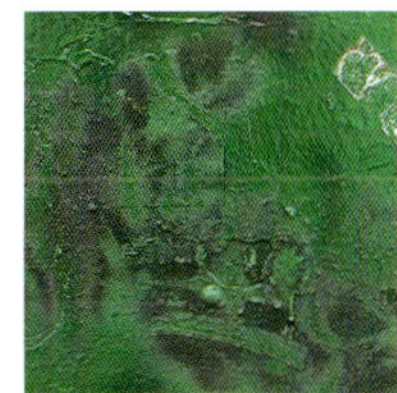

W. Hubbard Street,
River North

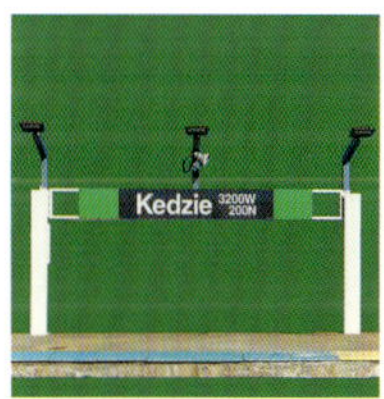

Kedzie CTA station,
Kedzie

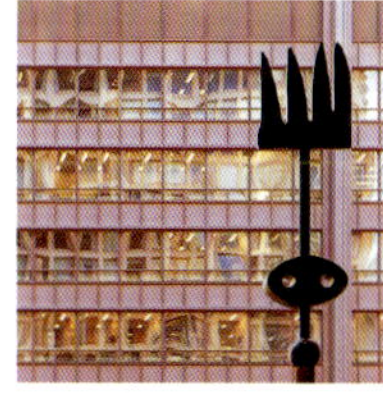

W. Washington Street &
N. Clark Street, the Loop

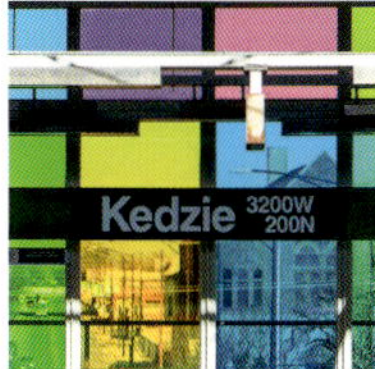

Kedzie CTA station,
Kedzie

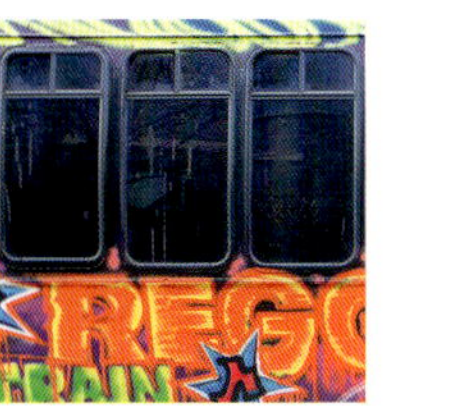

Reggies Chicago,
South Loop

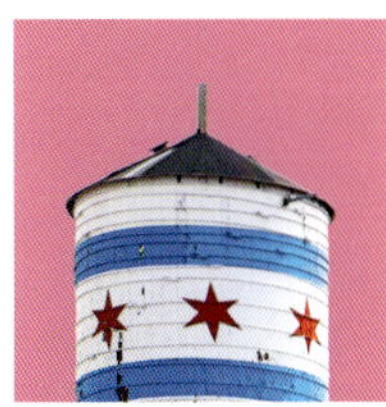

N. Ashland Avenue,
Wicker Park

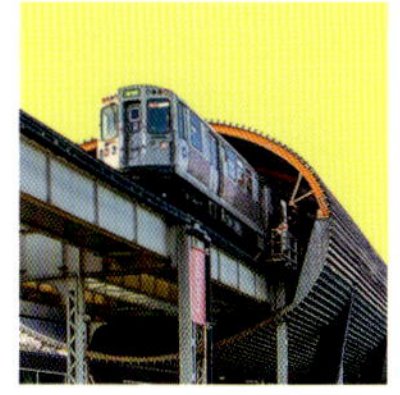

35th-Bronzeville-IIT
CTA station, Bronzeville

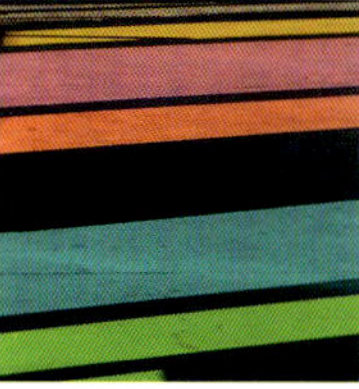

Kedzie CTA station,
Kedzie

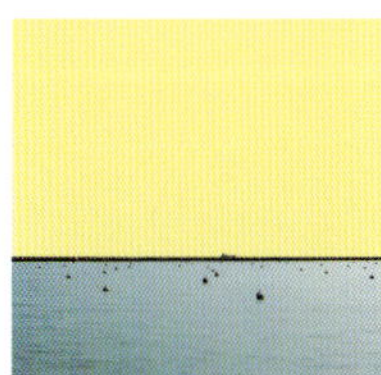

DuSable Harbor,
the Loop

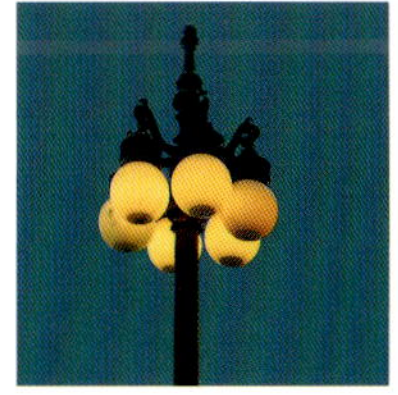

Street lamp, the Loop

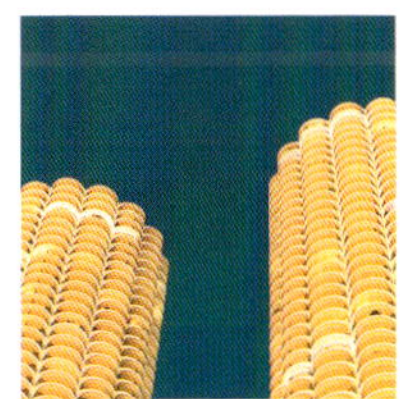

Marina Towers,
River North

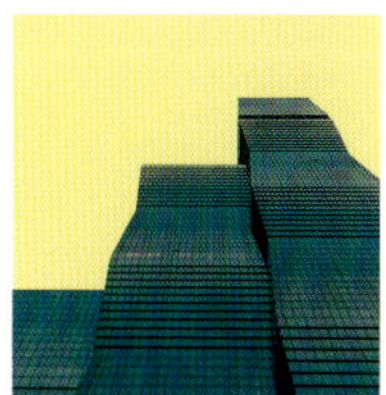

The St. Regis Chicago,
Lakeshore East

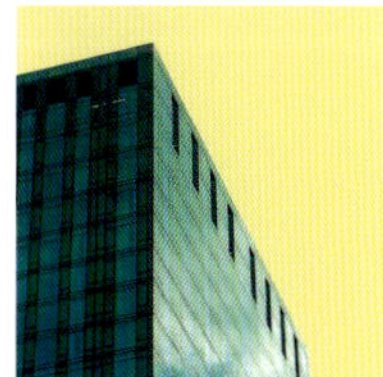

E. 11th Street & S. Wabash
Avenue, South Loop

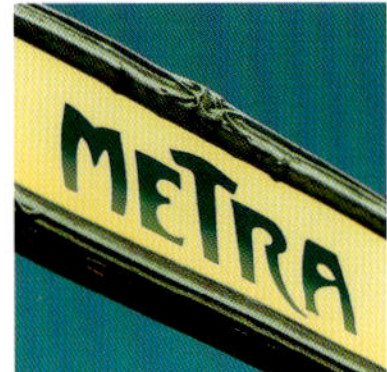

Van Buren Street
Metra sign, the Loop

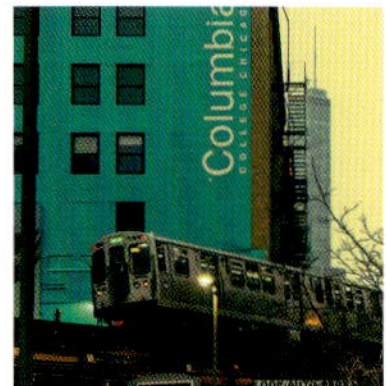

E. Harrison Street &
S. Wabash Avenue,
South Loop

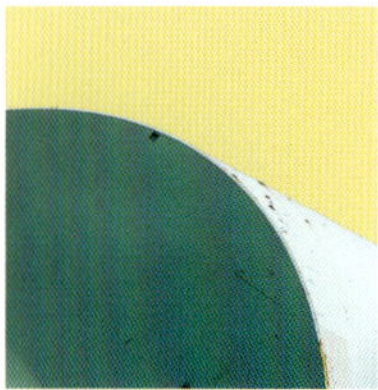

63rd Street Beach,
Jackson Park

63rd Street Beach,
Jackson Park

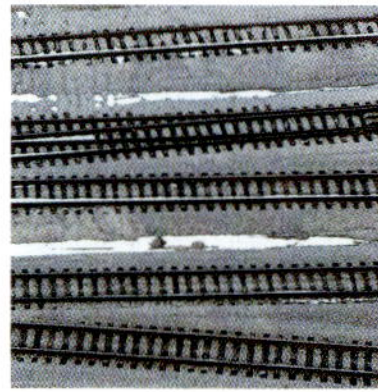

LaSalle Street Metra
station, the Loop

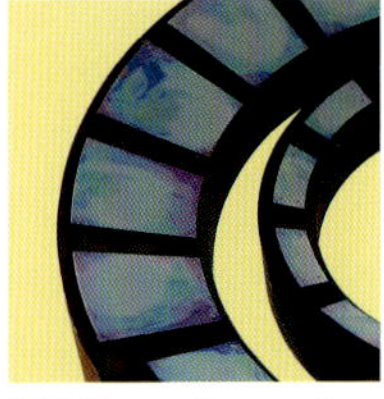

S. Baltimore Avenue &
S. Commercial Avenue,
South Chicago

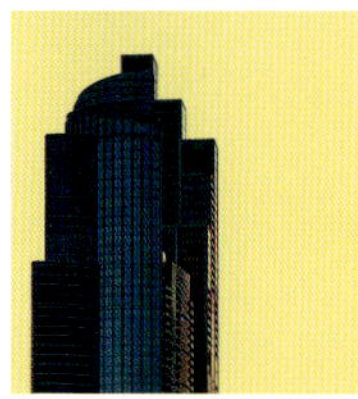

One Museum Park,
South Loop

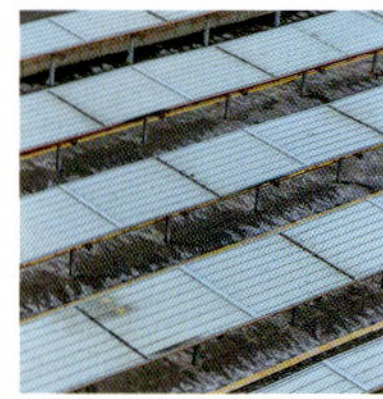

LaSalle Street Metra
station, the Loop

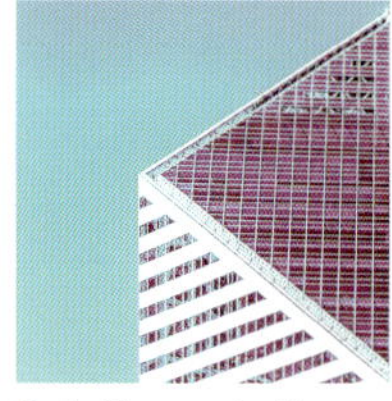

Crain Communication
Building, the Loop

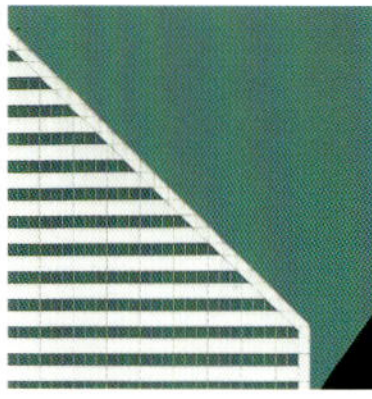

Crain Communication
Building, the Loop

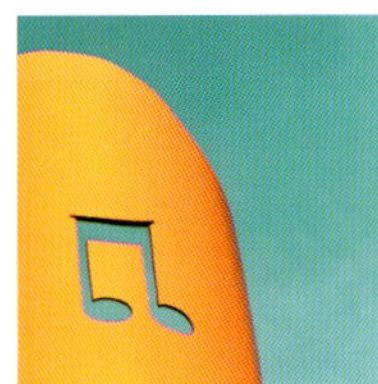

E. 47th Street &
S. Martin Luther King
Drive, Bronzeville

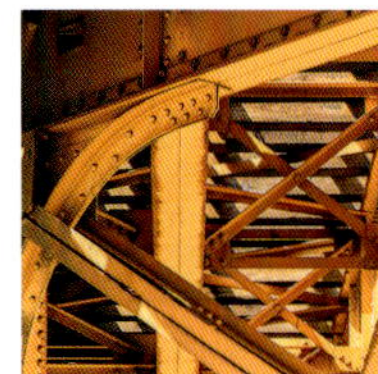

CTA tracks, Logan Square

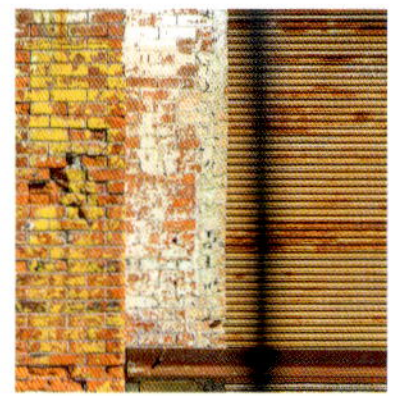

Pullman National
Historical Park, Pullman

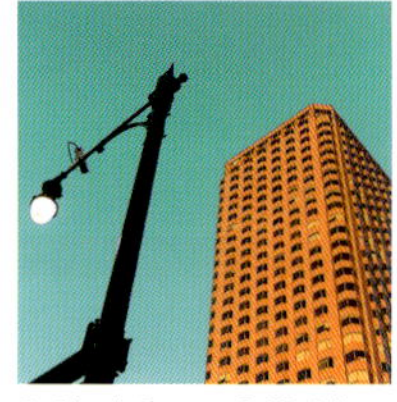

S. Clark Street & W. Ida
B. Wells Drive, the Loop

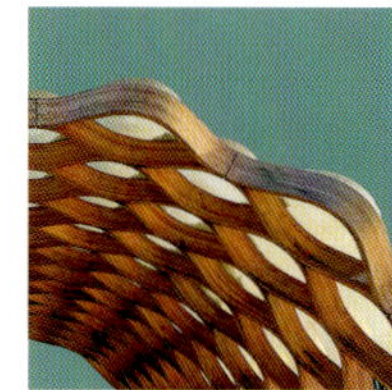

Peoples Gas Pavilion,
Lincoln Park

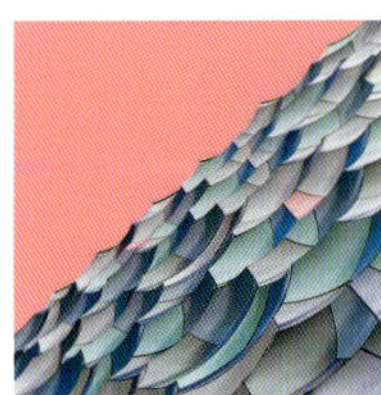

W. Jackson Boulevard &
S. Wacker Drive, the Loop

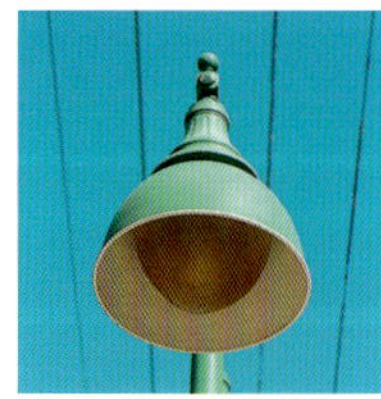

51st/53rd Street Metra
station, Hyde Park

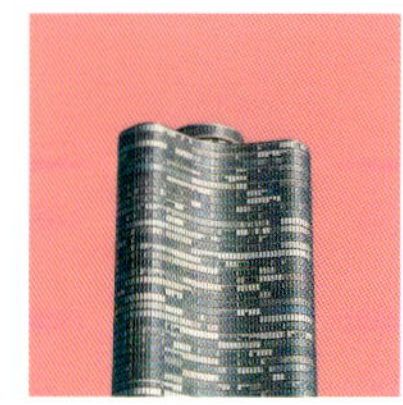

Lake Point Tower,
Streeterville

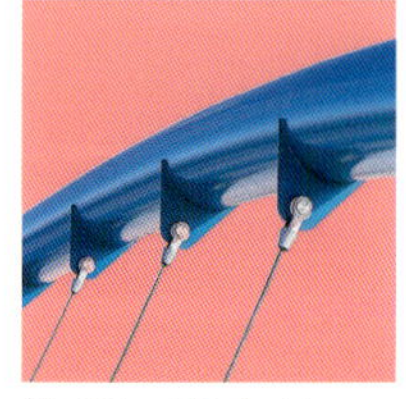

41st Street Pedestrian
Bridge, Oakland

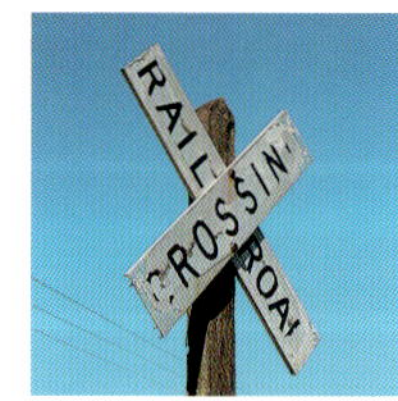

Union Stockyards Gate,
Back of the Yards

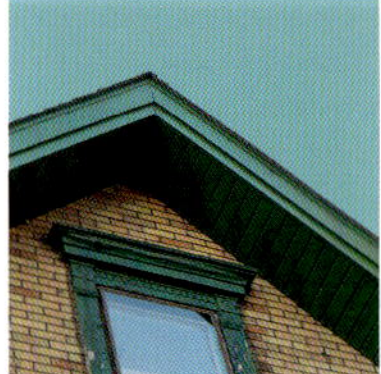

W. Irving Park Road
& N. Paulina Street,
Ravenswood

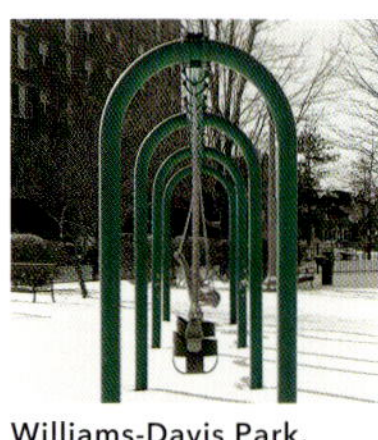

Williams-Davis Park,
Oakland

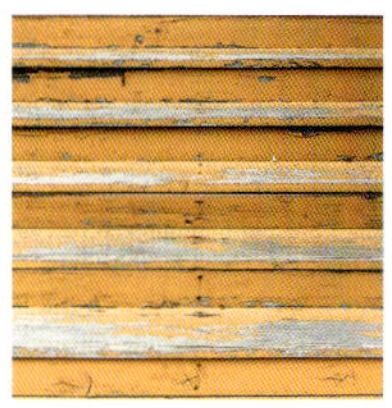

W. Montrose Avenue &
N. Greenview Avenue,
Bronzeville

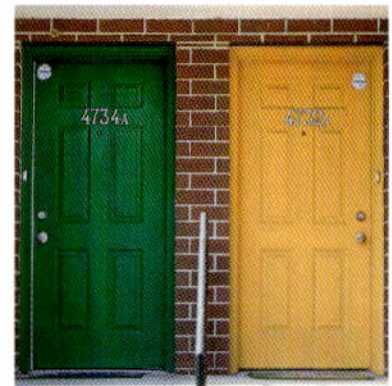

S. Indiana Avenue,
Bronzeville

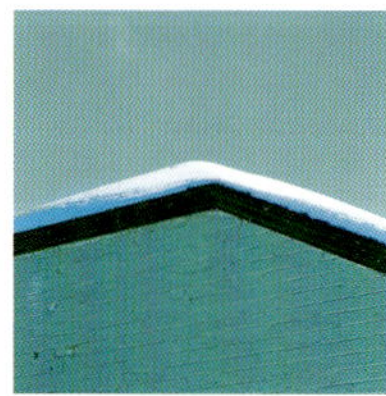

Lakefront Trail,
Hyde Park

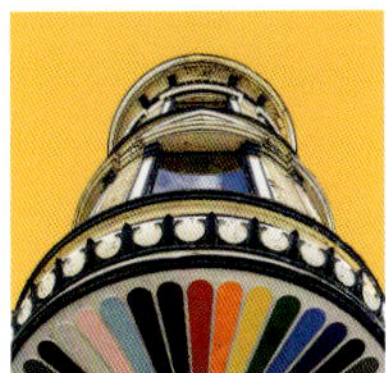

The SoFo Tap,
Andersonville

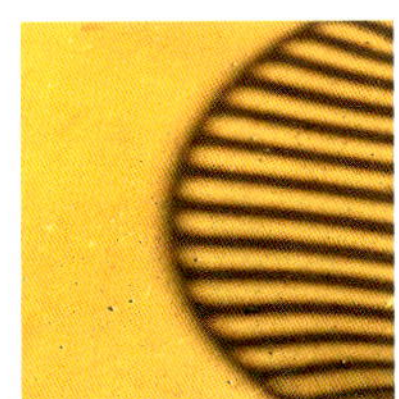

Kedzie CTA station,
Kedzie

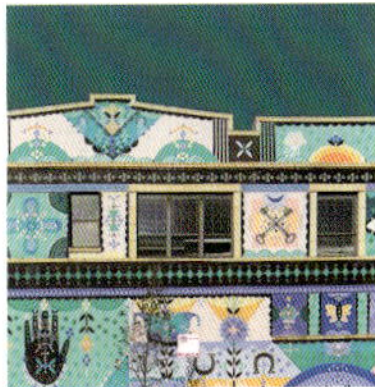

W. Surf Street & N. Clark
Street, Lakeview

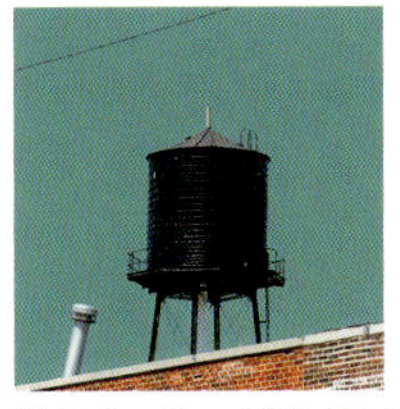

W. Fulton Street & N. Wood
Street, West Loop

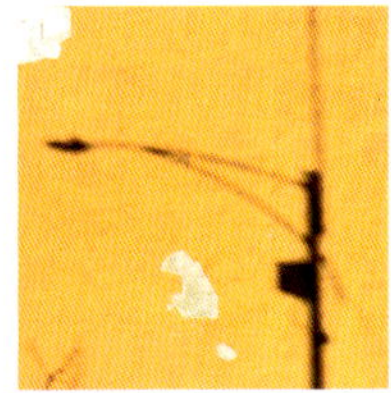

N. Kedzie Avenue &
W. Walnut Street,
East Garfield Park

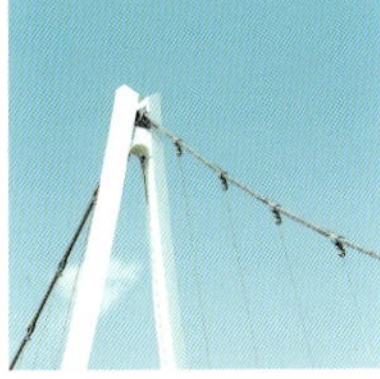

35th Street Pedestrian
Bridge, Bronzeville

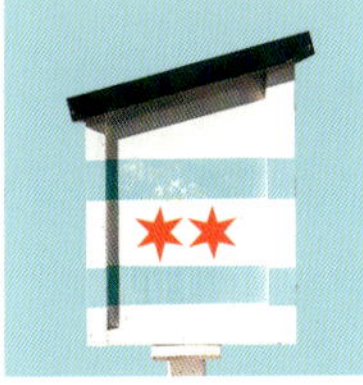

Park No. 571, Bridgeport

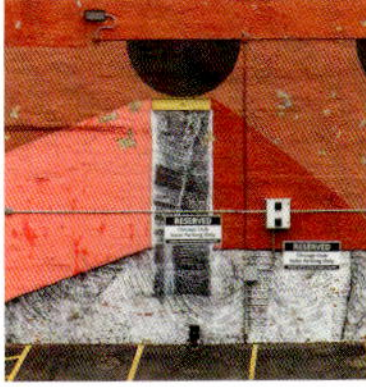

E. Van Buren Street &
S. Wabash Avenue,
the Loop

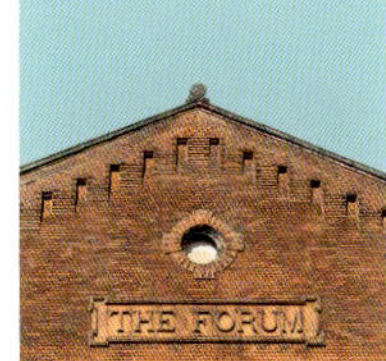

The Forum, Bronzeville

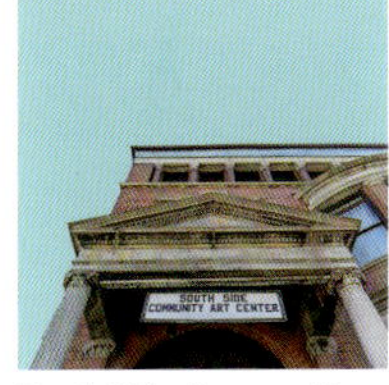

South Side Community
Art Center, Bronzeville

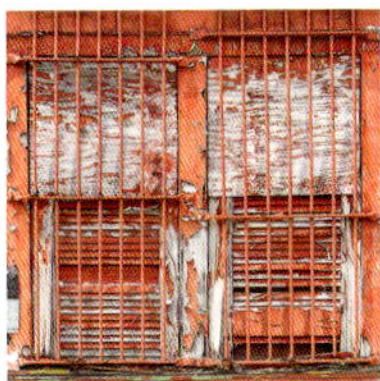

E. 83rd Street & S. Buffalo
Avenue, South Chicago

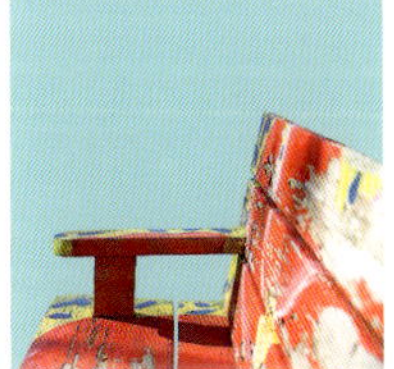

E. 43rd Street &
S. St. Lawrence Avenue,
Bronzeville

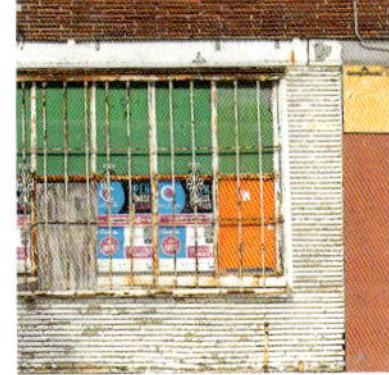

The Forum, Bronzeville

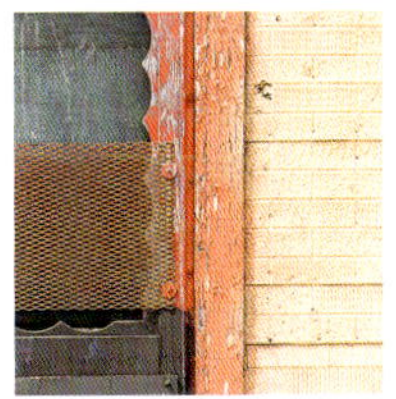

E. 83rd Street & S. Buffalo
Avenue, South Chicago

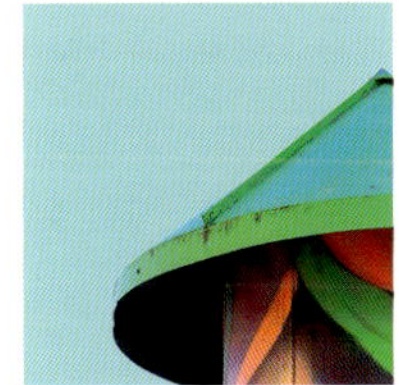

South Side Community
Art Center, Bronzeville

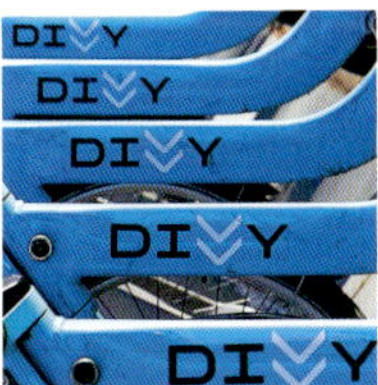

E. 47th Street & S. Lake
Park Avenue, Kenwood

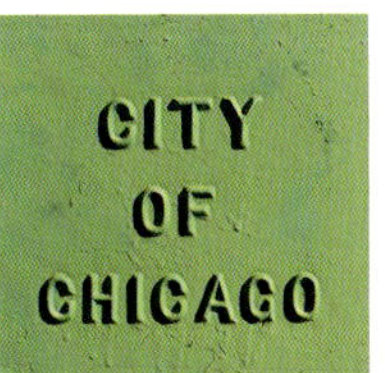

E. 47th Street &
S. Woodlawn Avenue,
Kenwood

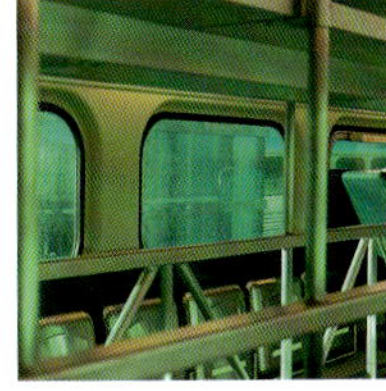

Metra electric train,
the Loop

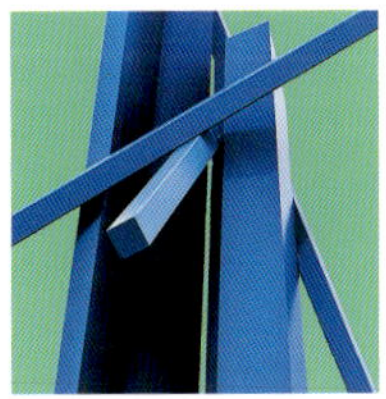

Chevron sculpture,
Lincoln Park

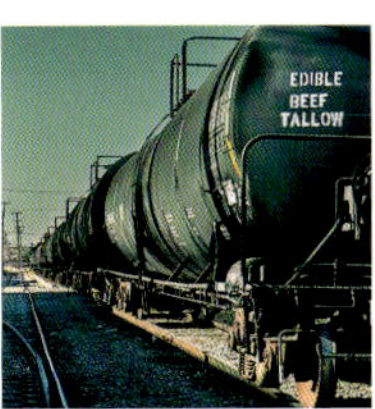

S. Morgan Street & W. 38th
Street, Bridgeport

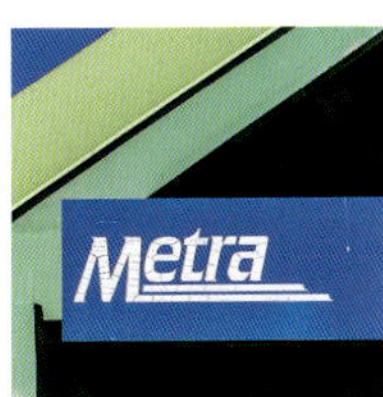

47th Street Metra station,
Kenwood

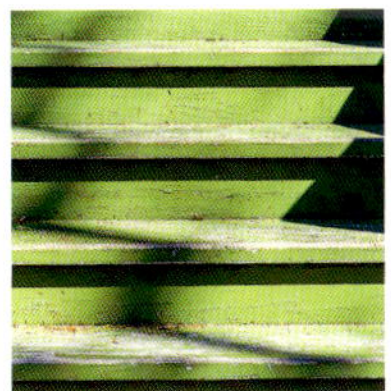

E. 47th Street &
S. Forrestville Avenue,
Pullman

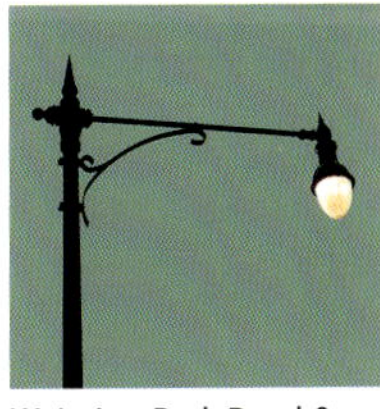

W. Irving Park Road &
N. Ravenswood Avenue,
North Center

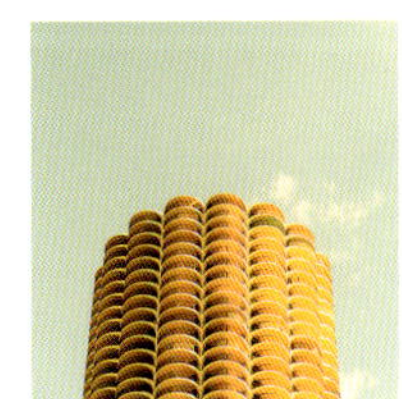

Marina Towers,
River North

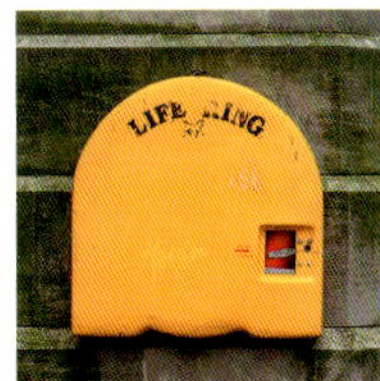

State Street Bridge,
the Loop

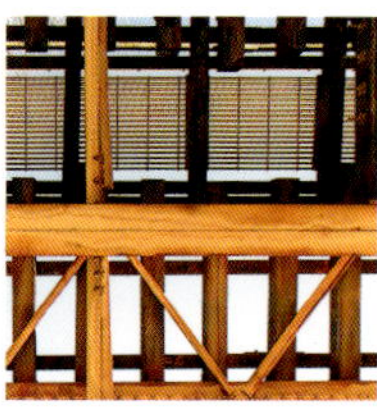

CTA tracks, Bronzeville

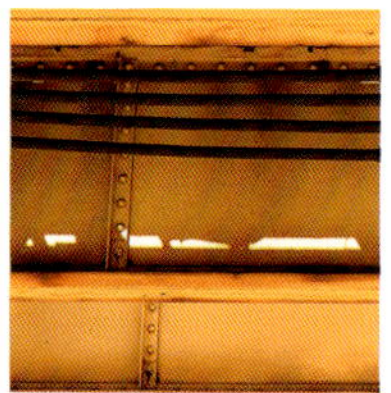

CTA tracks, Bronzeville

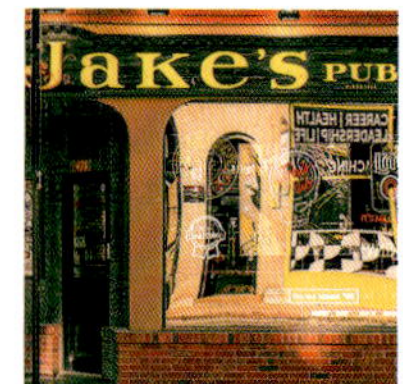

Jake's Pub, Lakeview

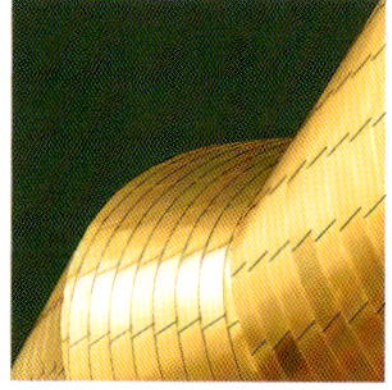

Jay Pritzker Pavilion, Millennium Park

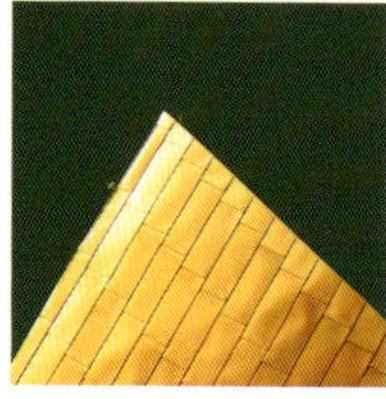

Jay Pritzker Pavilion, Millennium Park

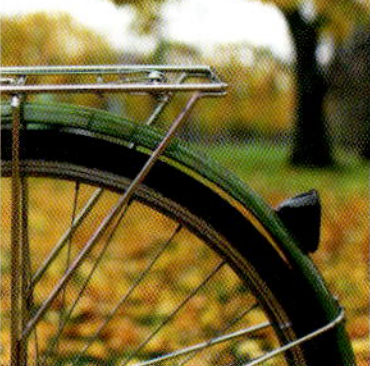

Washington Park

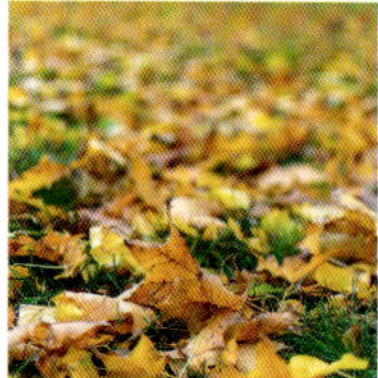

Washington Park

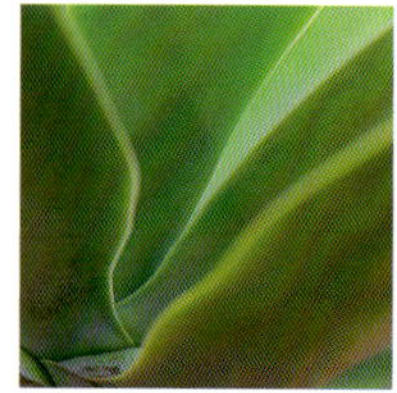

Garfield Park Conservatory, Garfield Park

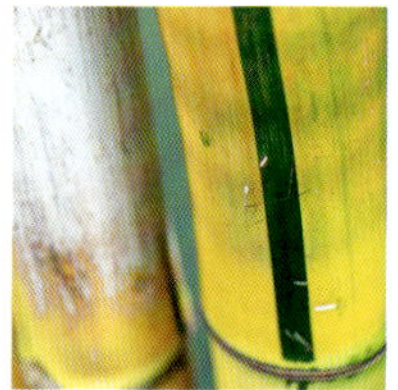

Garfield Park Conservatory, Garfield Park

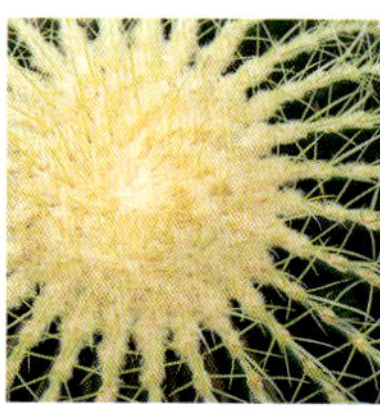

Garfield Park Conservatory, Garfield Park

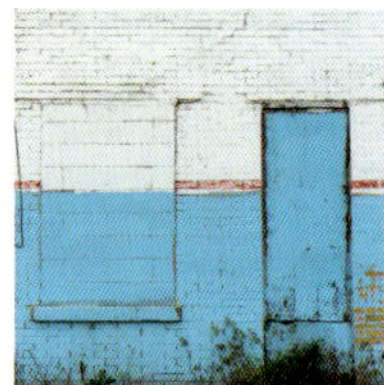

E. 75th Street & S. Rhodes Avenue, Chatham

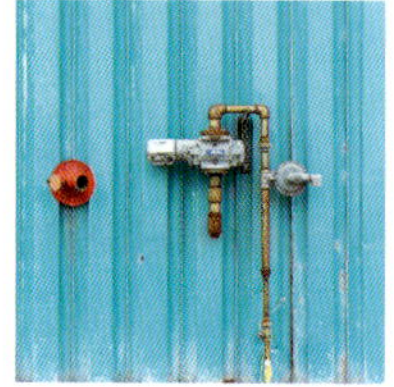

S. South Chicago Avenue & E. 69th Place, Woodlawn

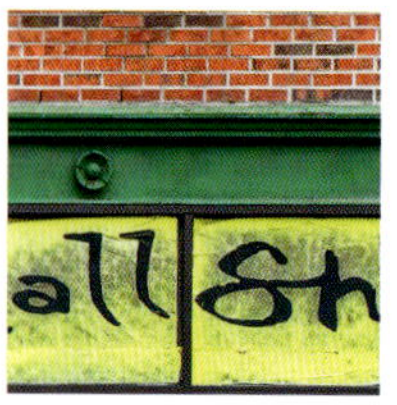

Small Shop Cycles & Service, Bronzeville

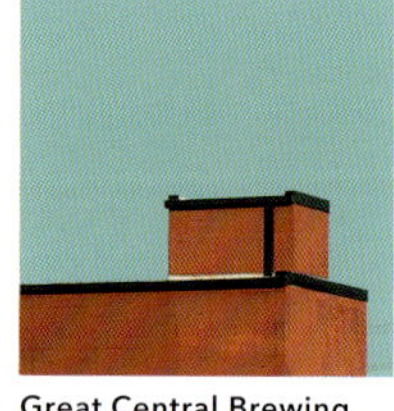

Great Central Brewing Company, West Town

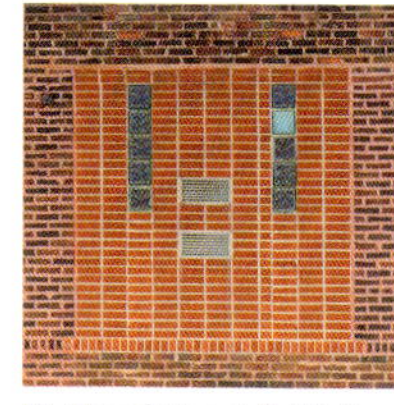

N. Wood Street & W. Carroll Avenue, West Town

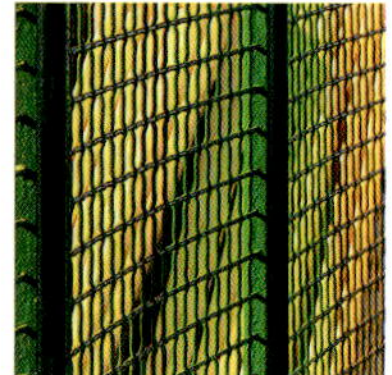

Kedzie CTA station, Kedzie

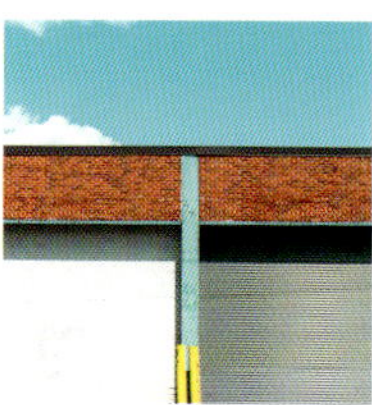

W. Fulton Street & N. Paulina Street, West Loop

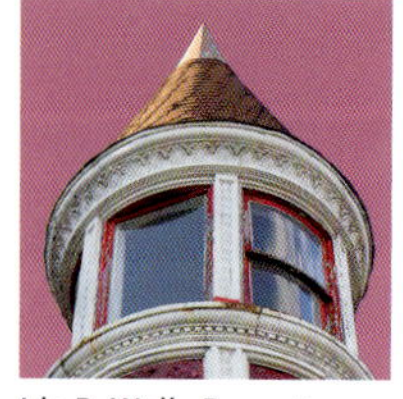

Ida B. Wells-Barnett House, Bronzeville

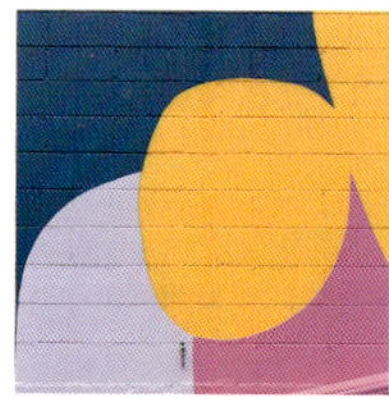

Kimball Arts Center, Logan Square

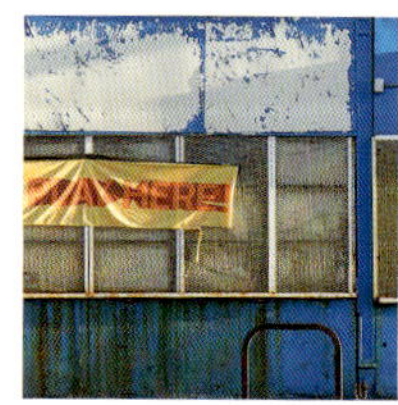

E. 47th Street & S. Forrestville Avenue, Bronzeville

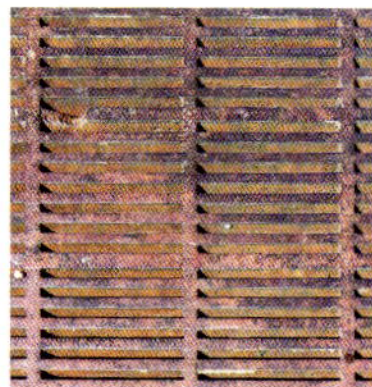

Grant Park, the Loop

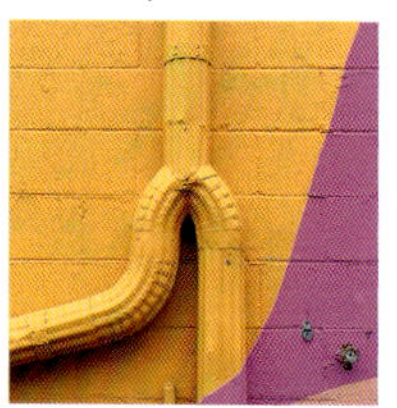

Kimball Arts Center, Logan Square

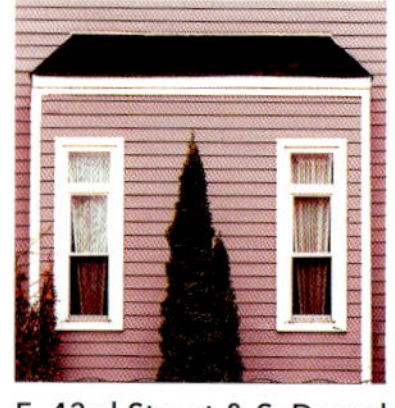

E. 43rd Street & S. Drexel Boulevard, Bronzeville

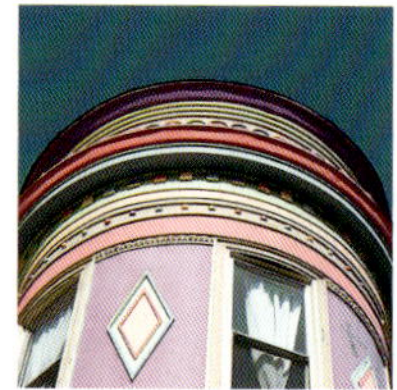

Carnival Foods, Lincoln Park

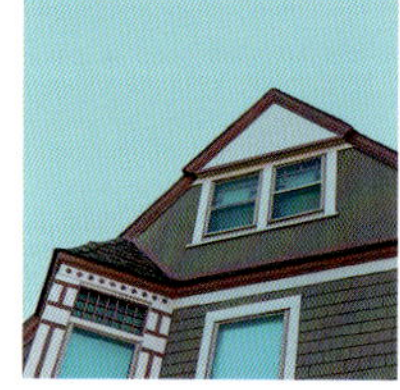

W. Fuller Street & S. Hillock Avenue, Bridgeport

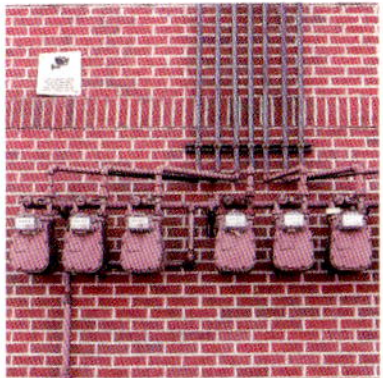

State Street Bridge,
the Loop

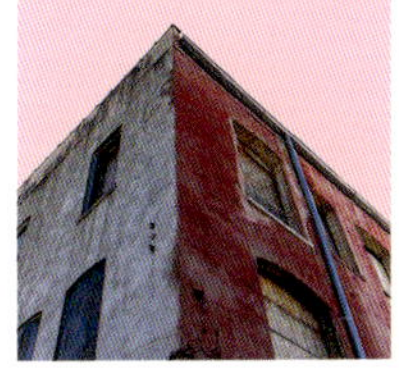

The Forum, Bronzeville

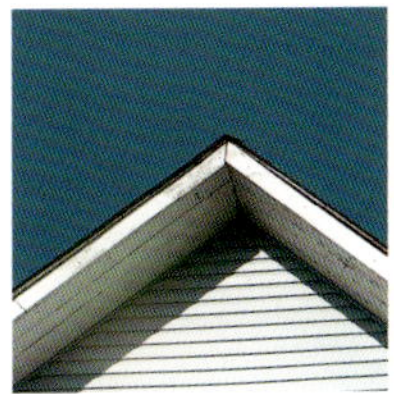

E. 44th Street & S. Evans
Avenue, Bronzeville

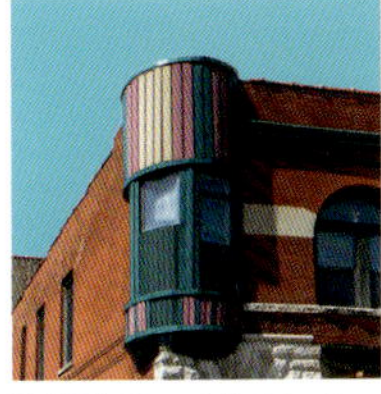

E. 45th Street & S. Indiana
Avenue, Bronzeville

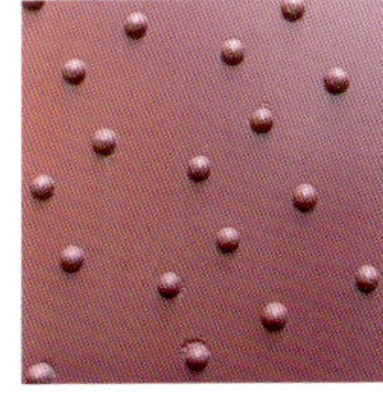

LaSalle Street Bridge,
River North

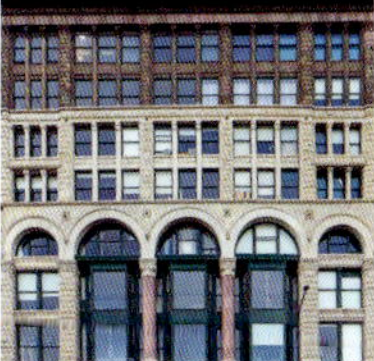

Fine Arts Building,
the Loop

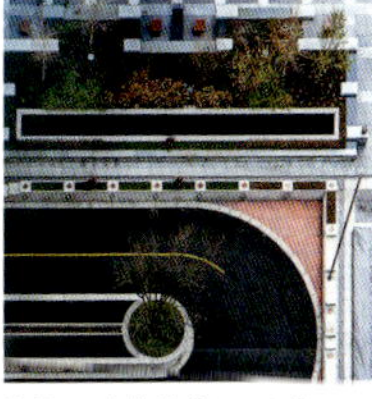

E. Randolph Street &
N. Columbus Drive,
the Loop

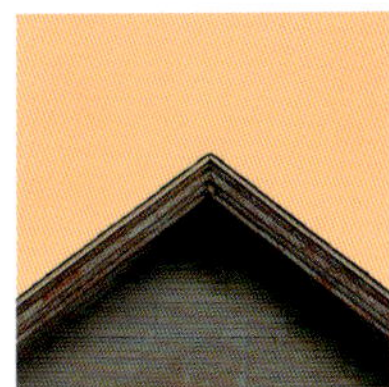

N. Sedgwick Street,
Old Town

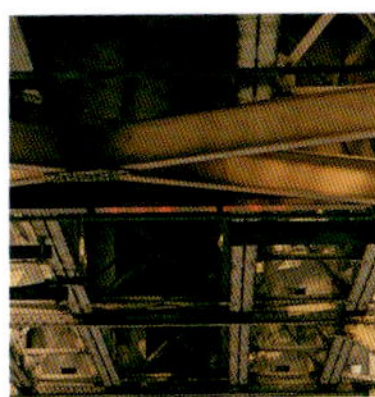

CTA tracks, Uptown

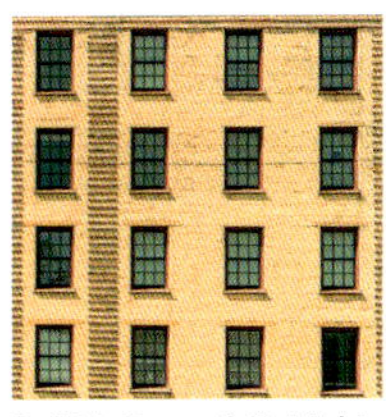

E. 47th Street & S. Michigan
Avenue, Bronzeville

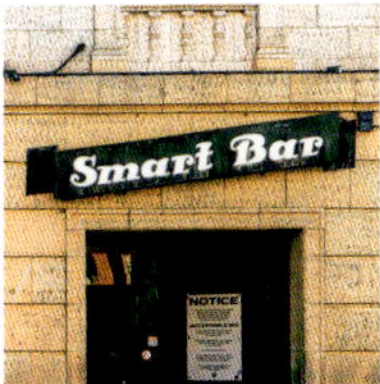

Smart Bar, Wrigleyville

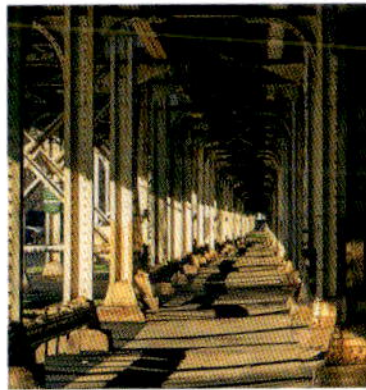

CTA tracks, the Loop

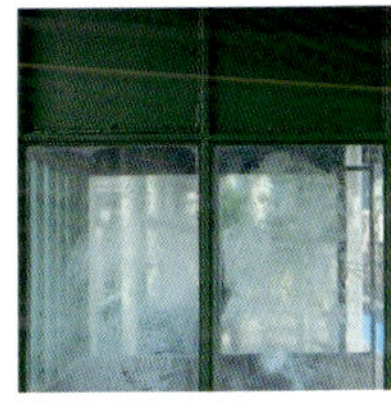

Ashland CTA station,
West Town

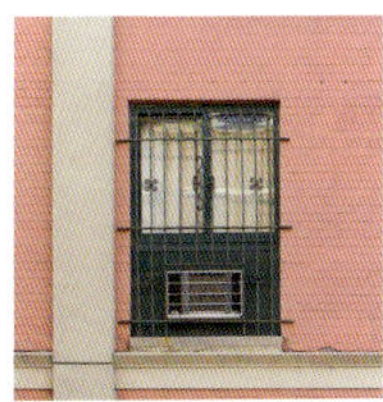

Amber Inn, Bronzeville

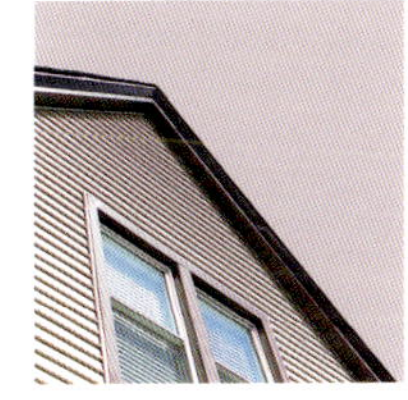

E. 46th Street & S. Indiana
Avenue, Bronzeville

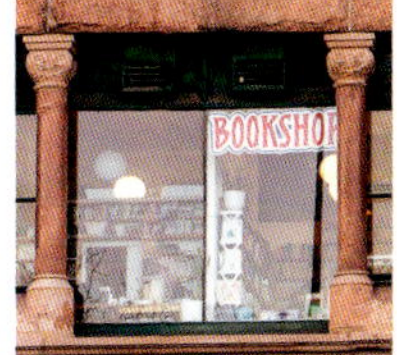

Exile in Bookville,
the Loop

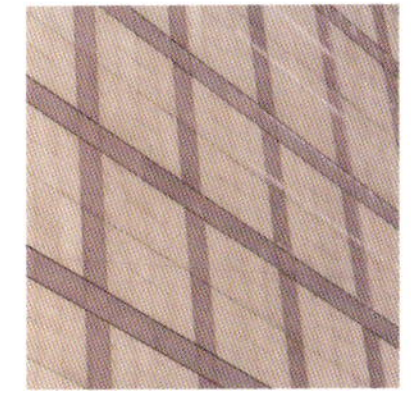

W. Kinzie Street &
N. LaSalle Drive,
River North

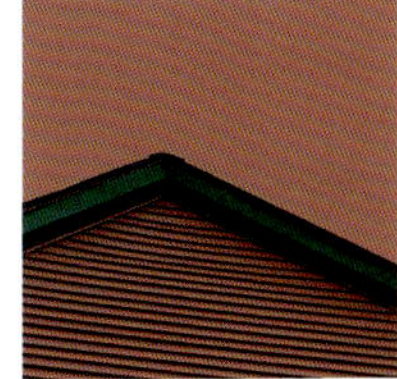

E. 42nd Street &
S. Vincennes Avenue,
Bronzeville

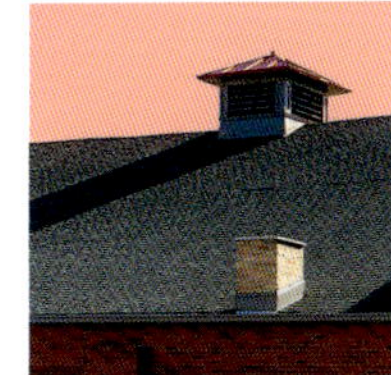

The Forum, Bronzeville

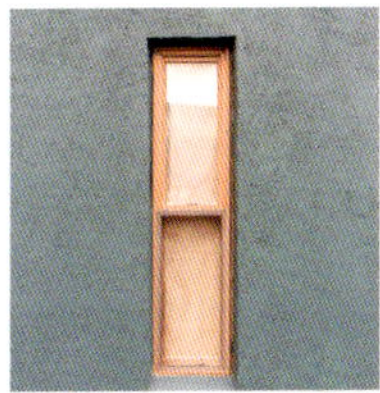

W. Waveland Avenue &
N. Lincoln Avenue,
North Center

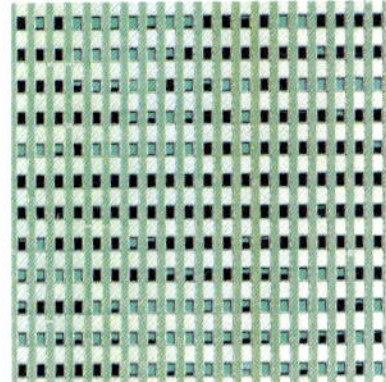

Prudential Plaza,
the Loop

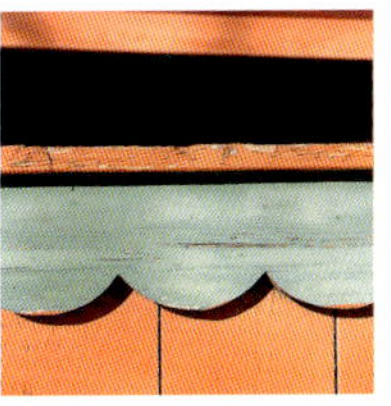

E. 37th Street & S. Giles
Avenue, Bronzeville

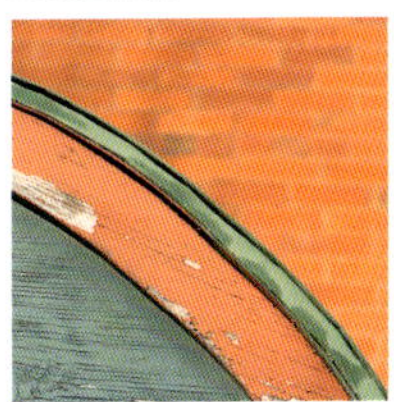

E. 37th Street & S. Giles
Avenue, Bronzeville

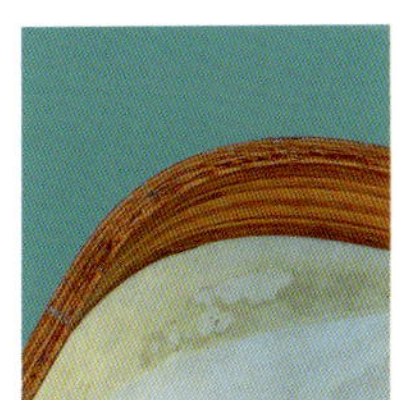

Peoples Gas Pavilion,
Lincoln Park

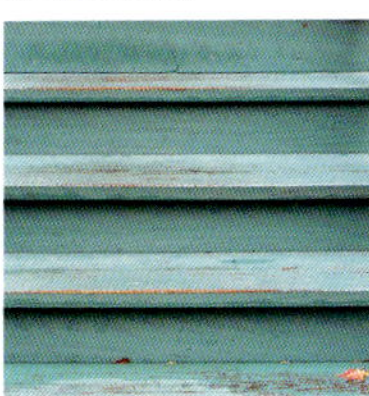

N. Ravenswood Avenue,
Ravenswood

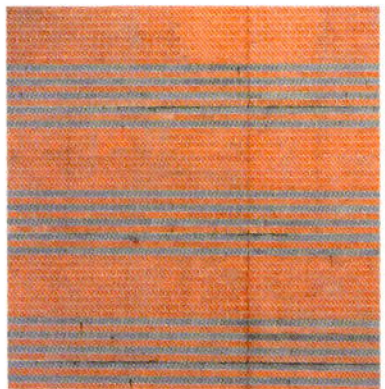

S. Wabash Avenue &
W. Adams Street, the Loop

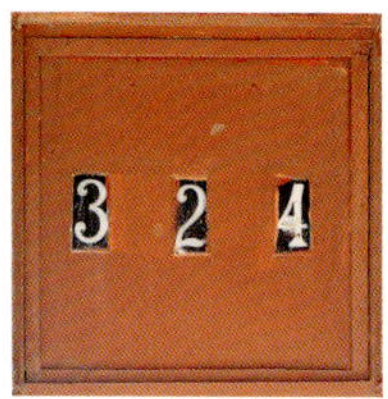

The Forum, Bronzeville

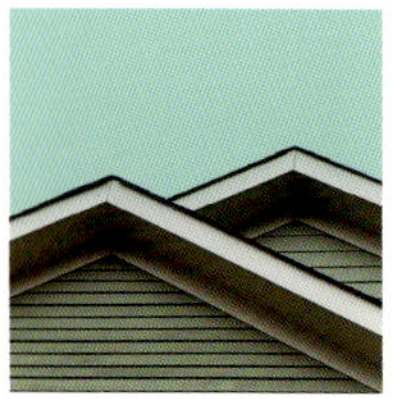

N. Ravenswood Avenue,
Ravenswood

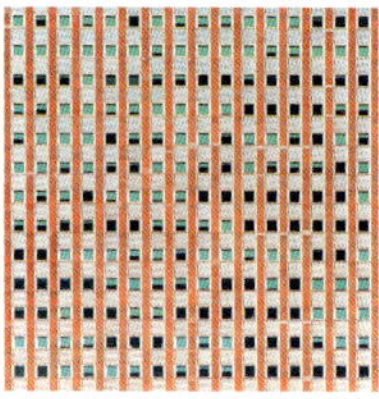

Prudential Plaza,
the Loop

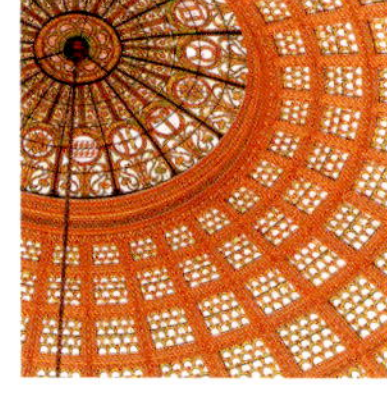

Chicago Cultural Center,
the Loop

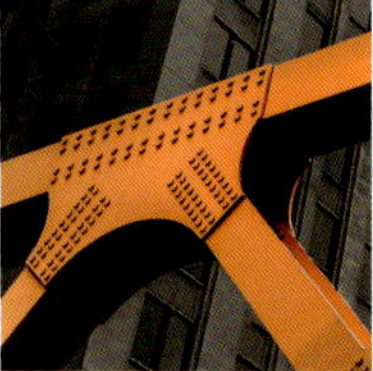

W. Wacker Drive &
N. Wells Street, the Loop

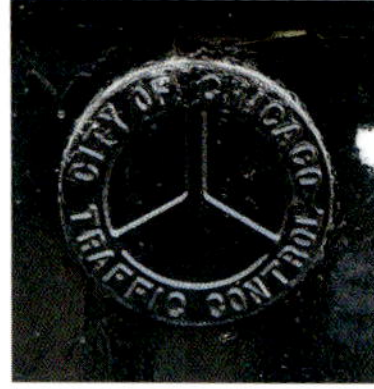

Kedzie CTA station,
Kedzie

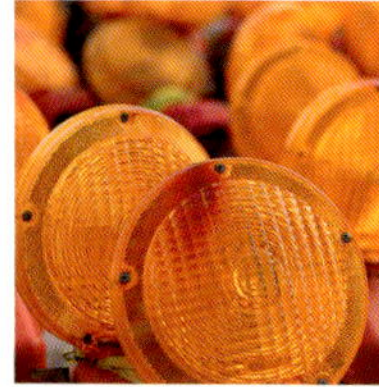

N. Southport Avenue &
W. Wellington Avenue,
Lakeview

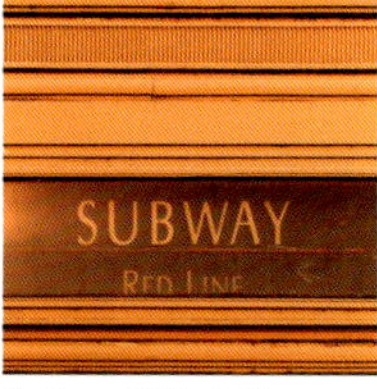

Jackson CTA station,
the Loop

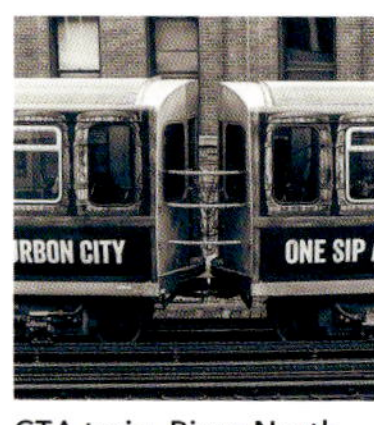

CTA train, River North

William P. Fahey Bridge,
the Loop

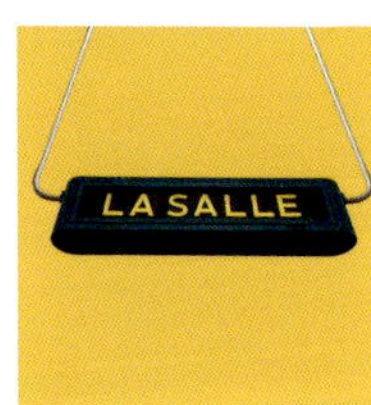

LaSalle CTA station,
the Loop

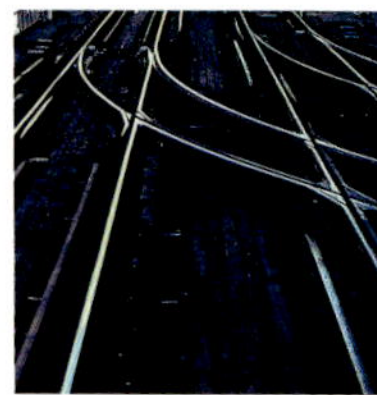

N. Wells Street & W. Lake
Street, the Loop

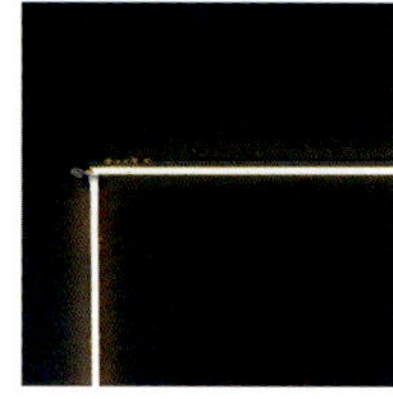

S. Michigan Avenue &
E. 13th Street, South Loop

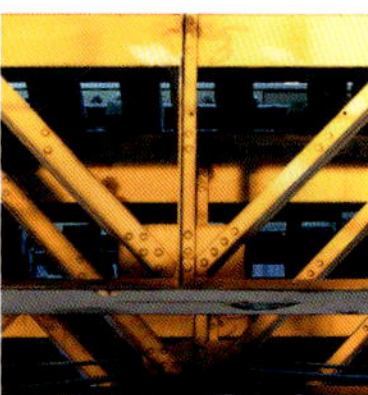

N. Wells Street & W. Lake
Street, the Loop

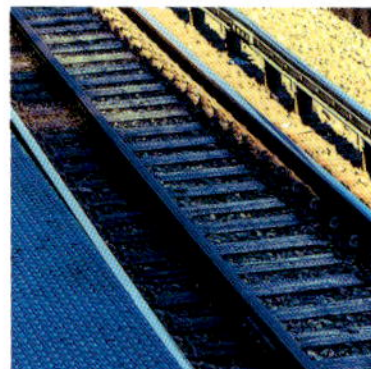

Garfield CTA station,
Fuller Park

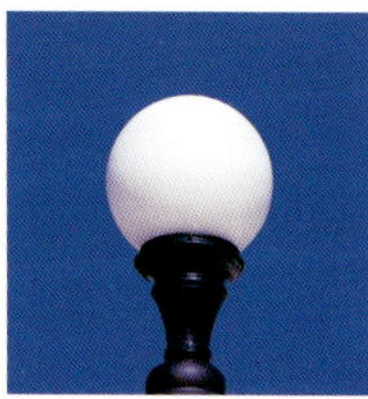

Pullman Park, Pullman

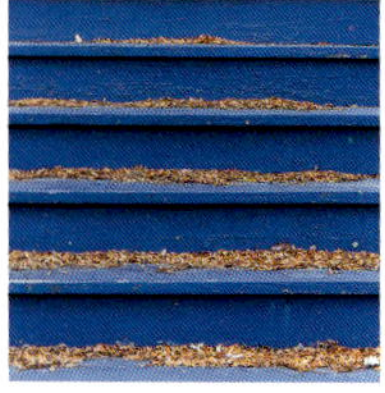

N. Ashland Avenue,
Ravenswood

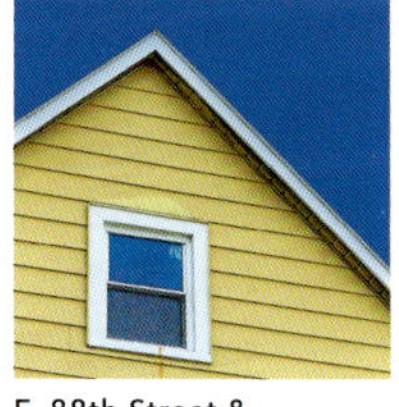

E. 88th Street &
S. Commercial Avenue,
South Chicago

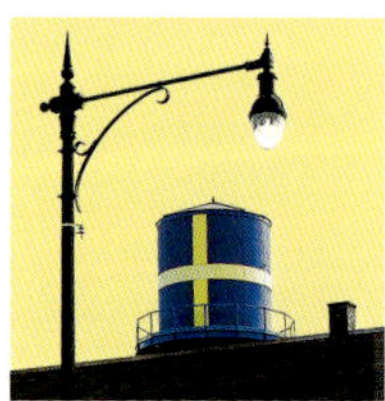

Swedish American
Museum, Andersonville

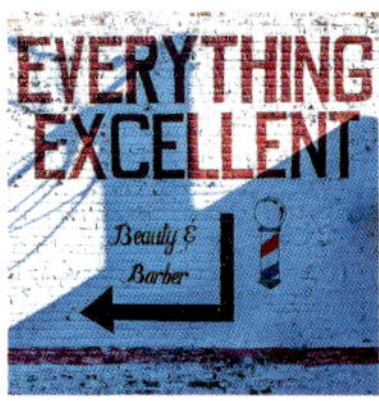

Everything Excellent
Barber and Beauty Salon,
Bronzeville

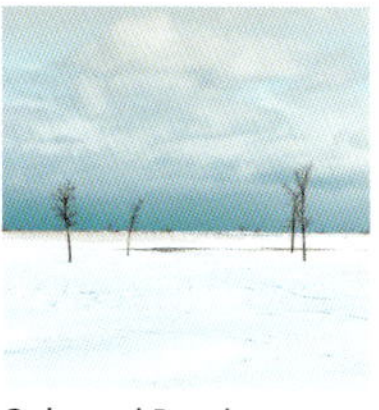

Oakwood Beach,
Oakland

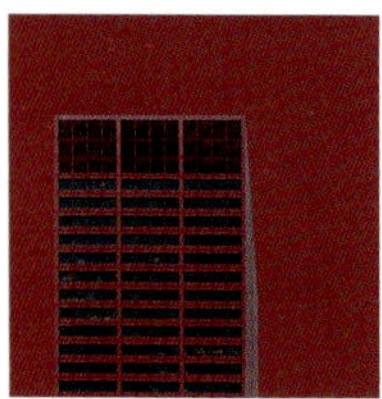

Richard J. Daley Center,
the Loop

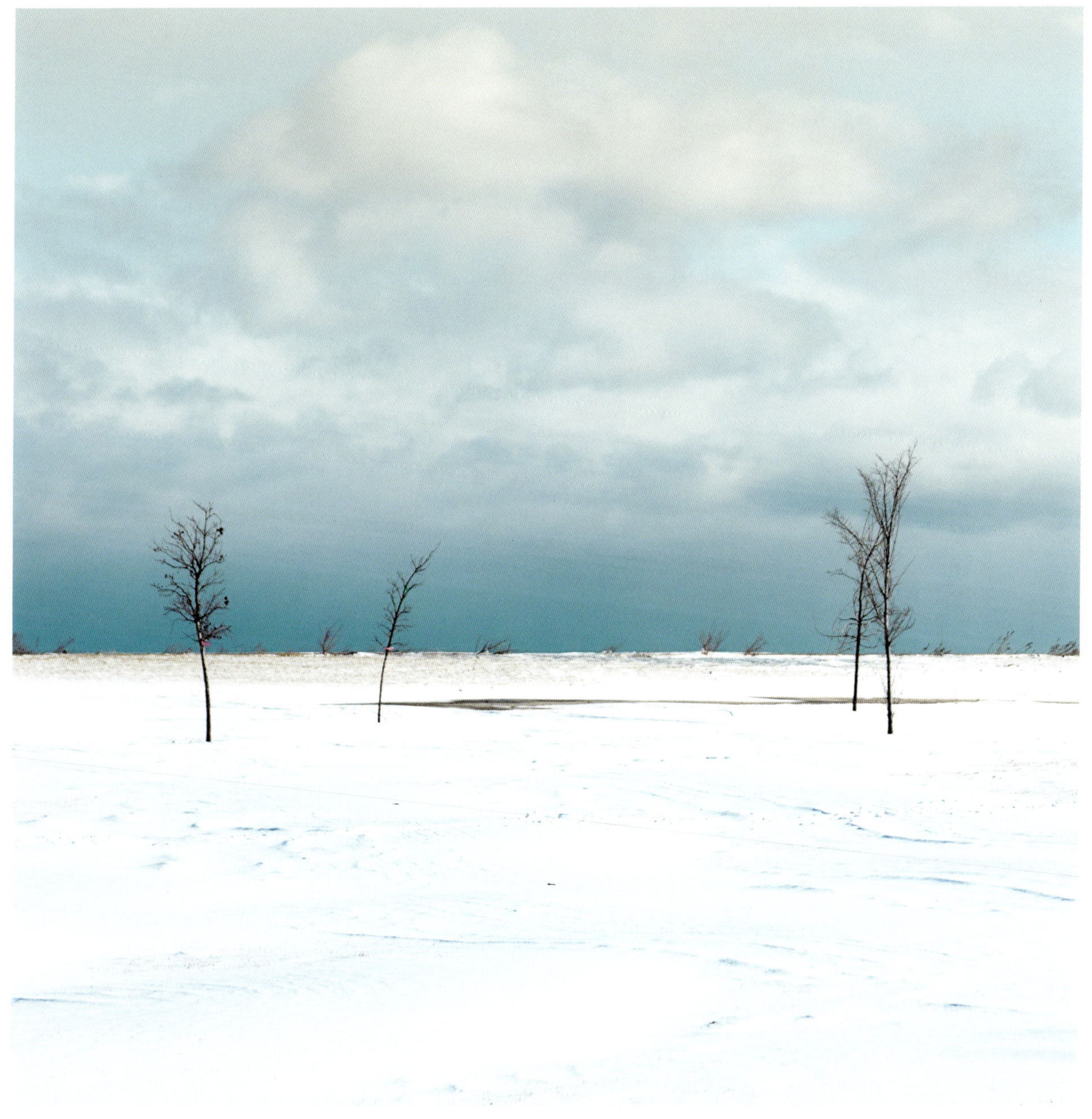

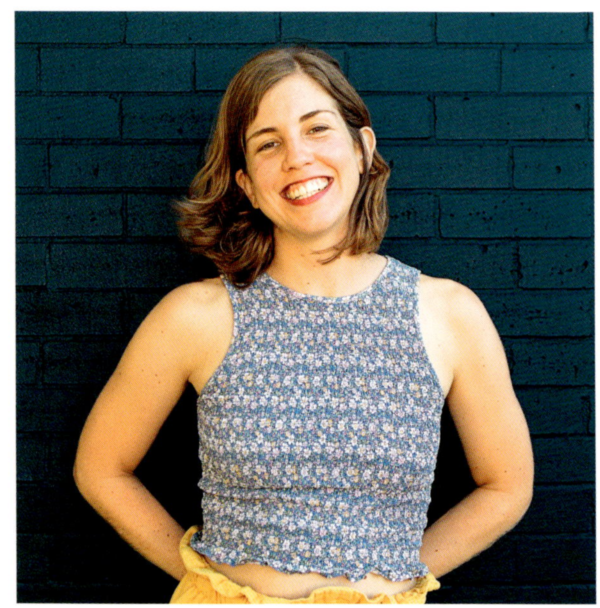
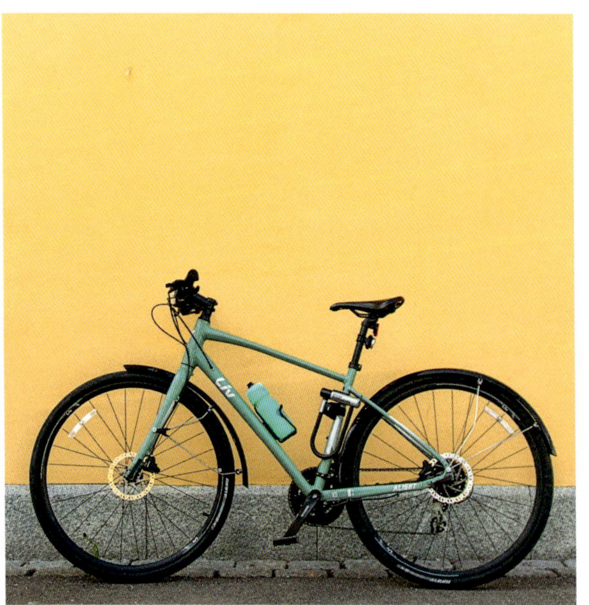

About the Artist

Judit Prat Martí has always loved taking pictures. Originally from outside Barcelona, Judit started taking classes at Richard Stromberg's Chicago Photography Classes school while a Postdoctoral fellow at the Astronomy and Astrophysics department at the University of Chicago. Judit loves how photography encouraged her to explore her new home of Chicago, exploring and getting to know the city and its various neighborhoods. Many Sundays, she would take her bike and her camera, and choose a neighborhood to explore, photographing everything that would catch her eye. Judit's studies have since taken her to Stockholm, where she is looking forward to exploring a new city and continuing to capture the magic with her camera.

LCCN: 2024937387
ISBN: 978-1-951963-28-6

Printed and bound in China
First printing, 2024

Trope Publishing Co.

The photographs from *Chicago in Color*
are available for purchase. For inquiries,
email the gallery at info@trope.com

+ INFORMATION:
For additional information
on our books and prints,
visit trope.com

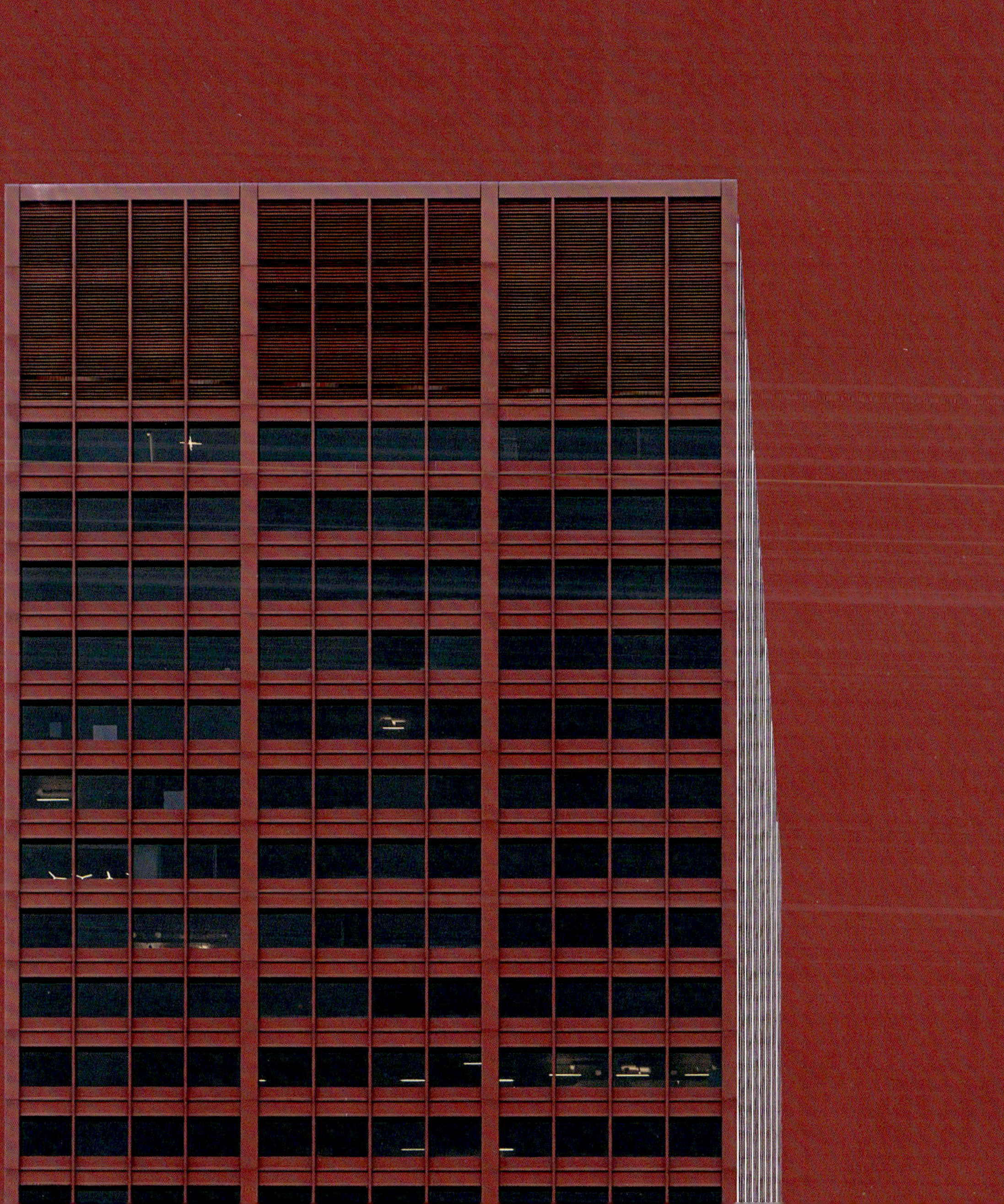

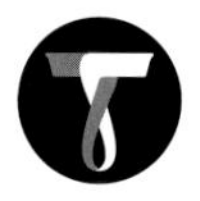

TROPE
PUBLISHING
Co.